Alfred P. Putnam

Old Anti-Slavery Days (1893)

Alfred P. Putnam
Old Anti-Slavery Days (1893)
ISBN/EAN: 9783743373716
Manufactured in Europe, USA, Canada, Australia, Japa
Cover: Foto ©ninafisch / pixelio.de

Manufactured and distributed by brebook publishing software (www.brebook.com)

Alfred P. Putnam

Old Anti-Slavery Days (1893)

OLD ANTI-SLAVERY DAYS.

PROCEEDINGS

OF THE

COMMEMORATIVE MEETING,

HELD BY THE

Danvers Historical Society,

AT THE

TOWN HALL, DANVERS,

APRIL 26, 1893,

WITH INTRODUCTION, LETTERS AND SKETCHES.

DANVERS:
DANVERS MIRROR PRINT.
1893.

[COPYRIGHT, 1893, BY THE DANVERS HISTORICAL SOCIETY.]

DANVERS HISTORICAL SOCIETY.

OFFICERS AND ASSISTANTS, 1892-93.

REV. ALFRED P. PUTNAM, D. D., ... *President.*
HON. ALDEN P. WHITE, ... *Vice-President.*
MISS SARAH E. HUNT, ... *Secretary.*
MRS. E. M. P. GOULD, ... *Assistant Secretary.*
DUDLEY A. MASSEY, ... *Treasurer.*
GEORGE TAPLEY, ... *Librarian.*
REV. WATSON M. AYRES, ... *Assistant Librarian.*
MRS. ISADORA E. KENNEY, ... *Curator.*
MRS. ANNIE G. NEWHALL, ... *Assistant Curator.*
EZRA D. HINES, ... *Historian.*
MISS MARY T. ROSS, ... *Reporter and General Assistant.*

DIRECTORS.

ISRAEL H. PUTNAM.   NATHAN A. BUSHBY.
MRS. LOUISA P. WESTON.   JOHN H. GOULD.
MRS. C. ADELINE HALE.   JOHN W. PORTER.
GEORGE A. PEABODY.   CHARLES H. MASURY.
            MISS SARAH W. MUDGE.

EXECUTIVE COMMITTEE.

HON. A. P. WHITE, *Chairman.*

ISRAEL H. PUTNAM.   JOHN W. PORTER.
GEORGE A. PEABODY.   ALFRED P. PUTNAM.

CONTENTS.

	PAGE.
Introductory Chapter, or Danvers and the Abolitionists	vii-xxv
THE MEETING IN TOWN HALL, DANVERS	1-61
Prayer by Rev. William H. Fish, Dedham	2
Address and Song by Mr. John W. Hutchinson, Lynn	4
Remarks by the President of the Society	5
Address by Mr. William Lloyd Garrison, Boston	6
Address by Rev. Samuel May, Leicester	12
Address by Hon. M. M. Fisher, Medway	18
Original Poem by Mr. George B. Bartlett, Concord	24
Song by the Hutchinsons, "*Car of Emancipation*"	26
Address by Hon. Parker Pillsbury, Concord, N. H.	27
Song by the Hutchinsons, "*There's no such word as Fail*"	33
" " " " "*The Slave's Appeal*"	35
Address by Rev. George W. Porter, D. D., Lexington	36
Address by Mrs. Lucy Stone, Boston	38
Address by Mrs. Abby M. Diaz, Belmont	42
Address by Rev. Aaron Porter, East Alstead, N. H.	45
Address by Mr. George W. Putnam, Lynn	50
Address by Mr. George T. Downing, Newport, R. I.	53
Address by Rev. Peter Randolph, Charlestown	55
Address by Miss Sarah H. Southwick, Wellesley Hills	56
Address by Rev. Daniel S. Whitney, Southboro'	58
Song by the Hutchinsons, "*The Old Granite State*"	59
Hymn, "*My Country, 'tis of thee*," offerings, etc.	60
LETTERS FROM FRIENDS	62-94
Hon. Frederick Douglass, Anacostia, D. C.	62
Mr. Charles K. Whipple, Newburyport	63
Mrs. Kate Tannatt Woods, Salem	65
Mr. Joseph A. Allen, Medfield	66
Rev. Thomas T. Stone, D. D., Bolton	66
Hon. Francis W. Bird, Walpole	67
Hon. Simeon Dodge, Marblehead	67
Rev. Joseph May, Philadelphia, Pa.	68
Mr. John Curtis, Boston	68
Rev. William H. Fish, Dedham	68
Rev. Robert Collyer, New York, N. Y.	69
Mrs. Caroline H. Dall, Washington, D. C.	70

	PAGE.
Mr. Wendell Phillips Garrison, New York, N. Y.	70
Mrs. Elizabeth B. Chace, Valley Falls, R. I.	70
Rev. Richard S. Storrs, D. D., Brooklyn, N. Y.	71
Mrs. Emily W. Taylor, Germantown, Pa.	71
Mrs. Ednah D. Cheney, Jamaica Plain	72
Mrs. Henry Ward Beecher, Brooklyn, N. Y.	73
Dr. W. Symington Brown, Stoneham	73
Mr. D. L. Bingham, Manchester, (with note about Mr. and Mrs. Daniel W. Friend)	73
Miss Anna L. Coffin, Newburyport	74
Mrs. Lillie B. Chace Wyman, Valley Falls, R. I.	75
Mr. Aaron M. Powell, New York, N. Y.	76
Miss Mary Grew, Philadelphia, Pa.	76
Mrs. Caroline M. Severance, Los Angeles, Cal.	78
Miss Mary J. Loring, Woburn	78
Mr. Francis Jackson Garrison, Boston	79
Mr. Cornelius Wellington, East Lexington	79
Mr. John J. May, Dorchester	79
Prof. Granville B. Putnam, Boston	80
Hon. Mellen Chamberlain, Chelsea	80
Mr. Lucian Newhall, Lynn	80
Mr. Gilbert L. Streeter, Salem	81
Dr. James C. Jackson, North Adams	81
Rev. William W. Silvester, D. D., Philadelphia, Pa.	83
Rev. William H. Furness, D. D., Philadelphia, Pa.	84
Mr. John M. Lennox, Boston	84
Mrs. Martha Waldo Greene, East Greenwich, R. I.	84
Mrs. Fanny Garrison Villard, New York, N. Y.	85
Mr. Daniel Ricketson, New Bedford	86
Mr. Walter B. Allen, Lynn	86
Mr. Robert Adams, Fall River	86
Mr. William D. Thompson, Lynn	87
Mr. George W. Clark, Detroit, Mich.	88
Dea. Joshua T. Everett, Westminster	89
Mr. William Stone, New York, N. Y.	90
Mr. David Mead, Danvers	90
Mrs. Anne E. Damon (with note about Mrs. F. E. Bigelow), Concord	91
Mr. J. M. W. Yerrinton, Chelsea	91
Col. Thomas W. Higginson, Cambridge	92
Mr. Theodore D. Weld, Hyde Park	92
Mr. Charles E. Graves, Hartford, Conn.	92
Rev. Samuel F. Smith, D. D., Newton	93
Mrs. Harriet M. Lothrop, Boston	93

	PAGE.
BIOGRAPHICAL SKETCHES	95–140
Rev. William H. Fish	95
John W. Hutchinson	97
William Lloyd Garrison	100
Rev. Samuel May	101
Hon. M. M. Fisher	103
George B. Bartlett	105
Hon. Parker Pillsbury	106
Rev. George W. Porter, D. D.	111
Mrs. Lucy Stone	112
Mrs. Abby M. Diaz	115
Rev. Aaron Porter	118
George W. Putnam	119
George T. Downing	123
Rev. Peter Randolph	126
Rev. Daniel S. Whitney	131
Miss Sarah H. Southwick	134
ADDITIONAL CONTRIBUTIONS.	
From Mr. Henry B. Blackwell, Boston	141
From Mr. F. B. Sanborn, Concord	144
From Charles A. Greene, M. D., Boston	147
From Mrs Catharine S. B. Spear, Passaic, N. J.	149
From a friend of Hon. Simeon Dodge	150
"The Liberator" in Danvers	151

Introductory Chapter.

Danvers and the Abolitionists.

The Anti-Slavery Commemorative Meeting of April 26th, 1893, whose proceedings, with Letters and Sketches, are published in the following pages, was originally designed to be of chiefly local concern, having its place in a general course of lectures for the earlier part of the year, under the auspices of the Danvers Historical Society. The deepening and widening interest that was felt in it, however, soon led to larger plans, and hence the more public character which the occasion finally assumed. Circulars of invitation were sent to hundreds of friends, scattered through various New England and other states, who were known to have been specially identified or in sympathy with the great movement for emancipation, but particularly, so far as their names and addresses could be ascertained, to those among the living who were earliest and most earnestly devoted to the cause. The favorable responses that came from all quarters were as prompt and numerous as they were hearty and gratifying, and the result was a Reunion that witnessed the presence of a surprisingly large number of members of the Abolition parties and organizations of former days, some of whom were among the most conspicuous and distinguished advocates of freedom for the slave a half century or more ago. It was a most impressive assemblage of the veterans; and those of the audience who had not shared in the labors or participated in the scenes of the momentous struggle, had a rare opportunity of seeing and hearing men and women who had been among the foremost in the fight and whose names will not be lost to the coming generations. Whoever of the throng had attended the memorable Anti-Slavery meetings of forty or fifty years before, could but have been struck with the remarkable reproduction or renewal, now, of their essential spirit, their salient features, and their peculiar characteristics and concomitants. A whole generation had elapsed from the time when the final victory was won, but here again were the old voices in both speech and song, the same old battle words and love of truth and justice, and the same unconventional ways, free and independent spirit, and intense interest and enthusiasm, with which some of us were familiar in the days when the strife was hottest and when the veterans knew so well how to do and dare for the right. But for the absence of all signs of angry dissent or violent opposition, one might almost have fancied himself transported back to the abolition meetings of the long ago which were so full of purpose, eloquence and life as to make well nigh all others seem tame and meaningless in comparison.

The Anti-Slavery enterprise, in its whole inception and aim, its progress and development, and its ultimate success, was, as has often and truly been said, one of the grandest moral movements in the centuries; and in view of the fact that it belongs to the history of our own country, while its effects and influences reach out, more and more, far beyond our territorial limits, it would seem that here indeed is a matter for inquiry and consideration on the part of such of our American societies as profess to be, or are supposed to be, devoted to the study of the past, however little, as yet, they have given their attention to it. No subject, no event, no epoch, no chapter of our national annals, can more properly claim their thought and research, and none can more abundantly reward investigation. But especially desirable and important is it, to gather up the necessary materials for the story, while so many of the real actors in the drama still survive and are able to give their testimony and relate their personal experience or recollections in relation to it. Such contributions are of exceptional and incalculable value. In the not distant future they may not be given as now, and it is plainly the duty of our societies, large or small, older or younger, to do what they can and may to procure and put on record facts or memories of the conflict which are more or less likely to be forgotten or neglected, but which should be made to live and fulfil their appropriate ministry. The Danvers meeting, while of course it rehearsed much that was already well known, had also the merit or distinction of eliciting much that was fresh and new, and thus of helping, in some humble way, to the desired result. Many of those who were there, thirty years after the Proclamation of Emancipation by President Lincoln, must have realized that they were gaining some better view and sense of the nature of slavery and of the power that contended against it and brought it to destruction, than they had had before they came together. Nor was the meeting less helpful to this end because it was so free and popular in its spirit and abounded so much in personal allusions and remembrances and earnest sentiment and feeling, instead of being occupied with some formal and labored historical or philosophical disquisition on the general subject. It answered its purpose best, because it was so vivid a *life-picture* of what it sought to recall and commemorate. As such, it was a true and genuine study of history itself.

Nor this alone. It was marked by moral lessons of the highest import and value. As there has been no greater service of man and God in our age than that which broke the chains of the three millions of our oppressed and degraded fellow-beings in the South, clothed them with the rights and immunities of American citizenship and made the nation free in fact as it was in name, so it was now seen, anew, what a noble thing it is for souls to consecrate themselves to a righteous cause and live for others; and it was seen, once more, that such devotion or work is never in vain, that no enmities or hostilities can avail to defeat it, that God is in it, and that in his own good time it shall vindicate itself and gloriously triumph. It was worth the while, for young and for old, to see and hear the confessors who had so loved the truth and who had so loved liberty for all, whose faith had known no fear and whose word had not been silenced, who had bravely met the frowns and jeers and persecutions of the world, and had still toiled on in trust and hope, and conquered at last. While the many were in quest of money, or pleasure, or office, or popularity, or power, or fame, these were willing to be poor, to forego the usually coveted privileges and delights of life, and to be of no reputation, yes, even to suffer, and if need were, to die, if only through their labors and stripes and sacrifices some comfort or deliverance might come to the trampled and the weary ones. Object lessons they were and are, to inspire men with more faith in the power of truth, and with increased zeal for personal excellence and for the universal weal. It is these and such as these, who have made it easier for others to believe and not to doubt, to hold to the right against whatever odds, to keep in sight the lofty ideals and to obey the heavenly vision, and still to press on until the cross is exchanged for the crown. It was good to be there, at the commemoration scene ; and the eager and unflagging attention of the audience to all that was said, and the vehement and prolonged applause which followed Mr. Garrison's very able and fine address and all the speeches that succeeded it, as well as Mr. Bartlett's poem and the songs of the Hutchinsons, showed how deeply their hearers entered into the the spirit of the occasion, and how well they seemed to take to heart the moral instruction and incentives of the hour.

And it was meet that such a Reunion should take place in Danvers itself. The old town was one of the early centres of earnest and active anti-slavery sentiment, and it lost none of its interest in the work of reform in subsequent times, but steadily and progressively gave its voice and vote in its behalf in the later days of the Free-Soil and early Republican parties. Not long after Mr. Garrison entered upon his great crusade, he found here, in the South Parish (now Peabody), as well as in the North, a respectable number of warm-hearted friends and sympathizers, most of whom continued to the last to give him their strong support, while some of them eventually connected themselves with political parties, the better to compass the object in view. The earliest distinct trace of them in South Danvers takes us back to the year 1834, when Isaac Winslow and his family, from Maine, were residing there, and when Joseph Southwick (one of the delegates to the Philadelphia Convention that founded the American Anti-Slavery Society of 1833) came with his family from the same State to reside with them, the two Quaker families being closely related to each other by marriage, and the Southwicks being descended from settlers in Danvers of about two hundred years before. Additional information concerning this interesting

circle of Friends is given in the address and sketch of Miss Sarah
H. Southwick, as published in subsequent pages. Together they
attended anti-slavery meetings and fairs in Boston, and constituted a nucleus of abolitionism in the place where they lived.
The Southwicks, having remained in Danvers but for a single
year,—though Miss Southwick somewhere refers to a subsequent
residence of three years (1853-56) in the same village,—removed
to the city in 1835, yet still continued their devotion to the cause
in company with the Winslows. It was doubtless in the southern
part of the town that was formed, April 7th, 1837, a "Danvers
Female Anti-Slavery Society," of which Mrs. Isaac Winslow was
chosen the President; Mrs. Richard Loring, Vice-President;
Miss Harriet N. Webster, Corresponding Secretary; Miss Emily
Winslow, daughter of Isaac Winslow, (Mrs. Emily W. Taylor,
now of Germantown, Pa.), Recording Secretary, and Mrs. Elijah
Upton, Treasurer; with Mrs. Eben Upton, Mrs. Amos Osborn,
Mrs. Benjamin Hill, Mrs. Charles Northend, Mrs. Abel Nichols,
and Mrs. John Morrison, as Councillors. The Society was evidently meant for the whole town and probably its sixty members
represented the North Parish as well as the South. Mrs. Abel
Nichols, not to mention others, was of North Danvers, and she
and her husband were among the best of abolitionists. Their
daughter, the late Mrs. Eben G. Berry, recalled with what fear
and trembling she was wont, as a young girl, to circulate anti-
slavery documents, and their nephew, Mr. Andrew Nichols, now
of Danvers, son of Dr. Andrew Nichols, remembers how he used
to be stoned in the streets for procuring subscribers to anti-slavery
papers. But among the men of the place who were earnest for
emancipation, there were—besides Isaac Winslow and Joseph
Southwick—Mr. Abner Sanger, whom Frederick Douglass so
deservedly honors in his eloquent letter; Eli F. Burnham, Amasa
P. Blake* and Andrew Porter; and Dr. Andrew Nichols and
Alonzo P. Phillips, both of whom were of the highest character
and came to be prominent and influential members of the Liberty
party. Some or all of these men, year after year, arranged for

* Mr. Amasa P. Blake died while these pages have been in press,
Sept. 5, 1893, at about the age of seventy. He was a native of Sheffield,
Vt., and came to Danvers about forty-five years ago.

evening meetings or Sunday afternoon lectures, secured the services of gifted and favorite speakers from abroad, and so kept the fires of freedom brightly burning in that neighborhood.

North Danvers, or Danvers as it now is, was still more, perhaps, a theatre of zealous and determined propagandism. About the time when the Winslows and the Southwicks first appeared in South Danvers in 1833-34, there seems to have existed here some kind of an association of anti-slavery friends (of which, however, no record is known to have been preserved) at "The Neck," or "New Mills," later known as Danversport.—having for its members, Jesse P. Harriman, Richard Hood, John Hood, Joseph Merrill, Hathorne Porter, Alfred R. Porter, John Cutler, William Endicott, James D. Black, William Francis, Henry A. Potter, Rev. Samuel Brimblecom, John R. Patten, Dr. Ebenezer Hunt, William Alley, Job Tyler, and Hercules Johnson, and possibly some other gentlemen, assisted and encouraged as they all were by good and faithful women, most of whom were of the same names and families, yet others of whom were such true friends of the cause as Mrs. Rachel Kenney, Miss E. H. Kenney, (afterward Mrs. Joseph Merrill), Miss Irene Kent, Miss Susan Hutchinson, and Miss E. H. Hutchinson, subsequently the Secretary of the Essex County Anti-Slavery Society. Only two of the men, whose names have been given in the list, still survive:—Henry A. Potter, now of Marblehead, and William Alley, now of Marlboro'. The latter, alone, was present at the commemorative meeting, occupying a seat on the platform. Mrs. John Cutler was also present, from Peabody. Mrs. James D. Black, who now lives at Lawrence, was unable to attend. Mrs. William Endicott was living in Danvers at the time, but in her greatly enfeebled condition she could ill understand the nature of the occasion, and she has since died. We are not aware that others of the wives of the original members of the Society of 1833, themselves all devoted to the anti-slavery cause with their husbands, were among the living on the 26th of April last. The widow of Dr. Hunt—that able and staunch Abolitionist who was at one time the candidate of the Liberty Party for Lieutenant Governor of Massachusetts—had, like himself, been previously married. She became his wife in 1844, and their only child is the present Secretary of the Historical Society. A daughter of John Page, Esq., of Danvers, Mrs. Hunt is remembered as having been from early life, not only a remarkably bright and interesting lady, but a warm friend of the slave and an efficient promoter of every benevolent work. She is said to have been one of the first two subscribers in the town for the *Liberator*, Col. Jesse Putnam, long since deceased, being the other. She and her husband welcomed to their home and hearts and helpful hands the fugitives from oppression. She still survives, but like Mrs. Endicott, she was unable, by reason of the infirmities of age, to recall, at the time of the Commemoration, the old anti-slavery days when she gave the rare beauty and strength and grace of her womanhood to the service of the poor and the wronged. It is such facts as these that impress us deeply with a sense of the fast diminishing ranks of the true and the faithful, and of the sure receding of the great drama and all who shared its fortunes into the calm and changeless realm of history.

It was perhaps a short time previous to 1833-4, that Oliver Johnson came to the town to deliver in the vestry of the First Church, of which Rev. Milton P. Braman, D. D., was the minister, what was probably the earliest Anti-Slavery lecture ever given in Danvers, a principal object of which was to combat the Colonization scheme which Mr. Garrison, in 1832, had mercilessly attacked and exposed, in a well-known pamphlet publication on the subject. It was probably in the year 1833, possibly 1834, that the writer of these pages, then about the age of seven, had the good fortune to hear, in the Baptist Church at "The Neck," an eloquent Fourth of July Anti-Slavery oration by James D. Black, who was at the time but nineteen or twenty years old. We well recall the earnestness and vigor of that excellent address, and the young man who delivered it, bright and gifted as he was, lived to be, not only one of the leading Abolitionists of the town, but also, in other ways, one of its most useful and honored citizens, whatever the injustice he suffered during his life. It has often been said of him that "he was the best moderator of the town meetings Danvers has ever known." Although Mr. Porter has not included him in his list of the "Seven Stars," yet, whether that designation was meant to express a certain definite number or not, our impression is that he really belonged to the galaxy, as he certainly deserved the honor. It was in 1834, also, that Rev. Cyrus P. Grosvenor,* an early and devoted champion of freedom, who should not be forgotten, came from Salem, where he was then settled, and likewise gave an Anti-Slavery address in the Baptist Church. In the same edifice, in 1835, a large number of people were privileged to hear the celebrated George Thompson of England. And in 1837, we learn from an old printed programme of the time, there was a Celebration of the Fourth of July by the "Danvers Anti-Slavery Society," Rev. Samuel Brimblecom being the orator of the day, and Alfred R. Porter the poet, both of them members.

The seed thus sown, took root and grew. From what soon took place, it is evident that the cause was gaining new friends and fresh strength. On the 26th of August, 1838, a meeting was held in the Universalist Church at the "Neck," at which steps

*The name of this early and eminent Anti-Slavery clergyman meets us often in the history of the great struggle. While writing, in 1879, a series of articles about Abolitionism in Danvers for the *Danvers Mirror*, I gathered from the late Dr. Henry Wheatland, President of the Essex Institute, some particulars concerning him, which may be of interest in this connection. He was a son of Rev. Daniel Grosvenor, who was born in Pomfret, Conn., April 20, 1750, and who, having graduated at Yale in 1769, was settled successively at Grafton, Paxton, and Petersham, Mass. The son, Cyrus Pitt Grosvenor, was born at Petersham. He graduated at Dartmouth College in 1818, afterward studied at the Princeton Theological Seminary, and was still later a Baptist minister at New Haven, Conn., 1825-26, at Boston, 1826-30, and at Salem, Mass., 1830-34. It was while he was at Salem, that the Essex County Anti-Slavery Society was organized in his own parlor, about ten or twelve persons being present. He was at Sterling in 1837, and subsequently he was President of Central College, at McGrawsville, Cortland County, N. Y. While at McGrawsville, he was Corresponding Secretary, says William Goodell's very valuable *History of Slavery and Anti-Slavery*, of the American Baptist Free Mission Society, which admitted no slave holding members and recognized no distinction founded on color. Said Dr. Wheatland: "He was a man of fine talents and scholarship and of unusual ability in the pulpit. He was decided and radical, but sincere, devout, and conscientious." He appears to have been foremost in really setting the Anti-Slavery ball in motion in Salem and Essex County. Subsequently he joined the Liberty Party. The *Salem Register*, of Mar. 3, 1879, had the following: "Rev. Cyrus P. Grosvenor, LL. D., died recently at Albion, Michigan, aged 86 years."

A. P. P.

were taken for reorganization, and Joseph Merrill, Thomas Bowen, and John R. Langley, were appointed a committee to draft a constitution for what was now to be "The Young Men's Anti-Slavery Society." The report of the committee having been presented and adopted on the following Tuesday, Rev. Samuel Brimblecom, the minister of the Universalist Church, was chosen President, (William Endicott being elected as his successor a year later), John R. Langley, Secretary, and Joseph Merrill, Treasurer. The list of members at once became enlarged, and included, not only the names already given as belonging to the earlier and less compact and efficient association, but also these: Thomas Bowen, John R. Langley, Jonathan Richardson, James F. McIntire, Moses Black, Jr., Elias Savage, John D. Andrews, James M. Usher, Charles W. Page, John Hines, Oliver C. Wait, James Kelley, Archelaus P. Black, Winthrop Andrews, George Kate, Joseph W. Legro, Benjamin Potter, Ingalls K. McIntire, Daniel Woodbury, Josiah Ross, Edward Stimpson, Jonathan Eveleth, Charles Benjamin, Samuel P. Fowler, Oliver O. Brown, Alexander A. Leavitt, William Needham, Elbridge G. Little, Ira P. Clough, Abner S. Mead, and Joseph Porter. Of the members of this new or reorganized society of 1838, as mentioned in the above two lists, only nine were living at the time of the Commemorative meeting; William Alley and Henry A. Potter, who, as stated above, also belonged to the earlier society; J. R. Langley, J. W. Legro, Winthrop Andrews, and A. S. Mead, all still of Danvers; and Daniel Woodbury, Jonathan Richardson and Jonathan Eveleth, of Peabody, Essex and Beverly, respectively. Messrs. Langley, Andrews, Mead, Richardson and Eveleth, were present at the Reunion, Mr. Andrews and Mr. Mead occupying seats on the platform, with Mr. David Mead (a brother of Abner), who is still a resident of Danvers, and like his friend, Parker Pillsbury, is 84 years of age, and who, though his name does not appear in either of the lists, was ever a most decided and uncompromising abolitionist. All the other members of the Society—there were forty-eight in all—are, it is believed, numbered with the dead. Some of them were variously represented at the Commemorative Reunion by wives and children:—Hathorne Porter by his sons

Frederic (of Salem) and Aaron; John Cutler and Moses Black by their widows, Mrs. M. M. Cutler of Peabody, and Mrs. Harriet N. Black of Danvers; William Endicott by his daughter, Mrs. Henry G. Hyde; John Hines by his son, Ezra D. Hines, Esq., historian of the Historical Society; Samuel P. Fowler by his daughter, Mrs. Clara F. Dubois; Dr. Ebenezer Hunt by his daughters, Katharine E. and Sarah E. Hunt; and doubtless there were others, the surviving members of whose families were present at the meeting.

But how well these young men of Danvers, back there in 1838, grasped the situation and dedicated themselves to the sacred cause of Liberty, when to do it was, to say the least, a sacrifice of social consideration and popular favor, appears in the language of the Preamble of their Constitution and in the various Resolutions which their society adopted. Says the Preamble: " *Whereas*, it is established by evidence and facts beyond all doubt, that American Slavery is a system wholly opposed to all natural rights and completely at war with the Christian Religion, and as such should be immediately abolished, we, the undersigned, do adopt the following constitution." And here, also, is one of their earliest declarations: " *Resolved*, that, whereas some millions of our brethren are held in bondage, are deprived of all their rights, political, civil, and religious, and are crushed to the level of the brutes, therefore we, as abolitionists, aim not only at their emancipation, but to restore them to their proper place in the scale of moral beings, which God has designed them to enjoy." And still again: " *Resolved*, that professing ministers of the Gospel who acknowledge Slavery to be a sin against God, but who neglect to lift up their voices against it, or to exert themselves in any way for its abolition, give the public strong reasons to regard them as time-serving men and unworthy of the confidence usually reposed in them."

All honor to those who thus, at the outset, bore their fearless testimony to the truth, and gave the strength, the freshness, the dew, of their youthful manhood to the service of the slave, nor counted the cost. They well deserve to be gratefully remembered. Possibly a few of them were destined, sooner or later, to fall back from their high moral vantage ground into old political relations with the Whig and Democratic parties of the time, in the vain and delusive hope that through one or the other of these instrumentalities the evil of slavery might most surely, however gradually, be mitigated, or removed. Others of them, like Dr. Hunt, Elias Savage and Winthrop Andrews, were to join the Liberty Party as the most direct and effective way in which the land might be redeemed from its curse and shame, while they would still hold to the Church, and make it the Bulwark of Freedom instead of the Bulwark of Slavery, as many deemed it to be. Associated with them in this attitude and action, were such men as Dea. Frederick Howe, Col. Jesse Putnam, John A. Learoyd and Peter Wait; and, in subsequent years, Allen Knight, Francis P. Putnam, Elias E. Putnam, Alfred Fellows, and others—all of whom, with their co-workers previously mentioned, were among the truest Anti-Slavery men in Danvers. But a large proportion of the later Society, and a still greater proportion of the earlier, were more and more persuaded that the church was irretrievably given over to complicity with the sin and iniquity of the Slave Power, and that to remain in connection with it under such circumstances would be to partake of its wickedness and guilt; while at the same time they regarded the Union and the Civil Government of the country as likewise the monstrous oppressor and enemy of the manacled and down-trodden captive, and therefore the exercise of the usual functions and privileges of citizenship under such a political system as a countenance and support to it, and consequently as wrong and inexcusable. Hence they withdrew from the church, declined to vote at the polls as they would also have refused to hold office, and disowned the Union and advocated its dissolution as a solemn duty and as the best means of setting at liberty the objects of their pity and compassion. They were "*Comeouters.*" Yet it was seen by others that one could not well live under such a political rule at all, could not at all remain in such a country and enjoy the ordinary intercourse of society and the manifold safeguards, opportunities and blessings which its laws made a common lot for the millions, without his being in some measure a party to the very Power that was called in question and defied. Absolute freedom from all entanglements would require self-expatriation. To pay taxes, to make use of the post-office, to buy and own and sell, to ride on the railroads, to share the general protection of courts, or of municipal or state or national enactments or appointments, was to acknowledge and respect the central and supreme authority, without which chaos would come again,—quite as much as if one should cast his ballot, or be a constable or congressman.

Yet the class of abolitionists to whom we refer were most conscientious in their action, and were as consistent as circumstances would allow, while virtually accepting the situation and living still under a government which they protested against and abjured. One can but greatly admire their high moral standard, their strenuous effort to free themselves from all responsibility for slavery in whatever way, and their willingness and readiness to bear whatever it might cost them to be faithful to their own honest convictions. And the cost was great. It was not without struggle or sorrow that they disowned the grand bequest of the fathers of the Republic, or renounced the church in which they were born and reared, however wicked or corrupt one or the other might be. Many of them were church-members, long and devotedly attached to the observances and sanctities that properly belonged to it; and they left it, not because they no longer believed in Christianity or could no longer engage in its appropriate forms of worship and communion, but because of the very strength and sincerity of their faith in it as such a pure and divine revelation and reality, that it must never suffer stain or profanation through the acts or words of its friends and adherents in excusing, or defending, or aiding, or encouraging gigantic crimes and the perpetrators of deeds of darkness. They were ridiculed and anathematized for it, but here they took their stand, and it must be acknowleged that it was lofty ground, however others might have deemed it the part of wisdom and duty to still abide in the Church, as well as in the Union, and fight the battle there, until each and both were "without spot or wrinkle or any such thing." And these men practically illustrated, in their character and daily life, the pure principles which they would fain make the

law of the land. Most of them were of humble pursuits and
circumstances. They were tanners, and curriers, and shoemakers,
and artisans, and tillers of the soil, yet were they possessed of a
high degree of intelligence, even as they were surpassed by none
of their neighbors in their reverence for God and his Christ and
in their aim and effort to do the will of heaven, while the work
upon which they entered and which so fully enlisted their sympathy and commanded their faculties and energies, had a wonderful
effect in educating them, in developing their mental and moral
powers, and in making them the bringers of light and life to
others. They held frequent meetings for talks, discussions, and
lectures. They attended conventions, far and near. They read
the Anti-Slavery literature, circulated papers and tracts, and
wrote for the *Liberator* and the *Herald of Freedom*. They
welcomed to their homes the Abolition orators, that the people
might hear them tell, in church, or hall, or schoolhouse, the story
of them that were in bonds and the one duty of the hour, paying
out of their own scant earnings the too meagre expenses. I well
remember hearing, as a lad, a talk from that sterling, indefatigable Quaker abolitionist, Benjamin Lundy, precursor of Garrison,
as, after his patient and self-denying labors in the cause throughout the country for more than twenty years, he made a visit to
Danvers (it could not have been long before his death at Lowell,
Ill., in 1839) and discoursed one evening to a few friends in the
old schoolhouse at "The Neck." But there came from time to
time, and again and again, Garrison, Phillips, Pillsbury, and
Douglass themselves, with Stephen S. Foster and Abby Kelly,
Sarah and Angelina Grimke, Nathaniel P. Rogers, Henry C.
Wright, Charles Lennox Remond, Lucy Stone, Thomas Parnell
Beach, Sojourner Truth, George Bradburn, and indeed well nigh
all the abler and more effective speakers of the old-line Abolition
party whom the people would throng most to hear. Richard
Hood (Mr. Hood was most prominent in arranging for all these
occasions, and both he and Harriman suffered imprisonment on
account of their anti-slavery principles and activities), Harriman,
Merrill, and the rest, rendered no small service to the town in
bringing to it such visitors and voices as these, as an inspiration

of liberty and life to its citizens, and as a contribution to its history which it will more and more be glad to remember and record. The cause nowhere had more constant and faithful servants than these men and their immediate associates. Mastered by one great idea, or purpose, so far as they could consistently with their secular avocations, they gave to it their time, their thought, their strength, their means, their life, in full and glad surrender. They kept the community astir. They made the people think and talk. They were moral agitators. There was no peace for the pro-slavery churches and political parties, and there were not wanting occasions when some of the more fiery spirits from abroad, like Foster and Beach and Maria French, seized with a consuming sense of the awful sin of slavery and feeling that the apathy of professing Christians and of the people generally was, to use the fit and forcible language of Mr. Garrison, "enough to make every statue leap from its pedestal, and to hasten the resurrection of the dead,"—invaded Sunday congregations in the hours of public worship, interrupted their services, rebuked them for their unfaithfulness, and threw them into indescribable confusion;—a method of warfare which, it should be said, the editor of the *Liberator*, with most of his noted associates and the great mass of the Abolitionists, did not approve, albeit many of them were inclined to excuse it. But however excusable the procedure under the unprecedented provocations which prompted it, it was plainly a violation of the letter and spirit of the law, and of the sacred and inherent right of all men, or bodies of men, peaceably to assemble themselves together and worship God in their own chosen way, or according to the dictates of their own consciences, with none to molest them or make them afraid, so long as they respect the public order and trespass not upon the common privileges and interests of their neighbors or of society. It was an essential right which the Abolitionists justly claimed for themselves, and never more than when their meetings were broken up by pro-slavery mobs or myrmidons.

Like all earnest reformers from time immemorial, who have been on fire for truth or right and who have been called to wage heroic warfare against the colossal sins and errors of their age, the Garrisonian party, so well represented by the Danvers friends we have referred to, were not seldom betrayed into various indiscretions and excesses which were but natural, if not inevitable. In such conflicts with intrenched and terrible wrong and injustice, brave soldiers of freedom cannot always deliberately weigh their words or carefully study propriety of action. Blows must rain thick, fast and heavy, and, as Edmund Burke said, *Something must be pardoned to the spirit of liberty.* The Abolitionists would themselves be the last to claim perfection and they have quite enough without the award. Yet even their faults or errors were not wholly without extenuation. If at times they were too indiscriminate and sweeping in their denunciations of church and clergy, and of political leaders and parties, and seemed to forget that there were amongst them thousands and thousands of true anti-slavery men and women, it must not be forgotten how furiously such organizations, or representatives of public opinion, denounced these friends of emancipation, and visited them with every vile epithet and every mark of proscription and disgrace, and how many of the best of such bodies and classes, by reason of their affiliations, were prone to disappoint expectations of their fidelity to freedom and to jeopardize its sacred interests, and therefore needed constant watch and warning. And if it shall be said that they were narrow and exclusive in spirit, indulging the fond conceit that only those who walked with them or stood on their particular platform could be counted as genuine Abolitionists, and not realizing how difficult it was, for those who dissented from the disunion, non-voting, anti-church, and other theories, which they connected with their anti-slavery gospel, to work with them and so share with them the general responsibility,—it must be remembered, also, that not a little of this lack of co-operation was largely due to the mere fact that here was a despised, unpopular and persecuted band of reformers; that much which the abolitionists associated with their appeals for the slave and which others than themselves then regarded as so irrelevant, is now seen to have been logically deducible from their fundamental principle; and that one, at least, of the proposed and related, but obnoxious measures, is now marching on to assured victory. So that, with reference to more than one of the reform movements which were urged by the Garrisonians, it may justly be said that the latter were not so much in the wrong in their attitude and teaching and work, as they were simply in advance of their time. Even with regard to their advocacy of the dissolution of the Union, if the impious and enormous plans and schemes of the South had still gone on unchecked, and it had been indisputably evident to the masses that ours was a nation that was in danger of soon becoming permanently the one great slave-holding empire of all history, their platform would have been crowded indeed, and millions instead of hundreds or thousands would, in due time, have joined their ranks and demanded the annulment of the covenant. God meant it otherwise and kept North and South together, that in the death-grapple of Freedom with Slavery, the Right should prevail and the Wrong should perish forever. The Union which many thought was the sure Fortress and Strength of Slavery, proved to be its sure Destruction.

The future will make small account of any shortcomings which men may see in the old Abolitionists. It is their everlasting honor that, at the time when millions of our fellow-creatures were groaning under insufferable bondage within our borders, and church, state, and people were alike deaf to their cries and were devoted to selfish gain and pride and fashion and pleasure, they were the first and foremost, as a class, to see the dreadful nature of slavery, to call the nation to repent and do works meet for repentance, and to rouse the public to a sense of its duty and to the needed action, giving themselves no rest until the beginning of the end had come. In an age of moral blindness and obliquity, of base compromises with the eternal right and of general worldliness and sin, they kept themselves pure and free from the evil, and maintained the highest character for strictness and even sternness of personal rectitude, whatever the exceptions. Their mission, their warfare, was a moral one. Their one supreme object was immediate and universal emancipation ; and to agitate and still to agitate the subject, and, in the service and for the sake of it, boldly to face and bravely endure the mockings and cruelties of their guilty countrymen, until their work was accomplished, or until others should enter into it and complete it, was the task which in the providence of God was assigned them, and to which they were faithful unto the end. It was not theirs indeed to fulfil it. Others were to take it up and carry it on to triumph. To these, as well, belongs the meed of praise. Without them, slavery, so far as human vision might foresee, would not have been abolished. But the animating principle of their highest endeavor and their crowning achievement came from those who had wrought before them, and without whom, also, Freedom had never won the victory. These were they who inaugurated the enterprise and breathed into it the breath of life, and however they might disapprove the methods of their successors, or however justly they might not hold themselves responsible for the consequences of their own honest words or deeds, yet all the same is it true, that the great original and solemn declaration of their purpose and principles, to which they so steadfastly adhered, meant and necessitated the Liberty and Free-Soil and Republican Parties, with Joshua R. Giddings and John P. Hale, Charles Sumner and Abraham Lincoln, Grant, Sherman, Sheridan and Farragut; and forts and iron-clads, and armies and navies and battles. Garrison might well have said, with the Reformer of reformers, " I came not to send peace, but a sword." Peace would come at last, but only through war and agony. The great work of the Abolitionists is seen, not alone in their own immediate labors, but also, and not the less, in the service of those who finally struck off the chains of the enslaved and made them free indeed; and again the Scripture was verified:—" And these all, having obtained a good report through faith, received not the promise, God having provided some better thing for us, that they without us should not be made perfect." They have renewed or perpetuated the line of the early Christians and martyr spirits of whom the author of the Epistle wrote, and " of whom the world was not worthy." A " Free-Soiler from the start," and still holding as aforetime to the Union as to the Church, we nevertheless acknowledge that not in American history has there been another conspicuous exemplification of such true Apostolic faith and practical Christianity as theirs; none which we believe will shine with such brightening lustre in the records of our past. Whatever change of religious opinion or feeling any of them may have come to share with others, in more recent years of such marked and general drift in the theological world as we have all witnessed, no fouler injustice could be done them than to say that in the course of their anti-slavery service they were inimical to the Bible, or to " the Way, the Truth, and the Life" whom it reveals. Garrison himself said—"Take away the Bible, and our warfare with oppression, and infidelity, and intemperance, and impurity, and crime, is at an end; our weapons are wrested away, our foundation is removed; we have no authority to speak, and no courage to act." As with the leader, so with his associates. We ourselves heard them all, from childhood up, and we never knew preachers who seemed more familiar with the Book of books, who had its truths and lessons more completely or readily at their command, or who more constantly, aptly, or powerfully applied them to the sins and the sinners of their day. Their appeal was ever to the spirit, the mind, the word, the example of the Christ, as if they knew for a certainty that, once His law of love and life should rule the souls of men, every fetter would break and every slave would be free. And who like themselves, in all the land, when Levites passed by on the other side, were the Good Samaritans to open their houses and hearts to the fugitives as they came, " wet, cold and hungry," or " panting, bleeding, and gory from the hells of the South," and to feed and clothe, and comfort and protect them, and send them safely on to the one sure refuge and rest, defying unjust and infamous law, with all its fines and imprisonments? All over the North were these numberless shelters of the hunted poor and friendless, and they were the homes of the "unbelieving" and "profane" Abolitionists! Had Christ been on the earth in those dark and perilous years, we know what he would have done and where he would have found his own. One of these days some other brilliant Macauley will take pen in hand and write of the Puritans of Puritans, of the old Anti-Slavery times. Meanwhile we may rejoice, indeed, that the source and cause of the nation's woe and humiliation is forever of the past; may still try to assuage the hurt of the people, of whatever race or color ; and while we yet remember the story and gather fresh materials with which to illustrate it and emphasize its lessons, may more and more cultivate friendly and harmonious relations between all sections and classes of a once distracted and endangered. but now free and glorious country, to realize the vision of which so many of the early confessors and martyrs toiled and waited in faith and hope, but died without the sight.

A. P. PUTNAM.

CONCORD, Sept. 6. 1893.

We give here the names of some of the friends who were present at the meeting, so far as we are able to recall them. We would gladly have extended the list. Those who were grouped on the platform are mentioned in connection with the picture, (with the exception of one whom we are unable to identify), with several others who, occupying a front seat in the audience, were caught unawares by the photographer. Others are as follows :—

Hon. Mellen Chamberlain, of Chelsea, Col. Henry Stone, of South Boston, Mr. and Mrs. D. L. Bingham, of Manchester, George F. Allen, of Manchester, Dr. Gaston W. Fowler, of Lynn, Mrs. Viola H. Campbell, of Lynn, Miss Kate L. Campbell, of Lynn, Abbie A. Flint, of Weymouth, Hon. and Mrs. Simeon Dodge, of Marblehead, Mrs. Aaron Porter, of East Alstead, N. H., Joseph G. Brown, of Lynn, Miss Helen Philbrick, of Salem, Miss Eliza Philbrick, of Salem. Mrs. Mary Philbrick Swazey, of Beverly, Climena Philbrick, of W. Somerville, Hon. and Mrs. Abner C. Goodell, of Salem, Emma M. Lander, of Newburyport, Lucian Newhall, of Lynn, Emma D. Newhall, of Lynn, Gilbert L. Streeter, of Salem, William D. Thompson, of Lynn, Lucretia Thompson, of Lynn, Miss Mary H. Stone, of Salem, Miss Caroline S. Rodman, of Wellesley Hills, Lydia M Tenney, William Austin Brown, Joshua G. Dodge, of Arlington, Robert Adams, of Fall River, Mrs. Lydia R. Putnam, of Boston, Miss Mary J. Loring, of Woburn, Dr. Mary L. Richmond, of Boston, Rev. O. S. Butler, of Georgetown, Miss C. D. Fales, of

Boston, Florence M. Atkinson, of Dorchester, Joseph A. Allen, of Medfield, Rosa S. Allen, of Medfield, John Curtis, of Boston, Abby Allen Davis, of W. Newton, S. Elizabeth Yerrinton, of Chelsea, Hon. John I. Baker, of Beverly, Dora Taft Brigham, of Boston, Edward L. Giddings, of Beverly, Charles Woodberry, of Beverly, Wilbur M. Waite, of Lynn, Daniel W. Friend, of Manchester, Julius F. Rabardy, of Manchester, Francis J. Garrison, of Boston, J. Russell May, of Boston, Mrs. Anna H. Weld, of Hyde Park, Louis D. H. Weld, of Hyde Park, Miss Cornelia A. Stickney, of Salem, Mrs. Charles Babcock, of Salem, sister of Charles Lennox Remond, Mrs. Mary O. Stevens, of Peabody, Hon. J. W. Berry, of Lynn, Miss Carrie E. Walton, of Salem, Miss Lucy H. Everett, of Plainfield, N. J., Hon. and Mrs. S. H. Phillips, of Salem, Hon. A. A. Putnam, of Uxbridge, Mrs. Emily P. Reed, and daughter, Miss Anne E. Reed, of Andover, Mrs. John Cutler, of Peabody, Nathan A. Bushby, of Peabody, Jonathan Eveleth, of Beverly, Jonathan Richardson, of Essex, Mrs. W. A. Gorton, of Providence, R. I., Mrs. Hannah Mansfield, of W. Peabody, Mrs. Clara Oliver, of Peabody, Mr. C. C. Alvord, of Philadelphia, now of Danvers, William E. Putnam, of Boston, Miss Margaret R. Putnam, of Concord, Mass., A. J. Archer, of Salem, Mr. E. Kendall Jenkins, of Andover, Mr. Aaron Nourse and daughter, of Salem, Mr. and Mrs. Frederic Porter, of Salem.

Among the friends present belonging to Danvers there were :—

Rev. and Mrs. E. C. Ewing, Hon. Alden P. White, Hon. and Mrs. Augustus Mudge, Mr. and Mrs. Ezra D. Hines, John W. Porter and son John Endicott, Mrs. Sarah P. Fuller, and her daughter Jessie, Miss Sarah W. Mudge, Mrs. Isadora E. Kenney, Miss Katharine E. Hunt, Dr. Warren Porter, Israel H. Putnam, Mrs. Andrew Putnam, Mrs. Ellen M. P. Gould, Mrs. Harriet N. Black, Mrs. Edwin Mudge, Mrs. L. P. Weston, Mrs. Lucretia D. Massey, Mr. and Mrs. J. R. Langley, Mr. and Mrs. Andrew Nichols, Mrs. John T. Ross, Mr. and Mrs. Thomas T. Stone, Mr. and Mrs. J. C. Butler, Mr. and Mrs. Alfred Fellows, Dr. and Mrs. C. W. Page, George Tapley, Miss Mary E. Kenney, Miss Oda

Howe, Miss Margaret Howe, Mrs. Parker B. Francis, Mrs. J. Warren Mead, Mrs. Annie G. Newhall. Miss Caroline B. Faxon, Mrs. Mary W. Putnam, Miss Bessie Putnam, Horace Ross, and daughter Miss Mary T. Ross, Rev. J. W. Hyde, Rev. W. H. Trickey, Rev. Eugene DeNormandie, Mr. and Mrs. Webster Putnam, Mrs. Henry B. Learnard, Miss Alice M. Putnam, Mrs. Joel Kimball, Mrs. Irad Goodale, Mrs. Augustus Proctor, and her sister, Mrs. Mansfield, Mrs. Fanny P. Gray, Mrs. Abby J. Woodman and Miss Mary E. Johnson from "Oak Knoll," Charles H. Preston, Mrs. Clara F. Dubois, Mr. and Mrs. G. A. Tapley, Miss Isabel Tapley, Mr. and Mrs. John A. Putnam, Mrs. Martha P. Perry, Miss Mary B. Putnam, Mrs. Alice Barnard, Miss Lena W. Trask, Mrs. David Mead, Mrs. Nathaniel Batson, Mrs. S. Lizzie Bradstreet, Miss Emilie K. Davis, Mrs. Daniel W. Woodman, Miss Addie Woodman, Miss Hannah P. Cheever, Mrs. Madaline L. Putnam, Mr. and Mrs. John Lummus, Charles H. Masury, Dudley A. Massey, Mr. and Mrs. J. Frank Porter, Miss Azubah Kimball, E. E. Woodman, Mr. and Mrs. Wm. A. Jacobs, Miss Mary A. Bomer, Miss Mary W. Nichols, William S. Nichols, Mrs. Nathan Oakes, Miss Betsey K. Warren, Mrs. Ellen B. Dodge, Miss Abby E. Richards, Miss Alice Richards, and William H. Weston.

Mr. F. E. Moynahan, Editor of the *Dancers Mirror* and representative of the N. E. Associated Press, Mr. Edmund Noble of the *Boston Herald* (whose name is incorrectly given on a subsequent page), Mr. Fred Tebbets of the *Boston Advertiser*, and other journalists, were present, and occupied seats near the platform.

1. Winthrop Andrews.
2. Miss Sarah E. Chase.
3. Rev. Peter Randolph.
4. Rev. D. S. Whitney.
5. George T. Downing.
6. Abner S. Mead.
7. John M. Lennox.
8. Rev. Samuel May.
9. Hon. Parker Pillsbury.
10. William Alley.
11.
12. Rev. George W. Porter, D.D.
13. Mrs. Abby M. Diaz.
14. Cornelius Wellington.
15. J. W. Yerrinton.
16. Miss Caroline Wellington.
17. Miss Mary Willey.
18. Mrs. Martha P. Fowler.
19. David Mead.
20. Hon. M. M. Fischer.
21. George W. Putnam.
22. Miss Lucy Chase.
23. John W. Hutchinson.
24. Rev. A. P. Putnam, D.D., Pres.
25. Rev. William H. Fish.
26. Lewis Ford.
27. Miss Sarah E. Hunt, Sec'y.
28. Mrs. Mehitable Sunderland.
29. Mrs. Lucy Stone.
30. Mrs. Marcia E. P. Hunt.
31. William Lloyd Garrison, Jr.
32. Rev. Aaron Porter.
33. Miss Anne L. Coffin.
34. George B. Bartlett.
35. Henry B. Blackwell.
36. Miss Sarah H. Southwick.
37. Mrs. Evelyn F. Masury.
38. Alfred F. Masury.
39. Mrs. Kate Tannatt Woods.
40. Rev. Samuel J. May.
41. William Lloyd Garrison.
42. Charles Sumner.
43. John G. Whittier.

OLD ANTI-SLAVERY DAYS.

THE MEETING IN TOWN HALL, DANVERS.

[REPORTED FOR THE DANVERS HISTORICAL SOCIETY BY MR. EDWARD NOBLE, AND OTHERS.]

One of the most remarkable meetings, commemorative of old anti-slavery days, ever held in this state or country, took place in the Town Hall in Danvers on the afternoon of Wednesday, April 26, 1893, under the auspices of the Danvers Historical Society. The gathering was a notable one from many points of view. It brought together veteran abolitionists of both sexes, who, on account of their extreme age, could never expect to come together again for a like purpose; it gave an opportunity, not only for a number of bright speeches from men and women who were engaged in the great movement aiming at the freeing of the the slave, but also for the exchange of personal recollections by actors in the stormy scenes that led up to emancipation; it focussed the interest and sympathies of abolitionist workers who, though unavoidably absent, could send letters of good cheer and congratulation to those who were present; and it did the excellent service for the young people, of whom many were seen in the audience, of refreshing their knowledge of a vital episode of the nation's history, and of inspiring them with a new enthusiasm for a great movement in the interest of human rights and universal brotherhood. The proceedings, which lasted from 1 to 6.30 P. M., were also made memorable by the sweet singing of the Hutchinson family, the members of which, led by Mr. John W. Hutchinson, sang a number of emancipation melodies and songs of liberty.

The people began to gather in the morning, and were brought into Danvers by various horse car, electric and steam railroad lines. Besides visitors from Danvers proper, friends came from Salem, Lynn, Boston, Amesbury, Newburyport, and other parts of Massachusetts or New England. On reaching Danvers they were entertained at lunch, served at noon in the rooms of the Danvers Historical Society, in the National Bank building. At 1 o'clock P. M., the commemorative meeting was opened in the Town Hall, the stage of which had been appropriately decorated for the occasion. Along the front of the platform were arranged a rich profusion of flowers and potted plants, and fine portraits of John G. Whittier, William Lloyd Garrison, Charles Sumner, and Rev. Samuel J. May, of Syracuse, N. Y., while the wall at the rear was handsomely adorned with the stars and stripes and other patriotic emblems or devices.

Rev. Alfred P. Putnam, D. D., President of the Danvers Historical Society, occupied the chair, surrounded by prominent abolitionists who were to take active part in the proceedings of the afternoon and by other well-known friends of the anti-slavery movement. The main audience included a large number of men and women from far and near who had long been devoted to the great work of emancipation, and many distinguished citizens besides, of Essex County and neighboring districts.

The opening exercises were somewhat delayed from various causes, chiefly to allow a photographic view to be taken of the group upon the platform by Mr. William T. Clark, of the Soule Photograph Company.

At about two o'clock President Putnam rose and said:

Gathering under such circumstances, friends, it is meet that we should give thanks to God for the great victory of Freedom which we have come together to commemorate, and should invoke his blessing upon this scene. I call upon Rev. William H. Fish, of Dedham, a well known veteran in the cause, to offer prayer.

PRAYER BY REV. WILLIAM H. FISH.

"Oh Thou, who art the unseen and infinite One, we rejoice that Thou art yet always present with us to bless us and guide us in our prosperities and our adversities, in life and death, as we need. Now we come to Thee, thanking Thee, Holy Father, for this bright and beautiful day. We thank Thee for the multitude that have assembled here at the call of this Society, drawn together as we trust by a moral and spiritual attraction. We thank Thee especially for the great and glorious cause, here represented and commemorated. We thank Thee for the great awakening power that it was in its day, for the work that it did, in thine own spirit, and for the many good things that have grown out of it for the welfare of man and woman. Father, we thank Thee for the noble leaders, baptized into the spirit of Christ, who inaugurated this movement and led it on so earnestly and so prosperously. We build monuments to them more durable than marble o: brass in our heart of hearts, and so may it be with all this nation. Though so many of them have gone from us, and vanished out of our sight, we are sure they are not dead. We cannot make them dead by any thought of ours. They believed that they should live on forevermore, and we hold them not only in our grateful memory and our deep and reverent affection, but as living and ministering spirits with us here today. We bless Thee for the reformers of that earlier time who are still in the flesh and are with us now, and who were so faithful in all their walks and ways. And we bless Thee for their children, and their children's children, so many of whom have had the spirit of their fathers and their mothers in their hearts. And we bless Thee, too, for those who consecrated to the service of the slave their gift of song and thus did so much to inspire the people with the love of liberty. And now we commend ourselves to Thee, praying that we who are nearing the eternal world, soon to pass away, may devote ourselves unto the end to whatever is promotive of the welfare of others. May we believe in Thee, because we find Thee in our deeper soul; and being united with Thee as children to a father, and having a calm and sweet confidence in Thee when we come to the close of this mortal life, may each one of us be able to say, "The Lord is my Shepherd, I shall not want. He maketh me to lie down in green pastures, he leadeth me beside the still waters, and though I walk through the valley of the shadow of death, I will fear no evil." And then may we be admitted to a glad and endless reunion with all the dear ones who shall have gone before us, to receive the positions and fulfill the duties which thou wilt assign to us, and so partake of a happiness which eye hath not seen nor ear heard nor heart of man conceived of. And unto Thee the all good and perfect One, in the spirit of Thy son Jesus Christ, we will offer thanksgiving and praise through all our days and in worlds unknown. Amen."

PRESIDENT PUTNAM:—We will now hear a song from the

Hutchinsons, whom we have asked to repeat some of the very words and music that so thrilled the old anti-slavery meetings for so many years, and in so many places at home and abroad. Our venerable friend, Mr. John W. Hutchinson, the sole surviving member of the famous quartet, will, however, first sing a song which he has written specially for this occasion and which he has adapted to a tune of his own. I hope he will preface it with some reminiscences.

Mr. Hutchinson then came forward and made the following remarks, addressed particularly to his former associates, after which he sang "*Few, Faithful and True*," accompanied in the chorus by his daughter, Mrs. Viola Hutchinson Campbell, and his granddaughter, Miss Kate Campbell:—

ADDRESS AND SONG BY MR. JOHN W. HUTCHINSON.

Dear Friends:—This is an impressive occasion and a momentous review. We bid you all a hearty welcome. To the few veterans whose life has dwindled to so short a span, let me say, we congratulate you that one more opportunity is offered that will yield sacred remembrances of joys we have tasted, and of true friendships we have experienced throughout the many years during which we labored in the vineyard of good will to all mankind.

Your joys are full, and our hearts are made glad this day, even though it should chance to be the last. We meet here upon ground sacred to the memory of our ancestors, who, two hundred and fifty years ago, settled and cultivated this soil, deriving title from the aborigines who had so recently vacated their corn fields and hunting grounds. Here seven generations, bearing the name of Hutchinson, have followed in due succession. From this place heroes of that and many another family went forth to the defence of liberty, and were among the bravest at the battles of Lexington and Bunker Hill and in the struggles of the Revolution. We, who have lived since that day of sharp conflicts with the foes of freedom, have rejoiced to hear again the sound of emancipation. And now, in our old age, we assemble with our countrymen here and commemorate the events that established the fact that the nation could live with chattel slavery entirely eliminated, and right made triumphant.

Familiar as household words shall be the names of Garrison, Rogers, Thompson, Phillips, Douglass, Weld, Quincy, Jackson, Burleigh, Sumner, Chase, Wilson, Birney, Brown, Foster, Kelley, May, Pillsbury, Putnam, Mott, Purvis, Chapman, McKim,

Whittier, Abraham Lincoln and Lucy Stone, with the Tribe of Jesse, and full many others.

The scenes and occurrences of anti-slavery days shall, in our social gatherings, be ever remembered. I cannot express, as I would, the sentiments I feel at such a gathering as this. The associations of half a century of experience mingle with these passing hours and fill me with delight, which I can only try to voice in song.

Mr. Hutchinson's spirited verses were sung with wonderful effect, and those who were present and who had heard him forty or fifty years before were kindled by him with the same enthusiasm as then and discovered no loss of his musical genius and electrifying power. We give the closing lines of his poem, as a re-echo of the opening stanzas, omitting the portions that touched more directly upon "The combat fierce, the battle long."

> "So, now, good friends, rejoice with me;
> The promised day we live to see;
> With grateful hearts and strong desire,
> We wait the summons, 'Come up higher!'
> Dear Comrades, faithful, tried, and true,
> Heaven is waiting for such as you,
> Your work on earth is fully done;
> Receive the crown that you have won.
>
> *Chorus*—Rejoice! Rejoice! Rejoice!
> The crown is won."

REMARKS BY THE PRESIDENT.

Ladies and Gentlemen:—As we have been delayed in our proceedings by circumstances with which you are familiar, I shall not long prevent you from listening to other speakers by any words of my own. But I may be permitted to say in behalf of the Danvers Historical Society that I warmly welcome all of you to this commemoration of old anti-slavery days. Especially do we welcome the veterans who are gathered here on the platform or who are mingled in the larger crowd before me,—veterans of many a well-fought battle, all or most of whom at the very outset dedicated themselves to the sacred cause of liberty and continued in the fight until the very end, subjected to persecution, to outrage, to wrong, yet faithful ever to the principles of truth and justice. We would fain do them special honor here and now, and thank them from our very hearts, for the service which they have rendered, for the example which they have set, for the influence which they have exerted, for all that they have done for our beloved country, and for the world at large. You have taught us, dear friends (the speaker looking around the platform), how to stand for the right, to stand for it consistently and uncompromisingly, and having done all, to *stand*. We are all of us the better, we trust, for what you have been, for what you have said, for the lives that you have lived. The blessing of them that were ready to perish is upon you, with the growing benedictions of a grateful people. Thinned and wasted are your ranks, and old age is with most of you, yet we rejoice to know that you are all still young and strong in thought and spirit, and love and faith. God grant that the time may yet be distant, when you shall go hence as have gone so many of your comrades in the memorable conflict. But be that day sooner or later, we are most happy to have you here, and hope to hear something from you of the immortal story. For better or worse, we have arranged for a single session only, and what with so many addresses that are to be delivered, so many letters to be read, and so many songs to be sung, each speaker is expected to be brief. We would gladly hear everyone at great length, but the hours fly fast and the committee have thought that the audience would prefer to hear numerous short speeches rather than a few very long ones, and they have made out the programme accordingly. I have the pleasure now of introducing to you a distinguished son of an illustrious father—a father who was foremost to enter upon the great warfare, to fling the gauntlet down at the feet of the slave power and breast the storm of hatred and abuse which he encountered—a son who worthily bears his name, and inherits his blood, and perpetuates his interest in every good and holy cause—William Lloyd Garrison. [Great applause.]

ADDRESS BY MR. WILLIAM LLOYD GARRISON.

I was invited by your President to speak, in the few minutes allowed me, upon the early anti-slavery life of my father. I could add little if any to the record of his authentic biography, and therefore elect to treat of a phase of the great movement still confused and generally misunderstood because of surviving prejudices and of personal antagonisms unforgotten or inherited.

To one baptized in the early spirit of the cause, and born into the circle of uncompromising abolition, nothing is more marked in the current attempts to write history than the utter failure of historians to grasp the secret of the anti-slavery reform, or to appreciate the undeviating policy of its leader. The distance is not yet great enough to allow the proper perspective, and the temper of the times is so swayed by the gospel of expediency that we must wait for the just recognition which is sure to come with the nation's ultimate moral regeneration. What Lowell has written of Lincoln is equally applicable to the pioneer of the anti-slavery cause:

> "I praise him not: it were too late;
> And some innative weakness there must be
> In him who condescends to victory
> Such as the Present gives, and cannot wait,
> Safe in himself as in a fate.
> So always firmly he;
> He knew to bide his time,
> And can his fame abide,
> Still patient in his simple faith sublime,
> 'Till the wise years decide."

But now, when a sacred treaty with a friendly nation, which recognizes "the inherent and inalienable rights of man to change his home and allegiance . . . from one country to another, for the purposes of curiosity, of trade, or as permanent residents," is basely broken,—when the days of the Fugitive Slave Law are reappearing with the Chinese for victims,—when the attempt to steal Hawaii recalls the fillibustering efforts to seize Cuba,—when a secret star-chamber treaty with Russia permits the Czar to drag back to death or exile the accused political refugees who naturally sought safety in the land of Washington and Lincoln,—when the injustice to the Indian and the southern negro is still condoned,—at such a time, what wonder that the popular estimate of the Garrisonian abolitionists is false and misleading!

Pick up the attempted histories which have been written since the civil war, bearing upon the causes and the struggles which led to the downfall of slavery, and read the authors' characterization of those impracticable men and women who contended for "immediate and unconditional emancipation" and demanded that the "covenant with Death and the agreement with Hell" be annulled. You gather from the portrayal that they were excellent and well-meaning but fanatical people, given to harsh language and using methods subsequently shown to be mistaken. That by their ultimate action in sustaining the Union, as against the South, they confessed the error of their early contention, and must therefore be considered less clear of vision than the statesmen of the Republican party. That, while they were of service in creating a moral sentiment against slavery, they must have been an uncomfortable lot to associate with, and the fact that society ignored them is sufficient evidence to that effect. In short, they were a necessary if disagreeable element in the great revolution, and cannot therefore be left out of the history, although it is frequently feasible to compress them into a few lines. Some "captain with his gun," who, but for these fanatics, would have slept in oblivion, commands more pages.

I shall aim to show with a forced conciseness, far too inadequate, that the very weakness alleged against the abolitionists was their tower of strength; that their direct language was their most effective virtue, that their refusal to take part in political organizations vindicates their claim to the highest statesmanship; that their unbending adherence to absolute principle made them more formidable than an army with banners; and, finally, that the "covenant with Death and the agreement with Hell" was annulled with the destruction of the old Union, leaving no barrier to their acceptance of the new.

In the initial day of anti-slavery, as at present, he who announced the moral law and proclaimed its constant and inevitable working, was forced to confront criticism and credulity and to see himself held in contempt by the so-called practical party-workers. Herbert Spencer, in his earlier and better day, has admirably characterized "people who hate anything in the way of exact conclusions," to whom "right is never in either extreme, but always half way between the extremes," who are continually trying to reconcile Yes and No; who have great faith in the "judicious mean," and who " would scarcely believe an oracle if it uttered a full-length principle." "Were you to inquire of them," he says, " whether the earth turns on its axis from east to west or from west to east, you might almost expect the reply.— 'A little of both,' or ' Not exactly either.' " And the wise philosopher bids us recollect "that ethical truth is as exact and as peremptory as physical truth," that " there can be no half-and-half opinions," and that in the nature of things " the fact must be either one way or the other."

Long before Spencer formulated this axiom it was apprehended and acted upon by Garrison. To his moral nature the question of obedience to the law could never arise, and, to his eyes, disobedience was fraught with danger and punishment. To affirm that slavery was wrong, was to him equivalent to saying that it must be abolished at once. "At once!" exclaims the startled expedientist. "Think of the danger and disturbance to follow!" The calm reformer replied, " Wrong can never be too quickly righted. The longer it prevails, the more terrible the judgment." No efforts to shake his position prevailed. On matters of mere opinion or expediency, no one was more accommodating than he, but on principle he stood like Gibraltar. So he was ever a landmark to steer by. Political promontories suffer geographical changes. What chart could locate a Webster permanent enough to prevent the shipwreck of mariners reckoning on his stability? Who can measure the drift from his Plymouth Rock speech to that of the 7th of March?

So the primal wisdom of Garrison was fidelity to an eternal principle. It angered men and parties who were incommoded by such stubbornness. Hence the charge of his unreasoning persistency. Well did Lowell understand it.

> "Men of a thousand shifts and wiles, look here!
> See one straightforward conscience put in pawn
> To win a world; see the obedient sphere
> By bravery's simple gravitation drawn."

Clear-sightedness controlled the reformer when he declined to trust either himself or his cause to a political party. It brought upon his head the angry denunciation whose echoes are not yet stilled.

It was natural for the Athenians to be weary of hearing Aristides called "the Just." While he stood as the recognized type of justice, the selfish and the unjust felt keenly their conscious disadvantage. If the standard-bearer of morality would not hold his emblem quite so steadily aloft, but would lower it now and then to accommodate certain circumstances or conditions, he would be less impracticable in the popular regard. Doubtless he was reminded, as all reformers are, that "the ideal is all very well, but that we must take things as we find them," and that "theory is one thing and practice is another."

Garrison never confused the functions of the reformer with those of the politician. One must keep himself in the clear atmosphere of abstract truth, the other must mingle in the strife of personal ambitions. As Theodore Parker well stated it, "In morals as in mathematics, a straight line is the shortest distance between two points." The course of the Garrisonian abolitionists was without deflection, and for the very reason that they had no elections to carry, no conservatives to placate, no fear of results. Results! A reformer who concerns himself with results loses his vision and his strength. "That is the business of Jupiter," not his. His to see and proclaim principles which, from their nature, can be trusted in their operation.

I remember once expressing regret to my father that he should differ with several of his anti-slavery friends on a certain question, and suggesting reconsideration in consequence. His reply was in effect, "If one would preserve his moral vision there are matters in which he should never consult with flesh and blood. The question is with his own soul, and to inquire how such or such a one thinks before deciding on his course is to lose discernment and to invite confusion. What matter if all the world differ?" That such an attitude should provoke expedientists is inevitable.

The course of the anti-slavery political parties was of necessity sinuous. Think of the crooks and turns of the party which, starting with James G. Birney for its presidential candidate, ended with Martin Van Buren! And, up to the time of the civil war,—brought about by the "irrepressible conflict" which the abolitionists ever preached,—its final candidate was blind enough to think that he might save the Union without destroying slavery. Fortunate was it for the reputation of Mr. Lincoln that his desire was overruled by omnipotence and his immortality ensured by the circumstances he would fain have prevented.

The future historian will have for a most pregnant chapter the no-union position of the abolitionists. As a moralist he will be bound to recognize that for them to take an oath supporting a pro-slavery constitution, which political action necessitated, would have stultified their conscience and impaired their powerful influence. To denounce slavery and then to agree to a constitutional compact recognizing it and consenting to its immoral compromises would have been an ethical paradox. The abolitionists attempted no casuistry to justify political action.

The old Union was dissolved by the shot fired at Sumter. To call States united, whereof half were busily engaged in slaughtering the other half, was to indulge in fiction. No dissolution could have been more decided. Conquest does not make a union. Poland in chains did not mean union with Russia. When "peace reigns in Warsaw," we know what kind of peace it is. A subjugated South was a nation tied by compulsion to the North, nor was the union restored at Appomattox. The uncompleted process has taken more than a quarter of a century and still goes on, but with slavery eliminated happily no obstacle exists to prevent the ultimate unity for which we so much long. History will yet recognize that the abolition cry for dissolution was the cry of conscience as well as of prophecy.

Let me illustrate the political anti-slavery creed that is vaunted as the practical and effective weapon which emancipated the slave. Listen to Richard H. Dana. In 1848 he declared that he was a Free Soiler by inheritance and because he disliked subserviency to the slave-holding oligarchy, adding, "A technical Abolitionist I am not. I am a constitutionalist, and in favor of adhering honestly to the compromises of that instrument. If I were in Congress, and the South should come with clean hands, keeping faithfully her side of the compact, and demand of us a fugitive slave law, I should feel bound to give her one." How long would it take such a propaganda to arouse a sleeping nation? The answer is "Until Doomsday." Slavery never trembled before such a platform as that upon which Lincoln was nominated. How it reads in the light of events! "The maintenance inviolate of the rights of the States, and especially the right of each State to order and control its own domestic institutions [slavery included] according to its own judgment exclusively, is essential to that balance of powers on which the perfection and endurance of our political fabric depends." What a trifling with conscience! What a contempt for the higher law! And according to current history it was such men and such party as this that abolished slavery!

How short are memories! Because in the storm and stress of civil war, and for self-preservation, the party of compromise and disbelief in abstract right were forced by military necessity alone to issue the edict of emancipation, to them is awarded the honor and the glory. Unwilling instruments, they forget the hand that used them for the mighty purpose. Ever ready to overlook the rights of the slave, so that an election might be carried or an office won, it is the partisans of such expediency who would belittle the pioneers. In the firmament of the century the telescope of real history will reveal clearly the fixed stars of abolition, and their names will be an encouragement to the idealists and a discouragement to the time-servers.

The calm verdict yet to be rendered will come at length from the race which was the victim of American Christianity. It will weigh carefully the men and the events connected with the freedom of four million slaves. Think you that it will find the language of the abolitionists harsh? That it will blame them for declining political affiliations which demanded a prolongation of the sum of all villainies? Will not the jury rather be inclined to consider the language far too inadequate to meet the situation? As for him who stood as the incarnate foe of oppression, advocating it with such fervor and feeling that men who had never seen him took it for granted that he was black, will the reflection of the jurors be, "Alas, that he was so impracticable! He might have been a member of Congress or the holder of a fat office, but he threw away his great chance because he was so impracticable that he could not forget them that are in bonds as bound with them."

At this stage of the meeting the Secretary, Miss Hunt, read eloquent letters addressed to the President for the occasion, from Hon. Frederick Douglass, Mr. Theodore D. Weld, Rev. William H. Furness, D. D., Miss Mary Grew and Rev. Joseph May, son of Rev. Samuel J. May, of Syracuse. Dr. Putnam spoke of the earnest and faithful devotion of these conspicuous anti-slavery champions, and, as Philadelphia, where several of them had long lived and served, was one of the most influential centres of Abolitionism by reason of their work and influence, he proposed that the following message should at once be forwarded to them and their co-laborers in that city:

"DANVERS, MASS., April 26, 1893.

The Danvers Historical Society and other friends of Liberty, now assembled here in commemoration of old Anti-Slavery days, greet with grateful affection and honor Mary Grew, Rosanna Thompson, William Henry Furness, Robert Purvis and their Philadelphia associates in the cause of emancipation."

The message was greeted with loud applause by the audience, and having been heartily and unanimously adopted, was sent by telegraph.

PRESIDENT PUTNAM: I have now the great pleasure of introducing to you, as the next speaker, one of the original and life-long co-workers with Mr. Garrison, one of the truest and best of the great Reformer's friends and helpers, who is widely known for his indefatigable zeal in philanthropic and Christian service, and who has given added lustre to a name which many others have made dear to lovers of God and man—the Rev. Samuel May, of Leicester.

Mr. May had a very warm reception as he rose to speak, and his words commanded the close attention and entire sympathy of his hearers.

ADDRESS OF REV. SAMUEL MAY.

The speaker said he should restrict himself to the allowed ten minutes. He thanked Mr. Garrison for the fine anecdote of his father, and said it reminded him of one of Wendell Phillips which he thought worthy to go with it. He had been similarly urged by a friend to moderate the severity of his speech: "You are hindering your work, Mr. Phillips; you will never abolish slavery in this way." "My dear sir," was the reply, "God did not send me into the world to abolish slavery, but to do my duty." [The further remarks of Mr. May are in the more extended form which he had prepared for the occasion.]

No more appropriate place than the County of Essex, for

holding a meeting to commemorate the overthrow of slavery, could be found. It was the birthplace, within a few years of each other, within a few miles of each other, of William Lloyd Garrison and of John Greenleaf Whittier.—two men who may be said to have created the movement, which led directly to the Abolition of Slavery in this land. There were abolitionists before their day; faithful souls who carried the burden of the slave's wrongs in their hearts 'all their lives; but they scarcely knew each other; and there was no concerted action among them. It was in every case an individual protest and a disregarded warning. Benjamin Lundy went on foot from state to state, from house to house, telling the shameful story; striving to awaken conscience and feeling; printing an edition of his paper now here, now there, and mailing it when printed to his few subscribers, and such others as his means allowed. Edwin M. Stanton, President Lincoln's able and fearless War Secretary, told me in his own office, just after the close of the War of the Rebellion, that Mr. Lundy was accustomed to make periodical visits to his father's house, in Ohio :—the wrongs of slavery his constant theme. That Woolman, Benezet, Franklin, Rush, Edwards, Lundy and others, prepared the ground and sowed good seed cannot be doubted. But the conscience of the nation seemed paralyzed. Its young people were hearing the fatal doctrines of slavery's constitutional rights from Calhoun and McDuffie, of expediency and compromise from Henry Clay and Edward Everett, from bishops and priests, from political editors and from theological seminaries. The noble words which Daniel Webster spoke at Plymouth Rock, in 1820, against the still active slave trade failed to arouse the American heart ; and he soon forgot them himself. Abject acquiescence with the slaveholding demands was everywhere. There was no open vision. There was no prophetic word.

But that word was to be uttered: and it came from a son of Essex County, Massachusetts. It said :—"I have determined at every hazard to lift up the standard of emancipation in the eyes of the nation, within sight of Bunker Hill and in the birthplace of liberty. * * I shall strenuously contend for the immediate enfranchisement of our slave population. * * * I am in earnest. I will not equivocate. I will not excuse. I will not retreat a single inch, and I will be heard." Thus did William Lloyd Garrison throw down the gauntlet, January 1st, 1831. That he took his life in his hand, we have all heard—some of us remember. The great command was on him. "Thou shalt speak my word to them, whether they will hear or whether they will forbear."

But it was the voice of one crying in the wilderness. Some listened and came by night, to inquire ; and a few joined openly. Twelve men gathered in a room in Boston, in 1832, and formed The New England Anti-Slavery Society. A Southern legislature in November, 1831, proclaimed a reward of five thousand dollars for the head of the Liberator, William Lloyd Garrison. Herod sought the young life to destroy it; and, as Whittier wrote, Pilate and Herod were made friends to accomplish it. Those who ventured to speak were assaulted, subjected to abuse and injury, cast into prison, their houses and halls burnt to the ground, not a few put to death. The rulers and all who sought to be such, conspired against them. Some, who ran well for a time, were bye and bye offended; forsook the cause and fled; and some betrayed it, to escape martyrdom themselves. It was among the plain people, the common people, that the call of Freedom was heard gladly by publicans and sinners, in the absence of saints, by a few Rabbis and lawyers, with now and then a man of learning, genius and eloquence. Sometimes one came who brought his wealth to Freedom's service. The mighty and the wise, with rarest exceptions, stood aloof or were hostile. It was the experience of all time. As Lowell wrote :

"Right forever on the scaffold, Wrong forever on the throne;"
But he added,
"Yet that scaffold sways the future, and, behind the dim unknown,
Standeth God within the shadow, keeping watch above his own."

It was the story again of the giant Goliah and the stripling with only a sling and a few smooth stones from the brook.

Every great effort for freedom and for truth discloses agencies, if invisible, yet mighty to the pulling down of Iniquity's strongholds. Fighting against God, no matter who or what the men, is a bad business and a losing one. The abolitionists said from the first, that "God himself was with them for their Captain."

But when will the victory come? "Not in our day," was, for long years, the prevailing answer. "There are two thousand millions of dollars invested in slavery, and it is in vain to assail it," said Henry Clay. That was American statesmanship then. The very power of slavery proved its destruction. Its arrogance led it to raise its hand against the nation. That act invited its doom. "Whom the Gods will destroy, they first make mad."

Our fathers of New England often spoke of the "Wonderworking Providence" which led them better than their own wisdom could devise. Could there ever be a more wonderful proof of a Power greater than man's, making for righteousness, than was evinced in the downfall of the great Babylon of American slavery? Yet it was no miracle. For thirty years the seed-wheat of God's mightiest truths had been sown fearlessly and in faith all over the northern lands. And when slavery, in its wrath and folly, lifted its murderous hand, it found a generation of men different from those who had bowed in servility so long. None the less was it felt that ~~that~~ it was with a mighty hand and a stretched-out arm that God brought his people out of the land of bondage; it was the almightiness of Truth and Eternal Right that had conquered.

Shall I say a word of my own connection with the Anti-Slavery movement? I was not of the earliest abolitionists. The first number of *The Liberator* was published on the first day of January, 1831. It was not until 1833, and the reading of Mrs. Lydia Maria Child's book, "An Appeal in favor of that class of Americans called Africans," that I found myself unable to be anything but an abolitionist. After my ministry, at Leicester, of twelve years, in which I had tried to treat the Anti-Slavery cause as an integral part of my Christian ministerial duty, I became, in 1847, General Agent of the Massachusetts Anti-Slavery Society and held the office to the end of the Civil War.

[margin: 1834-46]

You will be interested to hear of those who were then doing the anti-slavery work: men and women, whom the older portion of the audience have seen and heard. They were Abby Kelley, afterwards Mrs. Foster, Stephen S. Foster, Charles C. and Cyrus M. Burleigh, Parker Pillsbury (vigorous yet and with us today), Susan B. Anthony, Lucy Stone (with us today), Sallie Holley, Charles L. Remond, Wm. Wells Brown, Andrew T. Foss, Daniel S. Whitney (with us today); and later, Anna Dickinson, John L. Russell, George W. Putnam (who will bye and bye address you), E. H. Heywood and many more. Nor these alone. The cause had a reserve fund of unequalled power, who freely gave it [margin: men] time and labor of a value beyond price:—Mr. Garrison himself, Wendell Phillips, Edmund Quincy, James N. Buffum, Henry C. Wright, Edwin Thompson and others. Brave and truly Christian ministers, Theodore Parker, James Freeman Clarke, Adin Ballou, Thomas T. Stone, Jacob M. Manning, O. B. Frothingham, Samuel Johnson, Samuel Longfellow, were generous in answering calls upon their time. At the first open-air meeting of the Society which I attended,— it was at Waltham, July 4, 1847—James Russell Lowell was present. I asked him to "say a word" to the meeting; but he said "Oh, I cannot; I never said a word in my life." He *said* so many good words later; he had already *written* so many good ones; that his silence then was easily excused.

Let me name, too, those who were then officers and managers of the Massachusetts Anti-Slavery Society; not public speakers, but inspirers of those who were; the organizers, the clear-headed, stout-hearted, fearless men and women, quite as essential, quite as helpful, to the cause as any who have been named. First of them I speak of Francis Jackson, President of the Society, to whose house the Boston Female Anti-Slavery Society was invited, when driven by the mob of October, 1835, from their own rooms at 46 Washington street; Mrs. Maria W. Chapman, Mrs. Eliza Lee Follen, Miss Anne W. Weston, Dr. Henry I. Bowditch, James R. Lowell, John Rogers, Cornelius Bramhall, Charles K. Whipple, John M. Spear. Samuel Philbrick was Treasurer, Robert F. Wallcut, Secretary, Edmund Quincy, Corresponding Secretary. These, with Messrs. Garrison and Phillips, then constituted the Board of Managers. Of the twenty-six Vice Presidents, only three survive, Rev. Thomas T. Stone, now of Bolton, Joshua T. Everett and Wm. Bowman Stone. From the very first, and throughout, Ellis Gray Loring and Samuel E. Sewall were devoted friends and helpers.

It was at a later time that Theodore D. Weld came to Massachusetts, his health so impaired by his work in the Western and Middle states, that he has but seldom spoken here in public. In the earlier days of the Society, its principal agents had been Arnold Buffum, Samuel Joseph May, Frederick Douglass, John A. Collins and Loring Moody.

Ralph Waldo Emerson was at first critical of the Anti-Slavery societies. But that ceased, as the Fugitive Slave Law and the Civil War came on. He had previously given the principal address before a First of August meeting of the Society, held at Worcester on the hill where the State Normal School stands now. The address was printed in pamphlet form. We must recall today his well-known witticism, "Eloquence is dog-cheap in the Anti-Slavery meetings." Parker Pillsbury can tell you, better than I, of the help which that other Concord sage, Henry D. Thoreau, gave to the cause of freedom.

The cause had its poets. Who can fitly tell the service rendered to the cause of freedom by Mr. Whittier and Mr. Lowell? Thousands of tongues and pens have recently joined in doing honor to them both,—and yet there is room. Unending blessings, from all true hearts, will ever wait on their memories. Others there were, and among the earliest and bravest was John Pierpont, of Hollis street church, Boston.

The anti-slavery movement was an emancipating one, in another sense. It emancipated *its advocates* from the bondage of sect, the bondage of party, the bondage of creed. It brought together people whom the sects and parties had kept asunder and kept estranged, and made them brothers. It was a great reconciling power. It set free men's souls.

Then witness its high religious function and force. Never, in America, had practical christianity been so taught and so exemplified. No one who had heard its speakers, no one who had ever read its poets and scholars, can question this. At one of its great open-air meetings (at Abington, in Plymouth Co.) James Freeman Clarke said, "I find here in the anti-slavery meeting a church of Christ, a church in deed and truth."

Thirty years nearly have elapsed since the overthrow and downfall of slavery in these United States. But it is yet too early for that complete history of the movement, made up of many parts, which this meeting was called to commemorate. A full and reliable history, the most so of any now existing, is the memoir of Mr. Garrison by his sons. Its bulk has probably stood in the way of its being extensively read, but that is not objectionable to the thorough and conscientious student; nor will it ever cause regret to any one who takes it in hand in a truth-loving spirit.

We meet today in no boastful spirit. We rejoice, with exceeding great joy, in the triumph of right over wrong. Our only personal feeling is that of thankfulness that we had a part, however small, in lifting our country from the guilt and shame of slavery. As Mr. Garrison always said, so would we all say, "Not unto us, not unto us, but unto Thy name give glory, for Thy mercy and for Thy truth's sake."

PRESIDENT PUTNAM :—One of the early and most powerful agencies for forwarding the anti-slavery movement, was, of course, the old Liberty Party. It was the first of the great political organizations that were found necessary to carry into effect the essential truths and principles which had begun to take hold of the mind and heart of the people. It did a noble work in its time, and we have the good fortune to be favored with the presence with us today, of one of its most highly esteemed and useful representatives. He, too, is full of years and honors. He has told me that he has written what he has to say, and that, should his strength fail him before the allotted time has expired, he will pass his manuscript over to his grandson, Mr. Willis R. Fisher, who is with him. As we hope to publish all these speeches in pamphlet form, we shall expect to have the benefit of our friend's words in full, in one way if we cannot in another. Hon. M. M. Fisher of Medway will now address you.

(Mr. Fisher, having read a few pages of his manuscript, handed it to his grandson, who occupied the remainder of the ten minutes. The entire paper is herewith presented.)

ADDRESS OF HON. M. M. FISHER.

MR. PRESIDENT AND FRIENDS:—An old man is not much if not reminiscent. He either never knew much or has forgotten what he once knew. A very common soldier in the Anti-Slavery War of thirty-five years, from 1831 to 1865, must have had *some experience*; whether he can relate it so as to be agreeable to himself or to others is quite a different matter.

A few months before the death of our dear mutual friend Whittier I visited him at Newburyport. I read to him an extract of some twenty lines of equal measure from a poem, so called, written for and delivered in public on a graduation day of a High School in Medway in 1831. This was the time of my enlistment in the old conflict, and *he* said they were good.

On my seventy-seventh birthday he wrote me as follows:—' "As one of the Old Guard in the Anti-Slavery War I know well thy works of courage and devotion in the dark days of the great conflict." In this community where I am a stranger, and he so well known, I am quite willing, even proud, that such a friend should speak for me. Of these "works" doubtless he would refer you to the beginning of the slavery discussion in Amherst College, 1833, which ended in victory for free speech to the credit of the elder professor Hitchcock. He might speak of the opening of a colored school in that town and the incident of a young man who, on April 23d, 1834, sixty years ago save one, in a private carriage made a southern trip for his health, making a delightful call upon the Rev. Samuel J. May at Brooklyn, Connecticut, who received him with marked courtesy; and who would have also called upon Mr. Garrison and his new bride at Father "Benson's," only they had just left for New York and elsewhere—and who, at Mr. May's earnest request, rode over to Canterbury to visit Prudence Crandall and her colored girls' school, and who gave them as they needed a word of cheer. Then as he passed on to the first anniversary meeting of the American Anti-Slavery Society in New York and its thrilling incidents as published in the "Commonwealth" of Boston in 1885— going south to other meetings in Philadelphia, and then travelling through the slave states of Delaware, Maryland, District of Columbia, into Virginia and as a colporter distributing Phelps' Book on Slavery and other similar literature, conversing with slaves by the way and in their homes at Mount Vernon, learning their condition and giving them encouragement and hope in their grief over the recent sale of their children to the rice swamps and cotton fields of the far south, and also visiting the great slave pen of William Roby in Washington and hearing the tales of shame and grief from one to whom they were a daily and nightly experience. Again, he could refer to the first introduction, ten years later, of the slavery question into the great Missionary Board at Worcester, and to its final outcome in the withdrawal of many members and friends, resulting in the formation of the American Missionary Association in 1847, now so prosperous in the southern field in educational and missionary work; all of which may be found in the Boston Traveller of December 15, 1884.

These and other events with their many incidents in detail known to our friend Whittier, I suppose were the "works of courage and devotion" to which he referred in his very courteous letter he was pleased to send the writer on his seventy-seventh birthday.

But with due apology for so much by way of introduction, I must proceed to the second epoch assigned more especially to me, in the anti-slavery conflict—the organization and work of the Old Liberal Party, "all of which I saw and a small part of which I was."

The Liberty Party.

Mr. President:—As ideas precede action, so a sentiment of opposition to American slavery preceded all direct action for its abolition. This sentiment preceded and dominated the soul of Garrison before his spoken and written words, and like a voice from heaven kindled a like sentiment in the soul of many others. So ideas, voices and pens, in their natural order, preceded ballots and bullets in the great contest for the freedom of the slave. Early in the moral agitation and educational work by Garrison and Whittier, Channing and Phelps, Pierpont and Leavitt, Mrs. Childs and others, it was seen and admitted by discerning men, politicians, statesmen and common people, that before the slave could be free, the civil, if not the military power, must be evoked in his behalf. When and how to begin this necessary work was the supreme question. I well remember Henry Wilson in 1840 or a little later, with the true spirit of hatred to slavery in his soul, told me he could not vote for a slave-holder for President, but in 1844 he voted for Henry Clay, and as he wrote me he was better than Polk and favored gradual emancipation.

During the first ten years (from 1831 to 1840) of the moral agitation of the question, few slaveholders had been so convinced by the force of argument against slavery as to emancipate their slaves. Among the few James G. Birney, a prominent Christian lawyer in Huntsville, Alabama, was a conspicuous example.

Previous to this time candidates of the old political parties were solicited by letter to declare their position upon this question and received votes of anti-slavery men according to their answers.

The original platform of the National Anti-Slavery Society formed in December, 1833, was perhaps wisely reticent as to the necessity or use of the civil power in the prosecution of a work destined to shake the nation to its very centre. Relying upon the supreme justice of their cause, the intelligence and conscience of the American people, the united voice of the platform, the pulpit and the press, they hoped the great reform would be accomplished.

When concerted action in the use of the ballot by a new political party was suggested by some of its prominent members, there was unfortunately a large division of opinion. Complicated with other social questions, such as non-voting in politics, secession from churches, admitting women to the platform and the pulpit, questions new and unsettled in the social order, it seemed for a time to the conservatives that the very foundations of society were being or likely to be subverted. Amid such throes and convulsions the Liberty Party was born. It was soon found that the new abolition societies and the resultant Liberty Party for concerted political action were as earnest and potent forces against slavery as any agency which simply made moral and educational forces a specialty, and that both combined working in their chosen way would ultimately secure the desired result.

Though the struggle between the old and new order of things for a time was a little sharp, "when the new wine was put into new bottles both were preserved."

The birth of the Liberty Party occurred in 1840, on the eve of the most intense Presidential election of modern times, resulting in the election of William Henry Harrison by an overwhelming electoral majority. Only men of the most stalwart convictions on the slavery question could stem the tide that set so strongly toward the candidates of their old affiliations. Great inducements were personally given to anti-slavery men supposed to be at all ambitious for political favor to vote with the old parties just this once more, and next year their calling and election in the old parties would be sure. But with a few men the die was cast and under the banner of the Liberty Party they went to the polls and cast their votes for James G. Birney and for the doom of American slavery. A ticket for Presidential electors, state officials and members of Congress, was voted, I think, in ten, at least, of the free states. In my own town, seventeen votes only were cast for it and Medway was the banner town of Norfolk County. In the whole state there were only 1081 votes, and in all the states there were found "seven thousand who had not bowed the knee to Baal," a small vote to be sure, but significant. In 1844 the vote in Massachusetts went up by successive steps to 9635, a tenfold increase in five years, and to 60,000 in all the states. The smallness of the vote in 1840 was a disappointment, of course, and a subject for ridicule in the old party newspapers, and the prophecies of a short life and ignoble death were expected to procure their own fulfilment.

But such men as Hon. William Jackson of Newton, Samuel E. Sewall of Roxbury and Gen. Appleton Howe of Weymouth and men of their stamp, were made of sterner stuff than to have "put their hands to the plough to look back," and they pressed on under their chosen banner to victory.

During the next few years the anti-slavery sentiment pervaded the old parties; the churches and religious organizations began to crystallize into more emphatic forms of protest against the slave power. Salmon P. Chase in 1841 and later ex-Governor Morris, both of Ohio, and John P. Hale of New Hampshire, Governor Slade of Vermont following soon after, allied themselves to the fortunes of the rising young party. The Wilmot Proviso Democrats, and the Conscience Whigs, under the lead of Charles Francis Adams and Henry Wilson, stimulated the older parties to take higher ground against the domination of the slaveholding oligarchy.

It needed a party exigency of some magnitude to disrupt the party ties that began to menace a large depletion to both and a sure defeat to one at least of the old parties. This exigency came in the National Democratic Convention in 1848 that nominated Gen. Cass for President and in the Whig Convention that nominated Gen. Taylor,—a nomination that Mr. Webster said "was not fit to be made."

In this chaos of the old parties the wise men of the Liberty Party were not mere spectators. They saw in it the leaven of the truth hidden by Garrison and later workers in the cause, suddenly expanding the lump in unwonted proportions.

Mass meetings were at once called in all the free states. In June of that year, at least 5000 people assembled upon the Common in Worcester. The venerable and Hon. Samuel Hoar and his son, the ex-Judge, then a young man, Judge Allen and many others, were heard with intense satisfaction. A platform of principles was formed by a committee, Stephen C. Phillips, Chairman, of which Judge Hoar and myself are the only living members. The result of these meetings was the call for a national convention at Buffalo, Aug. 10, 1848, to nominate candidates for President and Vice-President for the Party of Liberty under a new name, The Free Soil Party, at that time especially appropriate as the slave power, was seeking the virgin soil of vast territories for its extension and perpetuity. The delegates to this convention were three from each county, one from each of the existing parties. It was the writer's privilege to be a delegate for Norfolk County with Charles Francis Adams and William J. Reynolds to this convention, over which Salmon P. Chase of Ohio from the Liberty Party was called to preside, while Charles Francis Adams from the Conscience Whigs presided over a mass meeting of many thousands. On a street in Buffalo I witnessed a scene I shall never forget. In the early morning a steamer from Cleveland had just arrived and hundreds of stalwart voters from the old "Western Reserve" in Ohio were thronging the street to the convention, and whom should they meet as they came up a cross street but Joshua Giddings, that war horse of Liberty and their old neighbor, with carpet-bag in hand, just arriving from the stormy scenes, as their Representative in Congress at Washington. Such a rush to grasp his hand in theirs fairly blocked up the street until he beckoned them to an open space where the multitude greeted him to their heart's content.

These conventions without doubt drew together the largest and most intelligent and earnest body of American freemen that ever assembled to protest against the domination and perpetuity of the slave power in this great republic.

The Convention of delegates cast 466 votes and Martin Van Buren received a majority of twenty-two and John P. Hale 181, with many scattering votes. The result was much regretted by the "Conscience Whigs," as they hoped to succeed in the nomination of Judge McLean of Ohio, but he sent a letter of declination on the morning of the Convention. Mr. Hale was exceedingly popular with the Liberal Party delegates and had been nominated in a previous convention of the party. But as a satisfactory platform was unanimously adopted and positive assurance given that Mr. Van Buren fully subscribed to it, the nomination was accepted with the full consent of Mr. Hale. Some old Liberty men with long memories and some prejudice feared that the cause in which they had labored at great cost was paralyzed, if not indeed "a lost cause." The leaders from the old parties first gave their adhesion to the nomination. David Dudley Field, a young and strong "Barnburner," from New York, now living, waxed eloquent over the nomination, beginning with a quotation from Richard The Third :—

> " Now is the winter of our discontent
> Made glorious summer by this Son of York :
> And all the clouds that lowered upon our house
> In the deep bosom of the ocean buried."

Stephen C. Phillips, I think, spoke for the "Conscience Whigs." Then a pause and silence was indeed expressive, until Dr. Leavitt, in behalf of the Liberty Party, rose to speak. He was a man of stalwart form, dignity of manner and speech. All eyes and ears were attentive. He referred to the cost and sacrifice made to sustain the Party of Liberty for eight years, to the devotion it had for its principles, and to John P. Hale their chosen standard bearer, and then in tone of lofty exultation and voice of thunder he exclaimed, "*The Liberty Party is not dead but translated.*" Such cheers and shouts as came from all parts of the hall when the Old Liberty Guard surrendered their name and their candidate for the *cause* were not surpassed by any of the memorable and thrilling incidents connected with this great body of earnest and devoted men.

After the nomination of Van Buren, Charles Francis Adams was nominated for Vice-President with great unanimity and enthusiasm. The old party (now but a memory) under its new name made great progress in some of the states. In 1848 sixty Free Soil Representatives were elected to our State Legislature. Two of your own citizens, William Dodge, Jr., and William Walcott, were among them. I now recall the fact that Hon. John P. King, another of your distinguished citizens, as early as 1844 as President of the State Senate gave his casting vote for a measure in the interest of the colored race and lived to be your Representative in Congress and died before he knew of their redemption from bondage at the south and from neglect and degradation in the north.

During the eight years of the Free Soil Epoch very distinguished men were elected to both branches of Congress, some Governors of States and members of State Legislatures. In 1851, Robert Rantoul, Jr., and Charles Sumner, Henry Wilson in 1855. Salmon P. Chase, John P. Hale and others to the United States

Senate; Joshua Giddings, Horace Mann and others to the House of Representatives; all devoted to the abolition of slavery upon the National domain and opposed to its extension to the vast territory upon the Pacific, and so, by cutting off its supplies of virgin soil, to starve it out of existence.

In 1856 the Party of Liberty took another departure in the change of its name to that of the Old Republican Party, and by the nomination of Fremont, the great explorer, and Dayton, the statesman, as their standard bearers. The name of Fremont, the son-in-law of "Old Bullion," as Benton was called, was a name to conjure with and inspired some hope of his election to the Presidency.

Although large numbers were added to the party, the hour for complete success had not arrived, but its speedy oncoming was but a question of time.

In 1860 the time had fully come and the men appeared and under the banner of Lincoln and Hamlin, and by the voice and vote of the American people and by the "favor of Almighty God," the pen of Lincoln and the sword of Grant, the haughty slave power was dethroned and the slave was free.

And so as John Pierpont said and sung of the ballot:—

"A weapon falls as light and still
As snow flakes fall upon the sod;
Yet executes the freeman's will
As lightnings do the will of God."

Mr. Fisher's address was listened to with marked attention and was followed by warm demonstrations of approval from the audience.

PRESIDENT PUTNAM:—The anti-slavery movement was full of inspiration and it was wont to voice its spirit and sentiment in song and poetry. We have with us here a very good friend of our Society, and everybody's friend, in the person of Mr. George B. Bartlett of Concord, who is a truly typical Concordian, and is not only an admirable lecturer and author, but a poet withal, as you will now see.

ORIGINAL POEM BY MR. GEORGE B. BARTLETT.

MR. GEORGE B. BARTLETT:—I have been selected for this task because I represent the very first town that ever sent a fugitive slave back to his master, the town of old Concord, Massachusetts! For when Rev. Peter Thatcher of Medford lost his slave, the latter, after being concealed in Cambridge, was discovered in Concord and carried back. As I always write in short meter I shall detain you but three minutes and a quarter. (Great laughter and applause.) I have chosen for my theme the imaginary audience who might be supposed to be listening to the glorious voice of the great singer who has pleased us so much this afternoon.

> Relics of the mighty past
> Sound the grand old bugle blast.
> Summon to their haunts again
> All these old historic men
> Who in Freedom's blackest night
> Dared to battle for the right.
> Garrison, that fortress strong,
> Refuge sure from every wrong,
> To the shelter of whose name
> Every hunted creature came.
> Phillips, on whose silver tongue
> Eager crowds enraptured hung.
> Whittier, who with mystic lyre
> Quaker souls could rouse to fire.
> Sumner, whose majestic head
> For the cause of Freedom bled.
> Andrew, who to victory sent
> Many a noble regiment.
> Craft, who stole himself away
> From the men who watch and prey.
> Burns, marched back to Southern hell,
> Past the spot where Attucks fell.
> Spring's best blossoms strew his way
> Whose presence was perpetual May,
> Who with consistent courage trod
> The footsteps of the Son of God.
> Parker, with his grandsire's gun
> From the Green at Lexington
> On that "ever glorious day,"
> Eager for another fray.
> Old John Brown, uplifted high,
> Saw the glory in the sky;
> What to him were pain and loss
> When the gallows gleamed a cross!
> These and twenty thousand more
> On the fair and shining shore,
> When our St. John strikes the chord,
> Chant the glory of the Lord.
> Whitest souls, with faces black,
> Fling the glorious tidings back
> From the resurrected land,
> Free from Slavery's iron hand.

The Hutchinsons were now again called upon and sang with all the old-time spirit and power, and amidst the greatest enthusiasm, the well-remembered song, "Ho, the Car of Emancipation," Mr. Hutchinson stating that it was written in its original form by his brother Jesse, during the progress of an anti-slavery convention in Faneuil Hall, and was sung by the family quartet on that occasion, and at numberless meetings afterward.

SONG—HO, THE CAR OF EMANCIPATION.

Ho! The car of Emancipation
Rides majestic through our nation,
Bearing on its train the story—
"Liberty is a nation's glory."
    Roll it along,
    Roll it along,
Roll it along through our nation—
Freedom's car, Emancipation.

*   *   *   *

Men of various predilections,
Frightened, run in all directions,
Merchants, editors, physicians,
Lawyers, priests and politicians;
    Get out the way,
    Get out the way,
Get out the way, every station,
Clear the track for Emancipation.

Hear the mighty car wheels humming,
Now look out, the engine's coming!
Church and Stateman, hear the thunder,
Clear the track or you'll fall under;
    Get off the track,
    Get off the track,
Get off the track, all are singing,
While the liberty bell is ringing.

All triumphant, see them bearing,
Through sectarian rubbish tearing;
The bell and whistle and the steaming,
Startle thousands from their dreaming;
    Look out for the cars,
    Look out for the cars,
Look out for the cars while the bell rings,
Ere the sound your funeral knell rings.

See the throngs that run to meet us,
At Danvers Hall the people greet us,
All takes seats in exultation
In the car Emancipation;
    Hurrah, Hurrah,
    Hurrah, Hurrah,
Hurrah, Hurrah, Emancipation
Soon will bless our happy nation.
    Come on, come on, come on!
    Emancipation soon will bless
    Our happy nation. Come on, come on,
    Come on—n--n—n—n!

It would be impossible to describe the stirring and thrilling effect of these words, so hastily written in the long ago amidst the excitement of one of the old abolition gatherings "by Jesse himself," as they were now sung again at the Commemorative Meeting. Only those who were present to hear them on this occasion, or who had heard them from the quartet during the great anti-slavery crusade, can fully realize their inspiring power, as thus rendered. The mention of "Danvers Hall" seems to have been happily introduced for the moment, instead of that of some other place, the singers probably having been accustomed to adapt the line to each new locality, wherever they repeated the verses.

PRESIDENT PUTNAM:—A rare treat awaits you. In one of the letters which our Secretary has read, Frederick Douglass referred to one of the old-line abolitionists as, more than any other, the terror of the slave power. The veteran soldier of Freedom is with us today. He has been in Danvers before, and some of us who heard him then, are not likely to forget his fearless and tremendous arraignments of a guilty Church and State in less peaceful days than these. He was then a man of war, and you will hardly be able to recognize him in the genial and beaming friend whom I shall now have the honor to present to you. Not one of us all is happier than he, and well may he be content and glad, since he has lived to see the cause for which he so long and heroically fought completely victorious; and all hearts are his at length. Though the fierce battles in which he engaged were so many, and though he is now 84 years old, you will find that Parker Pillsbury is still young, and he is always "Young for Liberty." (Great applause.)

Mr. Pillsbury, as he rose, met with a most enthusiastic ovation, and there was universal regret that his bright, pithy, eloquent and altogether characteristic speech was not much longer than it actually proved to be. In the course of his remarks he exhibited to the audience, as will be seen, various interesting mementos.

ADDRESS OF HON. PARKER PILLSBURY.

MR. PRESIDENT, LADIES AND GENTLEMEN:—I think it is no exaggeration when I say that this is perhaps the proudest, certainly the happiest day of my life. (Applause and cries of good).

How shall we compensate the Danvers Historical Society and its excellent president for giving us this foretaste of future and final bliss? (Applause). Perhaps among the oldest, if not the very oldest veterans of anti-slavery present, it is not unbecoming in me to say that certainly from my inmost heart and soul I thank that Historical Society. (Cries of good and applause). I hope it is not improper for me to say that although they have greatly honored us, I trust and think they have not dishonored themselves. (Cries of good and applause). But, Mr. Chairman, the moments that are passing at this time and under these peculiar circumstances, why, to me they are drops of time, falling into the ocean of eternity, more precious than all the jewels of the mines. And who am I, that I should by my voice here, almost at the completion of four score and four years—who am I that I should interrupt this beautiful current of thought and of music that has saluted our ears? I would that I were worthy of such an opportunity and such an occasion; but I shall keep before me the ten minute rule, inevitable, as seems to me, under these peculiar circumstances. And first I want to say that there are those who have been quiet workers in the anti-slavery movement and who have survived, and who have preserved some of the relics of those days, and they have entrusted to me the pleasant opportunity and duty of calling the attention of this gathering to them. Among the oldest that are presented is an oldtime daguerreotype of our famous friend whose name has not yet been spoken by any who have preceded me—I mean George Thompson of England. (Loud and earnest applause). I hold here the precious shadow of that mighty man. When I was travelling and lecturing in behalf of the slave I had the opportunity to possess myself of some of the shackles which slaves had worn, and one terrible whip, the five thongs of which were red with blood that had been drawn from the backs of slaves; and I had also shackles they had worn, and chains. Today I have but a single link presented by those same excellent women—the link of a chain that was worn by the slave Jerry who escaped and was finally secured by the abolitionists of Syracuse, N. Y., where our excellent friend, Samuel J. May, whose shadow is there before you, was Unitarian minister. There is the link of that chain worn by that slave Jerry, and if you harness your horses with chains to carry a ton or more, they would not be larger links than that, and that link was only got off his limbs by a blacksmith's file. He wore it out of slavery and before he could be emancipated the blacksmith had to cut it with his file because they had no key to unlock the padlock. I have one other little memorial of slavery. The name has been spoken of William Craft, the fugitive slave. Here is a picture of William Craft's wife. She was so white and so beautiful that she passed on their journey from Georgia to Philadelphia as the young son of a slaveholder, and her husband, who was quite a black man, was her body servant; and as body servant to the beautiful girl, he came with her safely through Georgia to Philadelphia. That is the photograph, or rather the photograph of the picture that was taken of her. Those of you who can perceive it can see that her arm is in a sling. You know it was necessary for travellers living south at hotels to register their names. But she, a slave, knew nothing of writing. But representing the son of a rich Georgia planter, she was of course expected to be educated, and her arm was put in that sling to give color to the pretext that she had inflammatory rheumatism and could not write! She was so beautiful on board the steamer as she came up that quite a number of both southern and northern young women actually fell in love with her. (Laughter and applause). I am glad to have found that picture, because at that time it was really a sensation. I hope it will be copied and circulated, and I thank the woman who brought it here and entrusted me with the pleasant duty of presenting it to this audience. (Applause.) Now I should like to say a few words for myself. But I do not know how I can, for I shall stand in the way of others who have a better claim to the ears of the audience than I. But here I am in my native County of Essex, and I am happy to say that my father and grandfather on both my father's and my mother's side, were also born here in the County of Essex—a county that gave Garrison and Whittier to the anti-slavery cause and the cause of freedom throughout the world. Honor enough for me to have been born in such a county; and indeed my ancestors from the year 1635, were all born here in the County of Essex. I have seen much of two hemispheres, but I never saw a county yet where I should so choose to be born as in this county. (Cries of good and applause). Then as to my work in the anti-slavery cause, I did what I could, and I want to say that in the service, Mr. Garrison had been in the field ten years before I entered. When I did come, it so happened that we had an opportunity to lay the axe at the root of the tree, and to justify ourselves in so doing. For the honorable James G. Birney, whose name has been mentioned here, and so creditably mentioned as the first anti-slavery candidate for the presidency, was a ruling elder in the Presbyterian church and a slave-holder in Kentucky, a Judge of the Supreme Court of that State and so high in literary culture and distinction that when the University was instituted there, he was appointed and given *carte blanche* to nominate the officers of the University. I should also say, and it was the crowning excellence in the estimation of the slaveholders, that he was the owner of forty-two slaves. Thus constituted and thus surrounded, he was encountered by one of our anti-slavery agents whose name has been mentioned in the letters read, Theodore D. Weld. He encountered this illustrious slaveholder in Kentucky, being there on some literary agency, and he arrested him with the question. "Where did you get your right to hold those slaves?" and he did not leave that judge's office till he had nailed the truth so hard and fast to his conscience that he never found peace, to borrow the parlance of the church, till he "found it in believing," and became a penitent slaveholder. The laws of Kentucky did not permit him to emancipate his slaves there, but he was able to bring them over the river into Ohio, and there he set them all free. I have named those considerations that gave him his distinction—his education, his office in the church as ruling elder, and high position as a lawyer and jurist, being a judge of the Supreme Court of Kentucky. But in that one act of emancipating his slaves of course he sacrificed every one of those distinctions, every one; and the persecution that he suffered in consequence was so intense that it drove him and his family out of Kentucky, and they came over into Cincinnati. There he established an anti-slavery paper, which was three times mobbed, press and type being thrown into the Ohio river. The leading influences in those mobs were the church and clergy of Cincinnati and the surrounding country on both sides of the Ohio river. It resulted in this, that he went to England and while there wrote and published the first church testimony against slavery—a tract of 46 pages, entitled, "The American Churches, the Bulwarks of American Slavery." Well, that moment I came into the anti-slavery field. That was in 1840. From that time I date my anti-slavery convictions and conversion; and, as I trust, my sincere repentance of any part I had had in the guilt of slaveholding. I want to say further, that we were logical in our conclusions. The church gave us that premise through Judge Birney. The anti-slavery men who became politicians did themselves honor of course in naming him for the President of the United States, as has been shown here. But in 1840, though he received some votes from anti-slavery men for the presidency, he was soon dropped out of sight, and certainly one of the most dishonorable of all the politicians that any party ever had, Martin Van Buren, was made his successor! (A voice: That's so.) And I think our friend Garrison has just illustrated, or rather illumined very clearly and forcibly the quality of political anti-slavery ever since. For that one fact, the repentance and redemption of Judge Birney, who really made a great many more sacrifices for his anti-slavery than even Garrison could make, he was nominated for the presidency. Garrison had no such sacrifices to make. He had no forty-two slaves, he had no political eminence, nor legal standing. He gave what he had. He was like the widow with her two mites. He gave more in himself than all the politicians. But Judge Birney had those possessions and beautifully and cheerfully and freely he laid them all on the altar of his convictions, and I do not know that he ever forfeited the confidence of the anti-slavery people of his time.

But I want to say that since that time, since that fall of those political abolitionists from James G. Birney to Martin Van Buren, it seems to me there has been no moral conscience in this country in any political party. (Laughter and applause.) I believe we have lost all knowledge of what right and wrong, positive right and wrong, in the divine sense, mean; and our trade and our commerce, our politics and our religion, are the whole of them, matters of convenience. And it is paying a good many of them a compliment to say even that. (Laughter and applause.) While we just now heard Garrison's position, I felt almost sorry that it was spoken, for I wanted to speak it myself. (Laughter.) Garrison took his stand and uttered his voice in memorable and emphatic words; "I am in earnest; I will not equivocate; I will not retreat a single inch; I will not excuse, *and I will be heard.*" (Applause.) He was heard. (Renewed applause.) As if the Almighty who spoke to the Hebrew prophet, had said to him, "Go thou and speak my word unto them; they will not hearken unto thee for they will not hearken unto me, nevertheless go thou and speak my word unto them, and it shall be known that there hath been a prophet among them." And was it not known? And has it not been known ever since? But we have no such conscience since. Why, the Baptist church, in its *close communion* doctrine, was the most consistent of all the religious sects at that time, in the country. We always called them the most bigoted, but they would not hold the Christian sacramental communion, and did not with Free Will Baptists even any more than with Congregationalists, although the Free Will Baptists were all immersed as well as themselves. I am not talking of the sincerity of any of them. The least said about that the better. There is no time for it now. But they would not hold communion with any man who had not been immersed, nor with anybody who would hold communion with anybody who had not been immersed, as would and did the Free Will Baptists everywhere. Now you see there was consistency, there was logic, there was a carrying out of principle. We have no such thing as that now. But the Abolitionists took the same ground that the Baptists did.

We would not vote for a slave holder, and we would not vote for anybody who would vote for a slaveholder. (Laughter.) And we were equally logical and and consistent in all our church relations. Garrison made himself heard. He said he would be heard and he was heard, and that was the reason. He would not go to the polls and vote, and he taught a good many of us, quite a good many of us who are here, and for forty years we did not go to the polls and vote, and I have never voted since, for I cannot vote any more for a government that robs and taxes and enslaves my wife and daughter without their consent and representation. (Cries of good and applause.) I have been consistent ever since. I have lived in Concord, N. H., since 1840, now three years more than half a century, and I have never seen a ballot box and never wish to see one. My wife, blessed be her very idea, fortunately for her has more to be taxed for than I have; but she cannot vote, and if she cannot, I am sure I will not. (Cries of good, and applause and laughter.) I am going to carry the principle out. I will tell you one reason the temperance cause has made no better advance. It is older than the anti-slavery cause. It was quite a number of years old when Garrison commenced operations. He began as a temperance man before he reached the matter of slavery. But the cause is working its way, and see what work is made of it. It has had no Garrison since 1879. It has not yet found a man or woman that will not budge a single inch, and will not excuse, will not equivocate, politically, nor religiously, nor in any way, and declares he will be heard. People do not know anything about principle, vital, moral principle; and in the common parlance of the street, "that is what's the matter." There is no man demanding temperance on the principle of Garrisonism. There is nobody demanding woman's suffrage on the principle of Garrisonism that I know of. I am trying to act on that principle myself. I will not vote for any government that taxes my wife without representation, any more than I will vote for any government that made slavery and returned fugitive slaves. But I am forgetting myself. I wish I could come down to my native county, and give you some anti-slavery reminiscences, but I thank you for listening to me so long. (Great applause.)

PRESIDENT PUTNAM:—However unfaithful to the interests of the slave were the vast majority of the clergy of the country, there were not wanting a large number of ministers who were among his truest friends. Of these, no one made for himself a nobler record than the now very aged and greatly venerated saint and apostle of Righteousness, Rev. Thomas T. Stone, D. D., of Bolton, Mass., formerly the pastor of the First Church of Salem. The feeble state of his health has prevented him from meeting you here today, but, ninety-two years old though he is, he has sent us a beautiful letter, traced with his own fine, delicate handwriting, which I will ask his honored son, Col. Henry Stone, of Boston, whom I see in the audience, to read for us.

Col. Stone cheerfully responded to the call, and read from the platform, and the letter, which was listened to with deep interest by all present, may be found with others in another part of the volume.

The speaking was then discontinued for a brief time to allow Mr. Clark, the photographer, to take a picture of the audience. The President improved the opportunity afforded while the necessary preparations were going on, to introduce to those present a grandchild of the venerable Theodore D. Weld, and to exhibit a piece of the strand with which John Brown was hung, in Virginia, a memento brought to the meeting by Mr. Charles Woodbury, of Beverly. After Mr. Clark had done his work, the Hutchinsons sang the following spirited song, composed by Mr. George W. Putnam, of Lynn, and formerly sung by them throughout the whole anti-slavery struggle and all over the North:

SONG:—"THERE'S NO SUCH WORD AS FAIL."

[Words by G. W. Putnam. Music by Asa B. Hutchinson. Of the six original verses the Hutchinsons usually sang these four.]

"Ridden by the slave power,
Crushed beneath the chain,—
Now has come our rising hour,
Lo! we're up again!
And voices from the mountain height,
Voices from the vale,
Say for Freedom's fearless host,
'There's no such word as fail!'

* * *

For this the songs of liberty,
Are ringing to the sky!
For this upon a thousand hills
Our banner waveth high!
And rallying 'neath its folds we call,
From mountain glade and glen,
All stern and fearless spirits forth,
Which bear the forms of men."

* * *

Free to speak the burning truth,
All fetterless the hand,—
Never shall the Yankee's brow
Bear the cursed brand!
Send the gathering Freemen's shout
Booming on the gale,—
Omnipotence is for us,
"There's no such word as fail!"

They're gathering on the mountain,
They're gathering on the plain!
And with the tramp of Freedom's host
The broad earth shakes again!
And this their glorious rallying cry,
Whose firm hearts never quail,—
God and the People! On for right!
"There's no such word as fail."

Another song being called for from the Hutchinsons, Mr. George T. Downing rose and asked permission to say a word. He said:—"In conversation with Mr. Hutchinson in the early stages of this meeting, we carried ourselves back to a building in the city of New York where the members and friends of the anti-slavery association used to assemble annually. At one of those gatherings a notorious man by the name of Rynders came there with his associates to break up the meeting. I was one of the number present. Mr. Hutchinson and his noble band sat in the gallery. The meeting became a complete scene of disorder, owing to the interruption of Rynders and his gang. Without any announcement, the Hutchinsons rose in the audience, or rather in the gallery, and with their sweet voices completely tamed the wild beast, as I recall him on that occasion, and they are about to give us the same song now, which they sang then.

Mr. Hutchinson:—It was not always convenient for us to be announced from the stage. We would manage to get among the audience, and when the opportunity came to do our duty, we did it. We did it on that occasion. It makes me feel like shedding tears of joy that we were privileged to serve and even to suffer for the great cause of Emancipation. It was when we were once with William Lloyd Garrison at Portland, and when the mob was so noisy that nothing could be heard, and he remained silent, and they would not allow him to speak, that he turned and asked us to sing. We arose and sang this very song. I would state that, of the two members of my family who are with me today, my daughter takes the place of my dear sister who was with me singing recently at the burial of our beloved John G. Whittier, who has gone to his glorious home above;

and her husband wrote me a letter which I received just before I came, in which he says, "Abbie and myself cannot be with you, yet we will be with you in spirit," and I believe it is so. We will sing, friends, the song "Over the mountain and over the moor, or "The Slave's Appeal."

Mr. Hutchinson and his companions sang this song from the platform, having sung the previous ones at the piano below, near the stage.

SONG:—"THE SLAVE'S APPEAL."

Over the mountain and over the moor,
Comes the sad wailing of many a slave;
The father, the mother, and children are poor,
And grieve with petitions their freedom to have.

Pity, kind gentlemen, friends of humanity,
Cold is the world to the cry of God's poor:
Give us our freedom, ye friends of humanity.
Give us our rights, for we ask nothing more.

Call us not indolent, vile and degraded,
White men have robbed us of all we hold dear;
Parents and children, the young and the aged,
Are scourged by the lash of the rough overseer.

Pity, kind gentlemen, friends of equality, etc.

And God in His mercy shall crown your endeavors,
The glory of Heaven shall be your reward;
The promise of Jesus to you shall be given,
"Enter, ye faithful, the joy of your Lord."

Then pity, kind gentlemen, friends of Christianity, etc.

PRESIDENT PUTNAM:—Few are those who can say that they were present and witnessed the scene when Mr. Garrison was mobbed in Boston and dragged through the streets to jail. Our revered friend, Rev. Dr. George W. Porter, of Lexington, late President of the Historical Society of that town and so well known to our own Society to which he has rendered so much service, and to this neighborhood in which he was born, is one of the number. He was a youth at the time, but his recollection of what he then and there saw is still vivid, as you may well suppose. Will he kindly tell us all about it, and tell us, also, of his personal acquaintance with that other noble champion of Liberty, Nathaniel P. Rogers, of New Hampshire?

Dr. Porter received a hearty welcome from the audience. who were evidently eager to hear about the memorable event from an actual eye witness.

ADDRESS OF REV. GEORGE W. PORTER, D. D.

Mr. President, Ladies and Gentlemen:—I was most happy to respond to the invitation of your president to be here today and to recount my recollections, first of a person, and secondly of an event, both of which were intimately connected with the cause we are here today to commemorate. In my early youth I was at a school in Plymouth, N. H. I found in that village a gentleman and his family who took a very kindly interest in me as a youth, and the interest between us was mutual and grew into friendship. That person was Nathaniel Peabody Rogers, one of the pioneers of the cause of human emancipation—a man of magnetic power, of logical mind, of fearless pen, and of great ability and influence in the cause which he had espoused. He became to me an inspiration, and my birth out of proslavery delusion into the light of emancipation began under his tutelage. He asked me to journey with him across the country some forty miles to the town of Canaan, where I had been a resident and where I think the members of this assembly will remember, an attempt was made to establish a school of higher academic learning, and that establishment was to be open to the colored people as well as to the white. Subscriptions were taken, the building was erected, and it was ready to be opened as a school of that character, when the feeling of the community became so aroused and the people became so adverse to the enterprise, that the farmers from the hillsides and the river banks came there with their yokes of oxen to the number of sixty, attached them to the building, drew it away, and left it in a swamp. By doing this I suppose they thought they had put an end to all abolition movements in that town and community. From that moment the cause of anti-slavery prospered and soon became triumphant in the community. So that I venture to say that within twenty years, possibly fifteen, after the date of this event, the whole community had changed its sentiment, and from being the advocates of slavery and of the ownership of slaves in the Union, became the advocates of anti-slavery. Mr. Rogers had a history of very great importance in the early period of the anti-slavery struggle. His influence was felt all over the state and perhaps largely over New England, and even beyond its boundaries. My recollections of him are very pleasant and only pleasant. As I said, he became an inspirer to me in the cause of humanity.

I will now recount my recollections of an event. That event was the mobbing of William Lloyd Garrison, in Boston, in the year, I think, 1835, and in the month of October. I, as a youth, was passing down Washington street and came opposite the Anti-

Slavery Rooms, as they were then called, where Mr. Garrison had his office as editor of *The Liberator.* I saw a crowd gathering. I asked the meaning of it, and I was told that they were gathering to mob George Thompson, a noted English advocate of American emancipation. That mob grew very rapidly. It was made up of very respectable looking men outwardly. Presently I saw them entering the building, which they did ruthlessly, roughly and violently, and then I heard that Mr. Garrison had escaped through a rear window of the building, and it was supposed that he had gone out to escape from the violence of the mob. It was seen very soon that the tendency of the mob was toward State Street. I was forced on with it and turned down State street. As I came near the corner of Wilson's Lane, I saw borne above the heads of the crowd the form of William Lloyd Garrison, with a rope around his neck. The mob was shouting and uttering maledictions and objurgations. It was a very violent crowd. State Street had already filled with a surging multitude. The mayor, Mr. Lyman, was at that time in the mayor's office, which was then in the old State House, and efforts seemed to be made by the friends of humanity, if possible, to secure the safety of the victim of vio'ence by placing him within the doors of City Hall. That was speedily done. Then a carriage was summoned. Then Mr. Garrison was brought out and put into the carriage, and the order was given to the driver to hasten with all possible speed to Leverett Street jail for the security of the victim of malice. The impression this scene made upon my mind was one that can never be forgotten by me. I have for the first time this afternoon had the opportunity of meeting with the son of that honored and illustrious father. I had no sooner seen him than I said he must be the son of his father, the resemblance is so strong between them. Mr. Garrison was of course in a state outwardly of great agitation. Inwardly, I trust, he had the peace of God and the consciousness of right within his soul. And as he was borne aloft his face was suffused with blood, and he was apparently choking under the violence of his enemies. In that way he was taken to the jail. I want you to remember that the mob was not an ordinary one. It was a kid-gloved mob, made up of the respectable gentlemen of Boston. There was no rough or very little rough element in it; and as the carriage was ordered to drive on, these men with gloved hands held onto the wheels of the carriage, resolved that it should not go. But with the help of the spirited horses, the still more spirited driver, and the still more spirited whip, the man conquered and the carriage went on. The mob went after it, shouting to make the welkin ring again; but taking a devious course which the driver was ordered to take, the carriage reached Leverett Street jail in safety and Mr. Garrison was therein safe for a while. He remained there until peace was somewhat restored, and was then taken into the country. The next morning I had occasion to go into the street where he lived and in front of his door there stood a gallows! The house had been ill-treated during the night, and that was the condition of Boston, friends, in the year of grace 1835. What is the condition now? I venture to state that ninety-nine persons out of every hundred are today what were known ignominiously at that time as abolitionists and friends of the slave. So God works wonderful changes in the consciences and minds of men. Illumination takes the place of darkness, and truth the place of error, and truth eventually under God is to conquer. (Applause.)

THE PRESIDENT :—The most persuasive voice that was heard in all the troublous years we are passing in review, was that of one you have long been waiting to greet. She needs no introduction. A pioneer in anti-slavery work and in so many other great and noble reforms, she has endeared herself to all true lovers of humanity, and you will be more than glad to listen to Mrs. Lucy Stone.

As one after another of these early and faithful reformers, so long ago famous, came forward to address the meeting, they could but realize, Mr. May, Mr. Pillsbury, Mrs. Stone, and the rest, how warmly and widely their earnest, self-sacrificing and long-continued devotion to the service of the oppressed was appreciated at last. Many who were present had often heard Mrs. Stone and others of the number plead the cause of enslaved men and women forty or fifty years before. It was a coveted privilege and pleasure to see and hear them again, and the manifestation of delight, on the part of all, at this reappearance of the favorite and most conspicuous advocate of the rights of her sex, with her accustomed brave words and winning voice and manner, was unmistakable. She spoke but ten minutes, confining herself strictly to the allotted time.

ADDRESS OF MRS. LUCY STONE.

I should like to add one word to what Dr. Porter said about the way in which Mr. Garrison was carried to the Leverett Street jail. One of the Essex County men, James N. Buffum, told me that he was there at the time of the mob. He said that when he saw the mob getting hold of the wheels and attempting to prevent the carriage from going, he had a spirited horse and he drove it on to them, and they had to let go for their own safety or else Mr. Buffum would have run them down. What I especially want to speak of this afternoon is the influence Mr. Garrison and the early abolitionists had in the cause of women at the time of the anti-slavery movement. There was then no such a thing as a woman having any part in public affairs. It was everywhere held that woman should be silent on such occasions. I remember many years ago that Elizabeth Stuart Phelps' grandfather, Rev. Eliakim Phelps, asked for any one to offer prayer. This was at the village prayer meeting. A woman knelt and prayed. When she ceased Mr. Phelps rose to his feet and said very solemnly, " Let your women keep silence in the church."

There was nothing like women appearing in public at that time, though Mr. Garrison and Wendell Phillips and others were telling us of the woes of mothers and of little babes sold on the auction block. It was not possible in such times for women to be silent. In the Friends' meetings, among the Quakers, freedom of speaking has always been accorded to women. Abby Kelly and the two Grimke sisters, three Quaker women, found it impossible to keep silence. I cannot tell you how it began, but they did come into the field of public speaking. Yet a certain class of abolitionists said they should not. Abby Kelly said: " Woe is me if I preach not this gospel of freedom to the slave." The anti-slavery society divided itself on the subject. Mr. Garrison and Wendell Phillips always stood in favor of the freedom of the public speaking of women. You can see by what Mr. Porter has told you, what the condition of public sentiment was in regard to anti-slavery. These men added to that, the odium of allowing women to do what they had not been allowed to do before—to speak in public. I remember when the sisters Grimke and Abby Kelly began to speak. The mob jeered at them and pelted them with bad eggs and even with stones, the newspapers ridiculed them and ministers preached against them. Abby Kelly once, in a town of Connecticut, went to church. The clergyman rose and took for his text, " This Jezebel has come amongst us also." Then he preached about her as though she was the worst kind of a woman. This brave Quaker woman had taken her life in her hands, and had gone out to help free the slaves.

The Women's Rights movement owes its inception to the anti-slavery cause. Look at the progress which has been made from the time when Abby Kelly was pelted with stones to the present time, when the women of the Columbian Fair have millions of dollars at their command from the United States government.

Well, all the progress made from Abby Kelly's time to this we owe to the anti-slavery agitation. (Applause.) I do not think we can conceive at this day of the condition of things then. Now when all doors are open to women, we find women managing the temperance cause, with Miss Frances Willard at its head, with her great army of 600,000 engaged in the temperance cause. But in 1853, there was a World's Temperance Convention in New York. One woman, Antoinette Brown, came there as a delegate. And the great body of the delegates to that convention, who were clergymen, turned themselves into a mob to prevent the woman from being heard. William Lloyd Garrison was there, and he said he had seen violent men in mobs before, but he had never seen anything like that, when for two or three days the great body of ministers clamored and banged with their heels and thumped with their canes, and did everything they could to keep a woman from being heard as a delegate. And in the year 1840, when there was a world's anti-slavery convention in London, and Mary Grew and Lucretia Mott went as delegates, the world's anti-slavery convention would not admit them, and Mr. Garrison said, "I am a delegate and these women are delegates, and if they cannot be received I will not be." So he sat in the gallery. It was the play of Hamlet with Hamlet left out, for they desired Mr. Garrison as a delegate more than any one else. But he sat in the gallery, taking his place with the women. (Applause). You will see what the condition was in those years by that very shutting out of women.

Now I come to a period later than that—1848 or 1849, or perhaps it was 1850. Rev. Samuel May then was agent of the Anti-Slavery Society. I went to Malden to hold an anti-slavery meeting. That meeting took place on Sunday at five o'clock in the afternoon. An orthodox clergyman was asked to give notice of the meeting, which he did thus, "I am requested by Mr. Morey to say that a hen will attempt to crow like a cock this afternoon at the Town hall. All those who like that kind of music will attend." (Laughter.) Now you can imagine, after all these years of Abby Kelly and of the sisters Grimke and of the anti-slavery fight, what the condition was in 1850, when a respectable clergyman could give such a notice. You can imagine from that what the anti-slavery men had to face when they took up this cause. I often think of Abby Kelly,—how she was hunted like a partridge on the mountain, and every woman thought she had a right to jeer at her. Men went with brickbats and stones to pelt her. I have often thought that if she had had to cut her way to the top of Mount Washington with a jack-knife it would have been an easier task than that by which she made a highway over which women now walk freely. When Galileo discovered the rotation of the earth, they pinched his flesh and he denied it, because he could not endure the pain. But Abby Kelly for twenty years bore all the cruel hurt to her spirit for the sake of equal rights. What do we not owe to those women as well as to the men! We can never measure what we owe. I remember the first time I attended an anti-slavery meeting in Boston. On the platform sat a woman. This was such an unheard of thing that I felt almost ashamed to see a woman there. It was my first experience. She had on one of those bonnets that came away out, so that I could not see her face, and she had a pale blue ribbon on it and at her wrist white cuffs. I wished to see her face to know what kind of a person she was. It was Eliza J. Kenny of Salem, who acted as Secretary of the Society for many years. The Anti-Slavery Society welcomed a woman to be its secretary, and helped to do away with prejudices. But the great thing the anti-slavery movement did was to emancipate the human mind. Before, everybody believed in a personal devil, with a hell in which there was brimstone and fire; but from the coming of the anti-slavery cause that movement set us free to question even the things held most sacred. When people said the Bible sustained slavery, Theodore Parker said "So much the worse for the Bible." The question had been opened whether the Bible was all that it claimed to be. We were taught that there was no thing and no claim, however sacred, which we had not the right to question. So this result of the anti-slavery movement was worth more to the world than even the freedom of the slave.

Mr. President, I thank you and the members of the Danvers Historical Society for the opportunity you have given me to come here and say a word and to look into the faces of those who are here. There are many wrinkled faces; yet many of us began with roses in our cheeks. Today we come young at seventy-four, young at eighty-four, and determined, as long as we can, to work to the end. (Great applause.)

The President next introduced Mrs. Abby Morton Diaz, author of many interesting books and stories, and prominent in the Women's Educational & Industrial Union, of Boston. "Her work," he said, "in numerous departments of usefulness, has resulted in a great deal of good, and promises to result in a great deal more. She will tell us something, I trust, of the Plymouth abolitionists, as she is a daughter of one of the most noted and worthy of them." (Applause.)

ADDRESS OF MRS. ABBY M. DIAZ.

I should like to say that a great many women here and elsewhere, engaged in money earning, have not the slightest idea how largely these extended opportunities have been made possible to them by the woman who has just sat down. I think I shall introduce myself as a relic of the anti-slavery times. I know that relics are looked upon not at all with envy, rather with pity; but I, as a relic, look with pity on the younger people here who did not have the opportunities which we had of being educated in principles. I am a relic, for one thing, of a Plymouth Juvenile Anti-Slavery Society, of which I was Secretary,—a relic of some Plymouth school girls who had become skilful in anti-slavery argument, and who circulated anti-slavery petitions on their way to and from school. The anti-slavery reading room was our daily stopping place. It was a free thought social centre. The sign of that anti-slavery room was mobbed and had the honor of being coated with tar. I am also a relic of an anti-slavery meeting held in Plymouth in an obscure church, the only one attainable. The meeting was mobbed, stones being thrown through the window. My father went to the sheriff, but the sheriff did not care to do anything about it. Then I am a relic of a party who went on to New York at one time in a steamboat, at the time when so many had been aroused by the enthusiasm of John A. Collins. The Graham boarding house engaged for the delegates would not contain us. We arrived in the morning early, and were sent to the St. John's Hall to get our breakfast, because the Graham boarding house could not take us in. But we had Graham fare. There were tables set up and down the hall and we had dishes of mush and other rations. There we took our breakfast. In the afternoon we ascended to an upper loft and partitioned it off with our shawls, so as to spend the night there, feeling it a great wonder that any owner would let us into his building. But later this owner came in great agitation, and said there was danger that the hall would be burned, and that we would have to go somewhere else. We picked up all our belongings and set forth. A crowd assembled in the street as we went out, and we heard the men say "Why, there are some very good looking women among them!" We did not know what to do when we got into the street. It was night, but darkness only added to the delight of the youngest of the party, because it was something very romantic to be thrown into the city streets late at night, and not to know where to go. We tried a great many places but nobody would receive anti-slavery people. At last we were taken in where we smelled supper getting ready.

We noticed some whispered conferences and presently the landlady came to us and said, "I cannot keep you. I shall lose every boarder I have in the house if you stay. You will have to go." So we had to put on our things at nine o'clock at night and go forth again into the streets of a strange city. At last in a tenth rate boarding house—it was very tenth rate—we obtained permission to stay, though rather than go to bed we lay down on the outside. There was one thing you can have no idea of. It was the enthusiasm, the utter devotion to the cause, of the young people of those days. Just as other young girls—"the world's girls"—looked forward to balls and parties and talked about their beaux, we of the anti-slavery cause looked forward to anti-slavery conventions, reckoned up the days that would elapse before the next, talked about the speakers, doted over *The Liberator* and some of us ate our bread bare of butter to save up money to pay half our weekly subscription to the Anti-Slavery Society, and knitted cotton garters to make up the other half, going around and selling them to get the necessary quarter a week. All we had a desire for was to put what money we could save into the contribution box. If any one of us had owned a watch it would have gone into the box. But this would not have been a sacrifice. It was a most delightful thing for us to do, and we were so absorbed in anti-slavery work that we had no wish for anything else. I remember that two girls were sent to Boston. Their mother had given them money to buy some shawls. "Now," she said, "I want you to buy good shawls." So they put nearly all their money into the contribution box, and went back with very poor shawls, to the great disgust of their mother.

There is one other thing that the anti-slavery people have done; they have given us labor-saving tools. As Marcus Antoninus says: "As physicians have always instruments ready for any case which may suddenly require their use, so do thou have principles ready for the understanding of things divine and human." I call principles labor-saving, because when any question comes up they save the labor of spending any time in talking about probable results, in consulting books, in listening to anybody in authority, whether in church or state. All you have to do is to bring that question to the judgment-seat of principle, and it is decided. The anti-slavery leaders taught us the use of these labor-saving tools, and you will find them very effective in shortening the duration—and the speeches—of your conferences and conventions. The Woman's Suffrage question would be settled in this way in about five minutes. Woman's Suffrage is not anything difficult after we have worked on anti-slavery. The rights of one human being decided, then follow rights for many and all human beings. The Woman's Suffrage question is decided on the principle of individual right of judgment and of settling matters of duty for one's self. I can prove that the anti-slavery people were not agitators, but that on the contrary those who opposed them were the agitators. The principle is this: As truth is infinite the human perception of truth must always be a progressive one. That being so, progress is in the divine order. That being so, those who wish to progress are in the divine order. The divine order was from slavery to freedom, and those who went on in this divine order were going on in the right way. Those who stopped them made the agitation. A stone in a stream makes more fuss and agitation than all the little boats that float with the stream. Thus I have proved to you by principles that the anti-slavery people were not agitators, but that those who opposed them were agitators. Then there is another principle to be considered, namely, that every new idea or every new presentation or plan has rights we are bound to respect. One of those rights is a careful investigation without regard to anybody's opinion, our own included, or to any authority however high and without regard to existing conditions. It must not be decided by any of these; it must just be brought down to a principle. And remember that "the new must be established in terms of the new." Also, that because a thing cannot be done now is no reason that it can never be done, and that the improbable is not on that account impossible. This Columbian era is a good time to say that. It was very improbable, all that came from what Columbus did, but although improbable, it has proved to be possible. One strange thing I have seen among people who have in a manner been liberated by these principles. I have seen it in the narrowness of liberalism as well as in the narrowness of conservatism; that when people have progressed a certain distance they say it is the end— thus far and no farther. The next thing that comes up they are not willing to accept or to thoroughly examine. They think they have got all there is. Many liberal people are more bigoted and narrow than conservatives. I have in my mind some very liberal and progressive people who have turned aside from things they were not familiar with, condemning without full investigation. (Applause.)

Here Mrs. Diaz found her time had elapsed.

Letters of great interest were here read from Rev. R. S. Storrs, D. D., Rev. Robert Collyer, Mrs. Henry Ward Beecher and Mrs. Caroline H. Dall. after which the President introduced Rev. Aaron Porter of East Alstead, N. H., the son of Hathorne Porter, one of the original and most deserving of the old Danvers abolitionists. "Some of the latter, by way of ridicule, were called 'The Seven Stars', by their proslavery neighbors. Perhaps our friend, whose father was one of the sacred number and who well remembers these lights of former days and other luminaries with them, will let us know how bright they were then and how they have shone since." (Cordial greeting.)

ADDRESS OF REV. AARON PORTER.

Mr. President:—I fully agree with the statement already made, that we are too near in time to the early abolitionists to dispassionately judge them on their methods. We are neither artists designing nor skilled workmen building their monument. We are only burden-bearers, bringing each one his share of the raw material which he hopes will have its place in the finished structure that we are all sure the providence of God will cause to be raised to their honor in the future. All who up to this time have been mentioned here are such as lived and wrought away from Danvers. Mine is the work of speaking a word for those who in this immediate locality—yes, within the circumscribed boundaries of "Danvers Neck"—illustrated their own peculiar anti-slavery faith, in everyday life; being "come-outers" from church and state alike, according to their own designation of themselves, and constituting according to the designation of others, the "Seven Stars" and the nucleus of the "School House Gang." When I first heard the terms "Seven Stars" and "School House Gang," my father read them aloud from a letter just received from William Endicott, while we were living in what is now North Randolph. Vt., where I lived for three years. Subsequently it was explained to me that the "Seven Stars" were represented by the following names:—John Hood, Richard Hood, Jesse P. Harriman, John Cutler, William Endicott, Joseph Merrill, Hathorne Porter. In his answer to William Endicott's letter my father wrote the following, which I extract from that very letter, kindly loaned to me by Mrs. Henry Hyde of Danvers, herself a daughter of William Endicott.

East Randolph, Vt., July 11, 1841.

Friend Endicott:—I received your welcome letter of the 5th inst. and was highly interested in perusing your vivid description of the scene in the anti-slavery meetings. If I understand correctly, those three meetings took place on the evenings of the first three days of July. I trust the "Seven Stars" shone with greater brilliancy on those nights and added new lustre to their accumulated radiance. I hope also that the "Seven Stars" have become fixed stars, fixed in the eternal principles of liberty, of truth and of humanity, and that they will continue to let their light shine to cheer the down trodden—lights to illumine the dark ways of oppression, and aid the children of adversity. This appellation, "Seven Stars," although intended as a term of reproach, will ere long be considered a title of honor. I had much rather be found with this faithful "Seven" who oppose American slavery and act consistently with their principles, than to be found applauding or approbating those who in 1776 declared that all men were born free, and of right ought to be free; and at the same time held hundreds of men in the most abject slavery. Reckon me then as among the "Seven Stars," with all the *aliases* annexed. Well, I am delighted with your report. I have some idea of how Harriman looked when he made the charge of voting for men thieves. I congratulate him and Bro. Hood and Sister Hood in their self-emancipation from the corruptions of a proslavery church. Where and how is Bro. Cutler, the *longest* "star" in the whole constellation? Let us hear about him in your next. How pleased I should be, had I been present. It would have done my heart good. Anti-slavery here in Vermont gains moderately. Although it is the busiest time of the year, yet there have been recently four or five conventions of abolitionists in this region, but I was unable to attend them. The time for labor in the cause here, is in winter when people are at leisure and when it is better travelling over these hills and mountains. There is indifference, perhaps ignorance, on the subject of slavery here, but not that bitter opposition—that determination to stop free discussion, which we have frequently seen exhibited even on old Danvers Neck. Here are no mobbings nor threats of mobbing, and there is not a church for miles around our region but would be freely granted for the discussion of abolition, if applied for. I have been invited to lecture in the Brookfield meeting house all day of a Sunday, and I think I shall try it in about three weeks. Bro. Henry C. Wright paid us a short visit and left last Monday for Boston. I have ten thousand questions to ask you, which I must defer.

     Yours for humanity,
       HATHORNE PORTER.

  Such were the "Seven Stars," as nearly as I can remember; but there come to me the names of others who were as worthy as these, perhaps, for the roll of honor. The early abolitionists were religious—profoundly and spiritually so—as religious as Carver, or Bradford, or Winthrop or any of the Puritans. As religious as Luther, or Melancthon, or Zwingli or any of the Protestant reformers; and so far as they were critical, and destructive and narrow, they were like all Pro-test-ants of every age. So religious and sincere were they that they made the mistake of thinking that essential religion could live by its own inherent and spiritual warmth without the aid of *any* extraneous forms. They said and rightly, that the common anti-slavery convention was a religious meeting; they said further,—and here they were mistaken,—that the religions forms of a religious meeting could take care of themselves; and so it came about, at last, that while provision was made beforehand, as to who should address the meeting, the matter of vocal prayer was left to be exercised on the spur of the moment, by any one who might volunteer so to do when the managers of the meeting announced the opportunity. Of course it soon followed that the opportunity was seldom improved. While I was away for three years in Vermont, occurred the intrusion of Beach and Foster and others upon the usual worship to deliver their testimonies for the slave, an intrusion of which many abolitionists—prominent among them, Garrison and Wendell Phillips—did not approve. Then also occurred for a short time, probably a year or so, the regular meeting on the Lord's day of these Danvers abolitionists in the school house, and hence the term, the "School House Gang." These meetings were at first opened with reading from the Bible, and with prayer. But soon these were discontinued, because they were regarded as formal, while the addresses and exhortations were considered practical. John Reed, one of the "Come Outers," was about my age, and when I returned from Vermont he was slowly dying of consumption. He and I talked over these things, and both of us wished the abolition meetings had kept in our time the old religious feature of the formal worship. John grew sicker. One night I sat up with him in company with his brother Augustus. How I longed to say something religious to him in connection with our devout anti-slavery feelings and hopes, but I was diffident and reticent and felt that his brother would not sympathize with his views, and possibly it might not be best. But I have been sorry that I did not, ever since. At his funeral the minister told of his *recent* conversion to Christ on his dying bed, after the fashion of the denomination to which his family belonged. Was not John converted to Christ when week by week he gathered with the "Come Outers" to remember those in bonds as bound with them, in the spirit of him who said, Inasmuch as ye have done it, or done it not unto one of the least of these my brethren, ye have done it or done it not unto me.

And here I wish to put in a few reminiscences of the "Old Anti-Slavery Days." The order in which I mention them is of my own memory, and may not be chronologically correct.

My earliest anti-slavery remembrance is of coming home from school and finding that Rev. ~~Alexander~~ A. St.Clair, agent of the American Anti-Slavery Society, was being entertained at my father's house. Next I remember a meeting for forming a Juvenile Anti-Slavery Society, held in the house of Richard Hood. He and Rev. S. Brimblecom, the Universalist minister, were the only adults present. The former offered prayer at the commencement and the latter at the close of the meeting. Next is the coming of the Grimke sisters to advocate anti-slavery views in the Baptist meeting house on a week day. They were born in the south and had emancipated their inherited slaves. The meeting-house was crowded. Next is an anti-slavery library, kept over William Alley's tailor shop, open every Saturday evening, with Alfred Ray Porter for librarian. He was my uncle, and often did I, at his request, officiate in his place. Then I remember one or two anti-slavery conventions held in the Baptist meeting-house on week days. Then the coming of the "Liberator," followed all too soon by a rival sheet, the "Emancipator," and then the "New Organization" with the woman question and the Sabbath question and the voting question! I suppose all these questions and discussions and cleavages were somehow necessary. They always have been. They came when Christianity separated from Judaism. They divided the church into Jewish Christians and Gentile Christians in Paul's time. They divided the church when Luther came. From them were evolved the Puritans and the Pilgrims. They are with us now in the "new departure" of modern Congregationalism and Presbyterianism. They still abide, but they do grow less bitter and unchristian. May these features of them disappear altogether in future progress. Whittier was on *both* sides after the division. So I suppose were Pierpont and John T. Sargeant and Dr. Hunt and John A. Innis. But can a man be rightly on both sides? I think he can, when, as was the case with the early abolitionists, the differences concern only methods of action and do not involve fundamental principles. I think there is a sense deep, true, spiritual, holy—in which Paul's saying about being " all things to all men that some may be saved" is to be apprehended and studied and practiced in conduct very Christian indeed. Paul was not a time-server!

I have followed with appreciation and interest the paper of

my friend, Mr. Garrison, in vindication of his honored father's Christian courage and logical consistency during those evil days when he stood so stoutly for the eternal righteousness. But the foundations on which the early abolitionists themselves builded were deeper and firmer than logical consistency or courage. They were, for their time, the true, the real church! And one's motive, purpose, spiritual desire, religious aim, must determine his anti-slavery standing. Before the inward majesty of these tests the verbal repudiation of church and state becomes external and incidental. Among the abolitionists arose a little company that declined to use the products of slave labor, particularly cotton. Mr. Garrison by one *ex cathedra* paragraph in his "Liberator" opposed their course and annihilated their organization. But why was not their aim as obvious and practicable as the moral battle cry, "No union with slaveholders?" Not that I condemn Garrison. I only seek to vindicate some whose methods he condemned. I, myself, heard Stephen S. Foster declare in Citizens' Hall, on Danvers Neck, "No man is an abolitionist unless he belong to the American Anti-Slavery Society or to one of its auxiliaries." Much as I would like to do it, I know no process of abstract reasoning or method of concrete devotion to those whom he represented, which can purify his saying from all taint of a bigotry and sectarianism as intense as any that has ever tainted ecclesiastical declarations. There is a moral and spiritual parallax for which we must make allowance ere we can determine the heavenly position of the "Seven Stars," and when we have determined it, as high as they, will shine such local abolitionists as Dr. Hunt and John A. Learoyd, to say nothing of such distinguished abolitionists as Rev. Charles Turner Torrey, who died in the Maryland State Prison, where he was confined for aiding slaves to escape; James G. Birney, first and only candidate of the Liberty party for the Presidency of the United States; Lysander Spooner, who tried hard to make the National Constitution what only the logic of the slaveholder's rebellion could make it—an anti-slavery document. And this the slaveholder's rebellion did through the rendings of the civil war, thus enabling the spirit of the framers of the constitution to shine through the letter of their immortal production. (Applause.)

The President next called upon Mr. George W. Putnam, of Lynn, as still another of the tried and honored veterans, who, from the beginning to the end, had been associated with the great anti-slavery leaders, and had done much and suffered not a little in behalf of the righteous, but once unpopular cause. Mr. Putnam, also, was warmly received. The audience had already heard the Hutchinsons sing one of his old Liberty songs.

ADDRESS OF MR. GEORGE W. PUTNAM.

Gray-haired and bent with age—we, a portion of the veterans of the "old guard of freedom" who still linger on earth, have come here today by the kind invitation of the Danvers Historical Society, to exchange our last greetings, and, with our fellow citizens to commemorate the most sublime event in human history, the abolition of American slavery and the emancipation of four millions of chattel slaves! Go back in memory only some sixty years and call to mind that, at that time, two and a half millions of slaves were held in bondage by a nation which made the heavens and earth resound with its boasted love of human freedom; a nation which stood forth a colossal hypocrite before the world; a nation whose "religious sense," the foundation of all human advancement, had been so long perverted by slavery, that it had well nigh become extinct; a nation whose Congress, state legislators, pulpit, forum, bar, press and people were all arrayed against the idea of the emancipation of the slaves of the country, then counted by millions, the most honorable exceptions to this being very few and far between. These things are hard and unpleasant to think of and to say, but we, the members who remain on earth of that "old guard of freedom," stand today too near our own graves to be willing to falsify history or to flatter anybody. But still let me say, I have spoken of these dark facts of the past mainly to impress on your minds the *tremendous* nature of that undertaking which sought, with every adverse element possible existing, to accomplish the stupendous work of the emancipation of the enslaved millions of America and by so doing to save a grand nation—the light and hope of the earth— from the inevitable perdition to which it was rapidly hastening. Who were the wretched victims in the case? I answer—they were the most poor, ignorant, degraded and helpless human beings on the face of God's earth! They had no grand history, no literature, no art, no civilization like that of Greece and Rome to fall back upon. Nothing in fact to arouse the interest and awaken the enthusiasm of the intelligent world in their behalf. Seized and brought to this land and enslaved! A hundred and more years of suffering, wretchedness, toil and degradation had been their lot at the time that the "yeomen went to Concord" on that never to be forgotten April morn and inaugurated that "Great Revolution" which created this nation and made it free and independent, but which, sad to say, brought to the faithful blacks who had done their part well in the war for Independence, no relief from their chains and their degradation! A few attempts at insurrection were afterward made by them, but they had failed and the insurgents were terribly punished. Occasionally some humane soul spoke a word for the slave. Jefferson said: "I tremble for my country when I remember that God is just, and that His justice will not sleep forever!" The good Benjamin Lundy and a few others made some efforts for the gradual emancipation of the slaves, but they had but little success.

About the year 1820 Rev. Samuel Worth was imprisoned in Kentucky for preaching the right of the slaves to their freedom.

"Darkness covered all the land
And gross darkness the people,"

when in the year 1830—a year never to be forgotten in the history of the world—a young man named William Lloyd Garrison opened at Boston his thunder batteries upon chattel slavery, and aroused the monster and its adherents north and south to the fiercest rage. Never will be forgotten the words of that young man when he said:—"I am in earnest! I will not excuse! I will not equivocate! I will not retreat a single inch and I will be heard!" and then in the name of God and humanity demanded the immediate emancipation of the American slaves. Very slowly came the friends of liberty to his support, but those who came were giants in their way, and the slave power south and north soon learned that Garrison and his faithful ones "meant business." Of the storms of rage, of the mobbing, rioting and murder, you all know well, and I need not recapitulate them here. The abolitionists were in earnest, and reaching far down into the darkness where lay the wretched slaves, they said, "Ours is a death grip! Take hold of our hands, and, God helping us, we will bring you up to light, life and liberty!"

What was the character of these early abolitionists? Were they all harmonious in their views and did they always agree? By no means. On the contrary, like all reformers who amount to anything, they had their sharp angles of character, and they disputed vehemently over the ways and means of carrying on their warfare with slavery. Some of them declared it the height of sinfulness to vote under the constitution of the United States, and others declared it a crime not to do so, and in their controversies they were often very sharp and severe upon each other. They reminded one strongly of the army of Cromwell. His soldiers were terribly in earnest and were "Theologians" to a man. By the light of their camp fires they read their Bibles, and they disputed violently in relation to the doctrines which they held of "election," "sanctification," "baptism," "original sin," etc. Their disputes were many and violent. "But when the trumpet sounded, they all went up to Naseby together!" So with the abolitionists; they disputed vehemently, earnestly and honestly in relation to the means of doing the great work they had undertaken. But every man and every woman had a dagger of some shape ready for the heart of slavery, and when the hour came they drove it to the hilt! The abolitionists earnestly desired that slavery should be abolished without bloodshed; but another and a higher power ordained it otherwise. The hour of retribution of which Jefferson had spoken had come at last, when for the boundless wrong and unspeakable oppression of the slave, the guilty south and guilty north had the "cup of trembling" presented to their lips by the hand of God, and were made to drain it to the dregs. Sad, indeed, it is to remember that the human race learn no lessons of justice unless they are written in human blood. We saw the vast paraphernalia of war gathered in our streets, in our valleys and on our hillsides. We heard the peal of thousand bugles, the roll of thousand drums! The parks of artillery thundered along our highways and the sunlight, from morn till night, flashed back from the long, long lines of northern steel gleaming on its southward way. We saw that unspeakably grand array,

"When the northern states, like giants,
Southward moved in awful form,
With voices of all nature
And God, behind the storm!"

what time the armed millions gathered to the "Armageddon," the great battle of God Almighty. And then, when the salvation of the Union was accomplished, when the earth and ocean had been reddened by the blood of white and of colored men, also, for they had done their part nobly on land and sea, the wide earth resounded with the crash of breaking chains, and the astonished nations saw four millions of most wretched and abject human slaves, *slaves*, come up from the pit of despair and, crossing as of old a crimson sea, take their places before the world, free men and free women forever! As to the noble character of the race thus redeemed from slavery, I have not time, nor words, even if I had the time, adequately to express it. Scarcely had the sound of clanking chains, the shrieks of the victims under the lash and the cries of the wretched ones separated at the auction block died away, when we saw, with astonishment, these newly emancipated slaves, *slaves*, in the schools and colleges of the land; many of these victims of slavery with the marks of the lash and the branding-iron still upon them, taking their places in the pulpit, the halls of legislation, in Congress, at the bar, in the jury box and on the judicial bench, and already vast amounts of wealth, honestly acquired, in their possession. Nothing like this has the world ever before witnessed. The colored race has shown a greatness of character and an innate power to rise from the load of cruel and miserable oppression which no words can fully express. And now for myself and all the old abolitionists present and absent, I would say that to each of us the remembrance, that in the hour of darkness when there seemed to be no help, God gave us strength to espouse the glorious cause of emancipation, and to rally with that "hope forlorn of liberty" which gathered upon these northern hills, is now, in our old age, the sweetest recollection of our lives. It was, indeed, but a cup of cold water which we had to give the wretched outcast, the chattel slave, but God knows it was given freely and with pure intent. A word more and I have done. There is a grand and glorious nation, the light and hope of the world, yet to be saved! The emancipation of the four millions of slaves, great as it was, after all was only the prelude of that unspeakably mighty work of saving this nation from destruction! Had slavery continued there had been today eight or nine millions of slaves in our land and the doom of our nation had been sealed forever. The tyrants of the old world are eagerly watching and longing for our downfall. But it must never come! This nation, again and again bloodbought, must fulfil the high destiny which the hand of God has marked out for it. The great struggle for human liberty must still go on. The blood shed upon hundreds of battlefields from Lexington to Yorktown, from Sumter to the Appomattox, must not have been shed in vain.

PRESIDENT PUTNAM:—We shall now have the pleasure of hearing Mr. Downing, of Newport, R. I., a colored gentleman who will very fitly represent his race in our meeting today. We could not think of holding a meeting like this, without some words from such a source. Known to all anti-slavery people, Mr. Downing is sure of your sympathetic interest beforehand, and he always has something worthy to say. (Earnest applause.)

ADDRESS OF MR. GEORGE T. DOWNING.

When I got the invitation from the Danvers Society I sat down and wrote a few remarks, knowing that there would be little time on such an occasion. I wrote my remarks down so as not to be led off by the thought suggested by such a gathering as this and that I might keep within the lines allotted to the several speakers. Aside from these remarks, I want simply to state that, while I am presented as a representative of the race that were freed through the efforts of the anti-slavery society, I myself was born free. Yet I feel that I may assume to myself the duty of speaking in behalf of the millions in the South who were once slaves, but who are now emancipated, and to say as their mouthpiece that they feel grateful for your work in their behalf.

My friends, I am here at your invitation, but not with that lightness of heart and freedom from care with which in all probability most of you have come; I come not with the fitting pleasure with which I would have come, but for a circumstance,—the most sad of all sad events that have occurred within many years of wedded bliss. I come in part to obtain some relief, I come, shall I not say, for an honorable diversion; to mingle with those having joyous feelings in connection with a moral accomplishment that reflects honor; that affords sweet satisfaction. My thoughts carry me in the direction of cemeteries, of monuments, of caskets which contain the remains of beauty, associated with love, with elevated virtues and most tender concern. But in my trend I stop—and worship at shrines that bring up happy recollections as to devotedness to truth and justice; to a self-sacrificing spirit, even unto martyrdom. I bend lowly on my knees on the grass, at this season of the violet and the lily, over spots where lie Garrison, Phillips, Sumner, Whittier, John Brown, Walker, May, Nell, Hayden, and other valiant defenders of the right; and dwelling there find an inspiring feeling come into me.

Our gathering of a small remaining part of the old anti-slavery guard is in many respects cheering. We can point to accomplishments, to having freed not only a race which is part of the nation from unjust servitude, but to the disenthralment of all its people; to their being freed from accountability in connection with a great and blighting sin that was upon the nation. It must not be forgotten in transmitting to our children that of which we are proud, that the obligation is upon us to consider not simply that our work, so far as it has gone, is highly commendable, but further, whether it is complete. I read the Constitution of the American Anti-Slavery Society; it tells me that all who allied themselves thereto pledged their lives and their sacred honor not only to labor without tire for the abolition of slavery, but to aid in passing the Freedman along and upward on the line of manhood and elevated citizenship without which attainment he is not in reality free. When William Lloyd Garrison and his followers declared for no alliance with political parties, because of a Sheolic agreement true of these parties, I admired their consistency; but when one is found outside of this fold and enters a political arena he can be justified as a moral adherent to party only in considering what is politic in aid of what is right.

I observe a party which has been regarded as being most deeply dyed in wrong, attracting to it as a reform party the sons of old abolitionists; a party to be made by the infusion of this young and fresh blood not only the defender of equality before the law, but the main guard of other just reforms. There is hope in the fact; there is satisfaction in its having selected as its chief executive a man who dares have convictions and to act thereon. I may have been wrong in advocating him; I may have been worthy of the censure that has been abusively used, but I have my convictions as to the same; I glory in them. I am willing to have them recorded with the rest of my anti-slavery record of which I feel proud. (Loud applause.)

THE PRESIDENT:—Mr. Downing was born free and was never a slave. Rev. Peter Randolph, of Charlestown, Mass., was born a slave but is now free. Such a man may fitly conclude the proceedings of this occasion. Most gladly do we welcome him, and it is not necessary for me to bespeak your interest in him and in what he may have to say.

Mr. Randolph was greeted with special sympathy and his simple and heartfelt words went directly home to the hearts of his hearers.

ADDRESS OF REV. PETER RANDOLPH.

Gentlemen, one word from me who was born a slave, not free. I will not detain you. I have been intensely interested in the speeches. When I received your invitation to be present at this meeting I was struck by a peculiar feeling that I was going to look into the faces of the heroes of emancipation, and I was glad when I received the invitation at the thought that I should see those men whose names were upon the programme. No one can speak of slavery. You can speak of it as an idea, but I could speak of it as a reality, had I time to talk to you. I want to return to you my sincere thanks, Mr. President, and the Society, and all these friends, for the noble work that you have done in behalf of my race. I remember all you have suffered for us, all you have endured. I remember listening to the speech of old Governor Wise before the United States Court, while I was serving as pastor in Richmond, Va., and a number of my people had gathered in the Court room. He looked and pointed his finger at us and said, "Thank God, there is the cause of the bone of our contention. Thank God it is gone." Yes, I bless God for all that you have done for us and all you have endured. All the insults that you have received, everything that has been spoken against you, was simply aimed at the black man, the colored race, and therefore I think you have stood between us and this terrible outrage, and it is due to you that we are free. I am now writing up a history of my work in the north and south, and I called upon an editor the other day and was repeating to him some of the topics I had written upon—and some of them about the race problem —and he said to me, "If you could solve those problems you would be Moses." I said "If you would hear what I have said, the problem is already solved. Over 1800 years ago God sent his son into the world to teach men the fatherhood of God and the brotherhood of men. That will solve the whole question and the problem of our race." That is the solution you have aimed at, my friends, and God bless you. (Applause.)

Other well known veterans on the platform the audience desired to hear, among whom were Miss Sarah H. Southwick of Wellesley Hills, and Rev. D. S. Whitney of Southboro', but there was no time. The former was obliged to leave for home during the later proceedings of the afternoon. Both of them afterwards kindly wrote out, by request, the remarks which they had it in mind to make, had they been called upon to speak, and their words are introduced here, like portions of other written, though unspoken addresses, as constituting a proper part of the testimony and recollections which belonged to the occasion and of which these pages are designed to contain a record.

ADDRESS OF MISS SARAH H. SOUTHWICK.

Mr. Chairman and Friends:—I have been asked to address you, but I cannot make a long speech. I will try, however, to say a few words. I was very glad to come to this meeting, for I am interested in anything that pertains to the history of Danvers and Salem. Danvers, which was in early times a part of Salem, was for two hundred and twenty-five years the home of the Southwick family—from 1630, when they landed at Salem and were given two acres of land by the Colony of Massachusetts Bay, to the death of my grandmother, Abigail Southwick, in 1856. I think there are not many families who have lived on the same land and carried on the same business for over two hundred years. They were tanners, and the old tannery still remains and I am told is still active. The history of the Southwick family too is almost the history of the persecution of the Quakers. That old house which stood till 1857, just opposite the Soldiers' Monument in Peabody, was the home of Lawrence and Cassandra, who were fined, despoiled, whipped, imprisoned and finally banished into the wilderness in the inclement winter of 1659, whence they found their way to the house of Nathaniel Sylvester on Shelter Island. Shelter Island is a small island at the easterly end of Long Island, where they died within three months of each other. This little island is owned by the family of the late Prof. Horsford who claim to be direct descendants of Nathaniel Sylvester, and it may interest you as it did me, when I tell you that in 1884 I received an invitation from Prof. Horsford to be present at a meeting of the descendants of Nathaniel Sylvester and of the "Friends" whom he had harbored, for the purpose of erecting a monument to their memory. And prominent among these were Lawrence and Cassandra Southwick. On that same place lived also their son, Josiah, who was also dreadfully persecuted, and Daniel and Provided, the two young people who were put up at auction to be sold as slaves to Virginia or Barbadoes and whom Whittier has commemorated in his poem of "Cassandra Southwick." It is from that Daniel that I am directly descended.

I have also heard my grandfather relate how his mother, Quaker though she was, took the hot loaves of bread from the oven and carried them and hot coffee to the soldiers, who were about starting, on the morning of the battle of Lexington, and who had congregated in the square at the foot of Boston Street, where the monument now stands just opposite their house.

At two different periods in my life, too, I have resided in Danvers. In 1834, when I attended Master Henry K. Oliver's school, whom many of you will remember as the educator of so many Salem girls; and again for three years preceding my grandmother's death, 1856, and I well know the value the Peabody Institute was to us.

Just after we moved to Boston, in 1835, occurred the mob in Salem of the house of Mr. Spencer on Buffum Street, where George Thompson was then staying and from whence he narrowly escaped, being sent to the house of Isaac Winslow in South Danvers. Then came, Oct. 7, the mob of "gentlemen of property and standing." Mr. Thompson had been invited to speak at that meeting of the Boston Female Anti-Slavery Society, but the threats of violence to him were such that the women sent word to

him not to come and it was in consequence of not finding him
that the mob attacked Mr. Garrison. I was not present at that
meeting, but my mother was. My sisters and myself were late and
encountered the crowd of men and were told we could not pass.
As we loitered the crowd parted and the women came through in
single file. We joined them and went to the house of Henry G.
Chapman, 11 West Street. There we were told that Mr. Garrison
was in the hands of the mob and every one was very anxious.
The meeting was turned into a prayer meeting and the prayers
you may be sure were very fervent.

At that time Mr. Thompson came to my father's house at 36
High Street, and remained there concealed for a fortnight, his
whereabouts being kept so secret that nobody but a few trusted
abolitionists were permitted to see him or know where he was
until he was sent privately to a sailing vessel bound to St. John
from where he went to Halifax and then to England. His wife
and family afterward stayed and were comfortably fitted out for
the return voyage in a packet ship from New York.

ADDRESS OF REV. D. S. WHITNEY.

MR. PRESIDENT AND ASSEMBLED FRIENDS:—On one occasion
when the taunt was thrown out that we had not freed the slaves,
Oliver Johnson promptly replied that if we had not freed the
slaves, we had freed ourselves. It is well at such a time as this
to give a little thought to what was accomplished in behalf of
themselves and the world by those who were so greatly absorbed
in the abolition of chattel slavery. Chattel slavery was a condition so horrible to humanity that, until it was removed, the lesser
wrongs endured by other sufferers were very naturally held in
abeyance. It was clearly seen by our noble anti-slavery women,
while they were giving heart and soul and life for the deliverance
of the slave, that they themselves and all their sisters were
suffering grievous wrongs, but with a magnificent magnanimity
they put their claims aside until the slaves were delivered. But
now that great undertaking is accomplished; the black curtain
hanging over humanity is raised. Before the law, the color of
the skin has no significance, and we can calmly look about to see
what remains to be done and what to do next before the point of
greatest perfection can be reached in our efforts to establish here
in America "a government of the People and for the People and
by the People." We ought never to lose sight of our peculiar
position. Providence has clearly appointed *us* to lead the
oppressed and benighted peoples up to Liberty and Light. What
is the next thing to be done? Clearly to restore her natural
rights to woman. What are her natural rights? The rights that

I claim for myself and that the law allows are clearly hers. I
know of no natural right that belongs to me that does not belong
to wife and daughters. But they cannot vote for the servants
whom we appoint from time to time to execute our laws. Why?
Because I and my brother, legal voters, hold the power to grant
that right and a majority of us refuse to do so. Year after year the
women have asked us to do this piece of justice, which our most
cherished political principles require of us. "Taxation without
representation is tyranny," exclaims Otis. Is it less so now than
a hundred years ago? If the man George, called King by the
vain ones, was a tyrant, what are we? O brother legal voters!

Let us hasten to right this great wrong and then we will see
what next to undertake. We may be sure, O brothers and sisters,
that there is a great work before us in this goodly land of
ours; but our working team is not yet fully made up. We have
the physical and intellectual force of men, but we need and lack
the moral and spiritual force of women, joined with the physical
and intellectual, before we shall do the best work for our country
and the world.

The Hutchinsons now favored the audience with still another
of their favorite songs, "The Old Granite State," which perhaps
was the most popular of all their pieces, unless the "Car of
Emancipation" was an exception. It had a special interest from
the circumstance that its numerous verses rang so much with
"The Tribe of Jesse," to which the singers themselves belonged,
and with the hills of the native home of the family. It was
largely composed by Jesse, one of the best known of the musical
brothers, in 1843, John adding some lines to the original form
during the war. We take from it the following characteristic
selections:—

SONG—"THE OLD GRANITE STATE."

  We have come from the mountains,
  We're come down from the mountains,
  Ho, we're come from the mountains
   Of the old Granite State!
  We're a band of brothers, etc.
   *   *   *   *
  And we love our glorious nation,
  Holding firm its lofty station;
  'Tis the pride of all creation,
   And our banner is unfurled.
  Men should love each other, etc.
   *   *   *   *

Yes, the good time 's drawing nigher,
And our nation, tried by fire,
Shall proclaim the good Messiah,
 Second coming of the Lord.
Heart and hand together, etc.

* * * *

Now, farewell, friends and brothers,
Fathers, sons, sisters, mothers,
Lynn people and all others,
 In the land we love the best.
May the choicest blessings, etc.

The meeting was brought to an end with the singing, by the Hutchinsons and the audience, of the favorite National hymn, "My Country, 'tis of thee," a copy of which, written by the author himself, Rev. S. F. Smith, was subsequently presented to the Society.

Other welcome offerings to the Society marked the occasion:— A fine portrait of William Lloyd Garrison, from his son, Mr. Francis J. Garrison; valuable anti-slavery books and pamphlets from Rev. Samuel May and Mr. Parker Pillsbury; a book on slavery from Mr. Lewis Ford, of Abington, of which he himself was the author; various anti-slavery tracts, given and sent by Mr. Charles K. Whipple, of Newburyport; newspaper articles about the Liberty Party by Hon. M. M. Fisher, of Medway, and presented by him, with photographs; a photograph of Mr. John W. Hutchinson, from Dr. Gaston W. Fowler, of Lynn; a piece of a slave's whipping-post at Charleston, S. C., from Mr. Luther S. Munroe, East Candia, N. H., and an ancient fire-screen that once belonged to Rev. and Mrs. Peter Clark, of Danvers, from Miss Mary J. Loring, of Woburn, a descendant.

Of the three other portraits that graced the stage, besides that of Mr. Garrison, the one of John G. Whittier was kindly loaned by the ladies of his household at "Oak Knoll," Danvers, that of Charles Sumner by Mr. Alfred Fellows, of Danvers, and and that of Rev. Samuel J. May of Syracuse, N. Y., by Mr. John J. May, of Dorchester.

The thanks of the Society were presented to these several parties for the interesting and generous gifts which they thus donated for its collections, and also to the many good friends from far and near who had by their attendance, speeches and songs, contributed so much to the success of the Commemoration. And grateful acknowledgments are also due and are here tendered to those of the members and neighbors, who tastefully decorated the platform of the Town Hall with flags and pictures, and flowers and plants, and superintended the tables and entertained the guests at the Society's Rooms; and also to the editors of the *Danvers Mirror* and other local papers for their helpful service and sympathy.

LETTERS FROM FRIENDS.

In response to the circular of invitation, a large number of letters were received from friends, many of whom were present, while others were prevented from attendance by previous engagements or by distance, or by illness or the infirmities of age. They are of so much interest that we have given place to a very considerable portion of them, or extracts from them. Nearly all of them are from men or women who were long identified with anti-slavery work, and not a few of those who here send their greetings or express their sympathy with the occasion, or relate their own experiences and recollections, were among the most conspicuous and zealous of the reformers. These letters, as well as the speeches, abound in pertinent facts and illustrations and seem to us strikingly representative of the faith and spirit of the earlier time.

FROM HON. FREDERICK DOUGLASS.

CEDAR HILL, ANACOSTIA, D. C.,
March 29, 1893.

I have duly received your kind invitation to meet in Danvers the few remaining veterans of the anti-slavery cause, and it would give me great pleasure were I able to respond favorably to that invitation. I should be happy to once more see the forms, look into the faces and hear the voices of those whom you have invited and who expect to be present at this, probably last of such meetings on earth.

Yes, I remember Danvers, and the Essex County Anti-Slavery Society, and the persons you have mentioned as active in those early days. Those times required men and women of strong convictions and of courageous and independent character, and there were many such. I remember my first visit to Danvers when I was made welcome to the home of Abner Sanger, a man of high standing, who, in the state of public sentiment then existing, could not entertain me without incurring from his neighbors much unfavorable comment. But he was not of the make to set aside his conscience and suppress his noble, humane sentiments in order to please his neighbors. He stood high above the prejudices of the hour and treated me as a man and a brother. I like, too, to remember the Merrills, the Endicotts, the Harrimans and others. Could I be with you, I would bear warm testimony to the manliness and brotherly kindness which met me in Danvers, in the earlier and darker hours of my career. To see Parker Pillsbury, the man who was perhaps the source of more terror to the proslavery church and clergy of his day than any other, and to see John Hutchinson, the only remaining one of the Hutchinson Family which gave its youth, beauty and transcendent musical genius to the cause of the slave, would compensate me for any trouble a long journey would require at my hands.

I am very sorry not to be able to be with you. There would be deep pathos in such a meeting, for we are all changed in body, if not in spirit. Some of our eyes are already dim, our hair white, our faces wrinkled and our bodies bent, and soon, as you say, there will be no more meetings on earth.

There will, however, be a bright side to your assembling. The recollection of deeds well done, of lives well spent, of wrongs successfully combated, and of a race redeemed from slavery, will make old eyes swim in young tears of joy. Believe me present with you in spirit, even if compelled to be absent in body.

* * * Mrs. Douglass joins me in wishing to my Danvers friends a happy and profitable meeting with the veterans of the anti-slavery cause.

FROM MR. CHARLES K. WHIPPLE.

NEWBURYPORT, Apr. 5, 1893.

I rejoice to hear of the proposed commemoration of old anti-slavery days by the Danvers Historical Society on the 26th inst., and am grateful for your courteous invitation to attend its meetings. It would be delightful to meet the old friends and fellow-workers who, you tell me, are expected there, but various circumstances combine to prevent my personal attendance. I will gladly, however, say a word of greeting and of suggestion to the friends who will assemble there.

In New England, from which most of the Abolitionists came, a new generation is arising who "know not Joseph;" to whom the names of Garrison, Phillips, Quincy, Weld, Burleigh, Foster and Pillsbury, and of those noble women, Abby Kelly, Lucy Stone, Maria Weston Chapman and Sojourner Truth are getting to be only names, with very little understanding of the difficulties and dangers they encountered and the heroism they displayed in laboring for the slave, when the chief representatives of Church and State, commerce and literature, were combining to obstruct their labors. To collect, preserve and diffuse the records of those labors for the instruction of future generations is one of the most important functions of a Historical Society. I hope the one in Danvers will not fail to obtain, while it is yet possible, such books as Richard Hildreth's "Archy Moore" and "Despotism in America;" Mrs. Chapman's "Right and Wrong in Boston" and "Right and Wrong in Massachusetts," and Theodore D. Weld's "Testimony of a Thousand Witnesses." Also, some of those school reading books which, in the early years of the present century contained dialogues, verses and stories, inculcating anti-slavery sentiments, such as the "American Preceptor" and the "Columbian Orator."

Since there still remain, at the north, as well as the south, persons disposed to misrepresent and calumniate both the abolitionists and the colored race, and since efforts of this sort still occasionally appear in our periodical literature, it is still needful to keep an eye on those manifestations, and to answer such of them as are worth answering. Work of this sort has been very faithful and judiciously done for many years past by our lately deceased fellow-laborer, Oliver Johnson of New York, as well as by Rev. Samuel May of Leicester; but the field is large, and many more such reapers are needed. One recent manifestation of the proslavery spirit appeared in an article in the September *North American Review*, entitled "Lynch Law in the South," by W. Cabell Bruce. This writer excuses the cruelties inflicted upon negroes by Lynch Law in the South on the ground (which he assumes as true) that the assaults of black men upon white women in that region are increasing in frequency. He proceeds to ask and answer as follows:—

"Why is it that the negro has become an habitual offender against female virtue in the South? * * * We answer unhesitatingly, much as we are gratified that the incubus of slavery has been forever lifted from the South, because the negro is no longer subject to the authority of a master, and is yet subject to *no other form of moral discipline* that can take its place to as good or better advantage."

Mr. Bruce here made the impudent assumption that the methods actually used by slaveholders before the war were "moral discipline," and also shows the desire to re-establish as much of it as may be practicable. Hoping to address the same audience in the *North American Review*, I wrote a rejoinder to Mr. Bruce's article, suggesting a probable explanation of the sensuality, and the brutal indulgence of it, attributed to the colored people.

After stating that the negro race are admitted to be especially imitative, disposed to copy the language, dress, morals, manners and customs of the class reckoned superior around them, I made an abstract of the abundant evidence that that superior class, for more than a century past, have deliberately and elaborately set before their imitators a model in regard to sexual indulgence as follows:—By habitual custom, sanctioned and fortified by legal statutes, and allowed to ministers and church members by the silent acquiescence of ecclesiastical bodies, they so organized their communities throughout the slave states *that any white man could ravish with impunity any colored woman.* These things being so, I asked:—Can you wonder that among the class who have been kept ignorant and brutal by the deliberate policy of the slaveholders through so many generations, cases should still be found of such extreme brutality as the slaveholders habitually practiced? And could a renewal of their form of "moral discipline" be expected to furnish better results?

As the editor of the *North American Review* declined to print my rejoinder, Mr. Bruce's article remains unanswered.

I request the Danvers Historical Society to accept, with my best wishes, four anti-slavery tracts, which I post to you with this letter.

I hope that all who join your gathering have read or will read an excellent article on "The Burning of Negroes in the South," by the editor of the Arena, in the April number of that periodical.

FROM MRS. KATE TANNATT WOODS.

"Maple Nest," Salem, Mass. April 7, 1893.

I am greatly interested in your efforts for the abolitionists' meeting under the auspices of our Danvers Historical Society. If this wounded limb of mine will only be *merciful*, I hope to be with you. Did you know that my parents when in New York city were shielders and protectors of *run away slaves* in connection with some good Connecticut Quakers?

Old "Aunt Dinah," whose story Mr. Garrison was fond of telling, was *my nurse*, a run away slave, cared for, loved, and humanly speaking, saved by *my own mother*. One of my first articles was the story of the "Coming of Aunt Dinah," and when Mr. Wm. Lloyd Garrison found that I was the author, he was ever after my kind friend. How strange it all seems that my gifted and handsome mother, who was fond of society and yet tenderly philanthropic, should be the rescuer of the poor slaves in the city of New York *without one of her own friends knowing aught of it!* How strange, also, that her child, who had never seen New England then, should come to be one of a committee, composed of Wm. Lloyd Garrison, Wendell Phillips, Lucy Stone, and other brave souls who were striving to emancipate woman, as they had done the black man!

If I am able to do so, I shall attend the meeting.

(Mrs. Woods was present.)

FROM MR. JOSEPH A. ALLEN.

NEWFIELD, MASS., April 9, 1893.

The letter of April 6, which you wrote to my brother, Nathaniel T. Allen of West Newton, was forwarded to me.

He is on a trip to California and he will regret very much, I am sure, being obliged to decline your polite invitation for the 26th.

Please accept my thanks for the invitation. I anticipate much pleasure in meeting some of the few remaining anti-slavery veterans.

FROM REV. THOMAS T. STONE, D. D.

BOLTON, April 10, 1893.

Few things could give me more pleasure than your invitation to meet the veterans of the anti-slavery conflict. But if there were no other hindrance, the age of 92 years may serve as an apology for my absence. And yet I can hardly forbear to write some of the thoughts which the occasion brings up. What a progress,—what a movement in evolution, as the word is now-a-days,—this nineteenth century has made, if it were in nothing but personal liberty. When it began, slavery was almost universal; its last decade is passing without a slave in Christendom. When within so short a period a revolution so great? We ought with all our hearts to thank God, and if we feel discouragement to cheer ourselves with the hope of sure victory for freedom and righteousness.

Not a slave, I have said, in Christendom. But the spirit of slavery and the influences which it has poured into the hearts and habits of men, naturally survive the institution. Among the outward and palpable effects which still remain, we cannot readily overlook the violence and the fraud by which our enfranchised countrymen are deprived of their political rights. Directly we can do nothing with these evils. But indirectly, and in what is the most effectual way, we can all of us do some thing; we can cherish in our own souls and express in our deeds and our words true love and earnest sympathy for those who are wronged, and can do all in our power to deepen the indignation which should glow in every heart and which could sooner or later reach the conscience of the oppressor. We may not live to see the end: indeed there is no end; when this and a thousand other evils are passed into oblivion, the Supreme Father will have other work for his children to do, putting away evils which are now hidden and striving for good of which we now have little foresight. So let us gird ourselves continually for each new conflict, for each new victory; for in this warfare there is never such a thing as defeat; seeming reverses often, but these are seen at last to be victories. The cross has become to us symbol of the greatest victory which has been won on earth. What was it before the one Sufferer made it the promise of God?

If I could well be with you at the gathering,—but let that pass; my heart is still with you, with all who in the darkest hour looked for the coming day. May we all be faithful to the last.

The blessing of the Highest be with each and all.

FROM HON. FRANCIS W. BIRD.

EAST WALPOLE, MASS., April 13, 1893.

It would give me great pleasure to attend the meeting for the commemoration of the old anti-slavery days. I like to refresh my fading recollections of those good times and good men. I could contribute but very little to such a gathering, but I should enjoy meeting those of fewer years and better memories than I am; but I could not be with you and get home before night, and I must defend my evenings.

FROM HON. SIMEON DODGE.

MARBLEHEAD, April 14, 1893.

Absence from home is the reason for my not receiving yours, dated April 6th, until today.

Please accept my thanks for your invitation to attend the meeting on the 26th, at Danvers Plains. I hope to be present on that occasion if I am in this vicinity at that time.

I think that all of the *early* abolitionists of Marblehead, with the exception of myself and wife, have either died or removed from town. There are others who came into the movement at a later date. I will notify them, or some of them, of the meeting.

FROM REV. JOSEPH MAY.

PHILADELPHIA, April 15, 1893.

I received the other day, in Boston, your kind letter about the interesting meeting you are planning. While everything connected with the grand movement for abolition is deeply interesting to me, for itself, and for its personal associations, and I should rejoice to attend the meeting, I am just now so very busy that I cannot think of it. I have assumed several pieces of extra work, which must, for two or three months, more than occupy all my leisure, of which I have little.

So I hardly think I can even write a letter as you kindly propose. I must be content to send only my assurance of deep sympathy in all that you do and in all the memories your meeting will call up. I esteem it perhaps the greatest good fortune in my own lot, to have been born and brought up under the influence of a movement, morally so noble, and of the group of men, not only morally, but intellectually, so able and inspiring. The personalities of all the leaders are most familiar to me—they all seemed like kinsmen—and I am deeply conscious of the indelible impression for good they and their cause made upon my character. I revere them and their pure, unselfish zeal.

FROM MR. JOHN CURTIS.

BOSTON, Apr. 16, 1893.

I am in receipt through you of an invitation from the Danvers Historical Society to attend a meeting on the 26th, commemorative of Old Anti-Slavery Days. You may be assured of my presence at so interesting an occasion as the assembling of the few veteran abolitionists yet spared from the destiny that awaits all mankind. It was my fortune to be simply a private in those stirring times, and though past "three score and ten," I have the most pleasurable recollections of the events and the renowned men and women who labored and led in the historical Anti-Slavery struggle. I trust your meeting will be most successful.

FROM REV. WM. H. FISH, SEN.

DEDHAM, April 17, 1893.

I am very glad and grateful that The Danvers Historical Society has had the thoughtful kindness to inaugurate a meeting commemorative of the Old Anti-Slavery Days, and to make generous preparations for it. At that meeting I hope to be present, having received a kind invitation to it from your committee of arrangements, particularly through my esteemed friend Dr. A. P. Putnam. I wish that my neighbor, the noble and faithful Theodore D. Weld, could also be present, but at ninety years of age, and quite feeble, this seems hardly practicable, if possible.

My interest in the Anti-Slavery cause and Garrisonism dates back almost sixty years—now eighty-one—and I am as thankful now as then that I was ever brought into a close and active union with it and with its representative men and women, especially in Massachusetts and New York—in New York in active association with those truest, noblest, divinest of men, Samuel J. May and Gerrit Smith, they themselves standing evidences of Immortality, for such men can never die, or cease to be.

I shall be glad of the opportunity to look once more into the faces and to take by the hand of an enduring friendship and fellowship, the very few of my generation and age that may be present at the meeting, as Samuel May and Parker Pillsbury—ever "faithful among the faithless found"—and to see also the children and children's children who cherish the faith and honor, the devotion and zeal of their pioneer fathers and mothers, the most of whom long since rested from their labors and entered into rest in the world "where the slave is free from his master," and their good works have followed them.

FROM REV. ROBERT COLLYER.

NEW YORK, April 17, 1893.

I would love to come to the gathering of the Old Guard of Freedom, but have no time or strength to spare just now or then. I should delight to see your faces, clasp your hands, and listen while you tell the grand old story so far as it may be told that day. My dear friend, Edward M. Davis, used to say that "the cause" had done more for you than you could ever do for the cause, and in what small measure I could be one with it along through the fifties, I know this was true. And it will be true always, but especially of the old abolitionists, be they among the living or those we call the dead.

"Those heroes who could grandly do as they could greatly dare,
A vesture very glorious their shining spirits wear."

They stand within the greatest movements on the life of the Republic while it has a name to live. If I could come and was worthy to say any word in such a gathering, this would be my word. I am sure it would not be needed, for the good scripture will be true of you all—"the word is nigh thee, even in thy heart."

FROM MRS. C. H. DALL.

WASHINGTON, D. C., April 17, 1893.

Into the midst of all the tiresome spring cares which beset those who live in hot climates, comes the circular of the Danvers Historical Society, like a refreshing northern breeze. When I stood with Mr. May and Mr. Pillsbury at Whittier's funeral when I heard Abby Hutchinson sing her swan-song for herself and the dead Poet, I thought I was standing for the last time with my old companions in Anti-Slavery work. It rejoices me to think that Danvers will not permit their memory to perish, that there are still men and women who hold the "Old Guard" precious and sacred. Those of us who lived through those perilous times cannot help smiling now and then, as we encounter on our roll names unknown or given only at the eleventh hour, and read the frequent assertion that Garrison and his men kept back the work and accomplished nothing. Let those laugh who will, for well we know who held the key of the situation! Much remains to be done before our country will hold the position before the world that all her true sons desire for her. Instead of Columbian Expositions I would rather see truth and honor in high places; instead of Palaces of Invention, I would rather see the upbuilding of a State whose foundations shall be laid in truth and righteousness. We are free—let us learn to be upright.

FROM MR. WENDELL P. GARRISON.

NEW YORK, April 17, 1893.

It would give me much pleasure to attend your commemoration Anti-Slavery meeting next week, and I desire to acknowledge with thanks the invitation extended to my wife and myself. But it will be impossible for us to attend, and for my own part I feel that ten years given to reviewing and reporting the history of the cause—so far as that could be done in the life of my father—entitle me to a long exemption from reminiscence, and certainly make it seemly to hold my peace for a while and let others take the floor.

FROM MRS. ELIZABETH B. CHACE.

VALLEY FALLS, R. I., April 18, 1893.

It is with extreme regret that I am obliged to deny myself the great happiness it would be to me, to unite with the dear old friends, and the friends of the younger generation, in commemorating the great struggle for human freedom, in which it was my blessed privilege to bear an humble part. But irrevocable circumstances make it impossible for me to share in this coming blessedness.

There is no portion of my life, to which, now, in my eighty-seventh year, I revert with more satisfaction, than that which I gave to the cause of the slave.

No guests were ever more welcome to my door, than were those who came in the darkness of night, to escape from the human bloodhounds who were seeking for prey. No ministers of the Gospel brought me so acceptable instruction as did the self-sacrificing teachers of the Gospel of freedom. To me, as to many others, it was a liberal education. There we learned the injustice, the degradation of the condition of woman, and were thereby prepared, when the slavery of the black man was abolished, to enter on the warfare for the emancipation, the enfranchisement and the elevation of the subjected, the dependent half of humanity. That so many of those early workers have passed away, will cast a shadow on the brightness of the occasion, but it is safe to indulge the belief, that, wherever they are, they are in full sympathy with it there, and are participating in the enjoyment thereof.

Those of us who still remain on the earth, but are denied the pleasure of this reunion, will miss the hearty hand-shakings and greetings of the day, but we will enjoy them in spirit, and we will wish for you all, the brightest of skies, the loveliest of southwesterly breezes, the warmest remarks of friendship, and the happiest remembrances of this memorable event.

FROM REV. RICHARD S. STORRS, D. D.

BROOKLYN, N. Y., April 18th, 1893.

How far away seem the days which you are to recall in Danvers! And what memories of eloquence, self-devotion, sacrifice, success, are awakened by your reference to them! I should be most happy to be present at your proposed celebration, even to take part in it in some subordinate way, but it will be as impossible for me to go to Danvers next week as it would be to carry thither the sunrise, in my hands. I can only thank you for your kind thought of me in connection with the occasion, and wish for your Society, in this work and all others, the largest prosperity.

FROM MRS. EMILY W. TAYLOR.

GERMANTOWN, PA., April 18th, 1893.

I have just received a circular inviting me to attend a meeting commemorative of old anti-slavery days, to be held at Danvers. Were it possible, I should delight to do so, to meet once more so many of the prominent speakers who are to be there and to recall memories of our three years' residence in Danvers when my father, Isaac Winslow, was very actively interested in the anti-slavery cause, harboring fugitive slaves at our house; also entertaining George Thompson at about the time that he was being watched for and hunted in Boston. I also recall with what interest my father aided in getting up a meeting at which his co-religionists, Sarah and Angelina Grimke, were to speak against the institution of slavery, in the midst of which they had always lived. Oh, those were days to which I look back with enthusiasm—days which were worth living in.

FROM MRS. EDNAH D. CHENEY.

JAMAICA PLAIN, April 18, 1893.

It grieves me very much that, owing to a severe attack of lameness, I cannot promise myself the pleasure of responding to your kind invitation in remembrance of old Anti-Slavery Days. I love these reunions of those who took part in that glorious struggle for right and liberty, and small as my part in it was, I am proud to be recognized as always having been with them in heart and soul.

But happy as we are in the great deliverance that was accomplished thirty years ago, and proud as we are of the wonderful progress, and admirable conduct of those who were then emancipated, the hour has not yet come when we can fold our hands in satisfaction without considering the evils that still remain, and threaten the permanence of the blessing we have gained through bitter conflict.

The outrages on helpless negroes at the South by lynch law, the indignities put upon them in defiance of the principles of the Amendment to the Constitution, the hindrances in their pursuit of various employments, in short the inhuman prejudice still powerful against them, ought to arouse us to vigilance and make us feel that we have not yet paid our debt to them, but must stand by them until they are really " through the woods."

If our hands are sometimes fettered in regard to direct work for them at the South, at least we can cast out the evil spirit from among ourselves, and by our own fidelity, send a current of bracing air ever down to those who are laboring for them at the South, and keep up the hearts of the new generation who knew not slavery, but who sometimes feel the degradation of their present condition as keenly as their forefathers did the miseries of actual bondage.

But you all feel and know these things, and so I need only say that I shall be with you in sympathy, and rejoice to know that you will be encouraged in your work by again joining hands in friendship and memory of old days.

FROM MRS. HENRY WARD BEECHER.

BROOKLYN, N. Y., April 18th, 1893.

It is very kind in you to remember me and invite me to this commemoration of the old anti-slavery days. Nothing could give me greater pleasure than to be present on an occasion so closely connected with the memory of my husband. But, if I can leave home and the work I have on hand, I am booked for the Pacific Coast, Puget Sound, where my youngest son is.

I may not accomplish all that I have planned, but as you can well imagine, long to see my boy and his family once more, and if I can compass that, I must not venture on any other engagements.

FROM DR. W. SYMINGTON BROWN.

STONEHAM, MASS., April 18, 1893.

Other duties will prevent me from enjoying the anti-slavery celebration on the 26th instant. I would like to see Parker Pillsbury once more, who, I believe, is the last of the old anti-slavery orators I delighted to hear.

When I came to the United States in 1850, I had letters of introduction to Wm. Lloyd Garrison, Wendell Phillips, and Theodore Parker; also one to Charles Hovey. They are all dead; but the sacred cause of human freedom still lives, and will never die. I still try to do the work it demands.

FROM MR. D. L. BINGHAM.

MANCHESTER, MASS., April 18, 1893.

We shall be most pleased, my wife and I, to attend the meeting commemorative of those old "Anti-Slavery Days," and to look once more in the faces of those who were true to God and humanity, when it cost—to be true.

In a letter written a few days later, (April 22), Mr. Bingham most properly asked if a circular of invitation had been sent to Mr. and Mrs. Daniel W. Friend, of Manchester, and stated that their home had once "gladly received" and greatly comforted and aided a poor fugitive slave, who had come to it, "wet, cold and hungry." In answer to a request for more particulars concerning the case, the following communication has come to hand. It records an act of certain "good Samaritans," which, like countless other similar deeds of the abolitionists, should be held in "everlasting remembrance."

MANCHESTER BY-THE-SEA, Aug. 8, 1893.

I should have answered your letter earlier, but my brother Friend was away, and I wished to hear again the story of the fugitive slave before writing. It was sometime in the fifties, in the spring of the year, the weather rainy and cold, when the poor fugitive came to the house of the Baptist minister. Brother Friend, going home in the gloom of the evening, saw the minister on the street, looking for one of the Selectmen to take charge of the poor wanderer, a very imprudent thing to do at that time. Brother F. said, "I will take care of him." The minister gave him supper, but was unwilling to shelter him over night. Brother Friend took him into a warm room, took off his soiled and wet clothes, bathed his feet in warm water, gave him clean, dry clothing, put him in his own bed, and treated him with hot drinks until he was warmed. He was trembling with cold when he entered brother F.'s house. The next morning brother F. came to me greatly pleased that he had violated an unjust law, by showing mercy. The fugitive was a good-looking, intelligent man, about 30 years old. He had been body servant to a wealthy Baltimorean. As he was thinly clad, my wife, Emeline Bingham, worked nearly all day Sunday, repairing an overcoat that happened to fit him. Mr. Thomas P. Gentlee, a near neighbor, came in Sunday evening with a purse of money. This was increased by brother F. I added some. So the poor man was in good condition to start for Canada very early Monday morning. It was Mrs. Hannah Friend, now dead, a most excellent woman, who helped receive the fugitive. But Mr. Friend's present wife was also "*in at the start,*" as I wrote. * * *

Respectfully and truly yours,

D. L. BINGHAM.

FROM MISS ANNA L. COFFIN.

NEWBURYPORT, Apr. 19, 1893.

When I was calling at Mr. Whipple's a few weeks ago, he spoke of the contemplated reunion at Danvers on the 26th inst., of the old abolitionists, and how much my father, the late Joshua Coffin, would have enjoyed such a meeting.

He was always a lover of freedom, showing it in his boyhood by buying caged wild birds from his mates and enjoying the supreme pleasure of freeing them; and in his early manhood by outspoken and earnest words against slavery. Later in life he joined the Anti-Slavery Society, risking his life by going from Philadelphia to Memphis in 1838, and rescuing from slavery a free colored man who had been kidnapped and sold. These events occurred before my recollection, but many years after he used to tell us about his "south-western tour," as he called it, always finishing by saying, "A war between the North and South will surely come and the slaves will be freed. I may not live to see it, but you undoubtedly will." To his great joy, and ours with him, he lived to see it. During all the dark days of the civil war he never lost his faith in the goodness of God and His over-ruling providence.

FROM MRS. LILLIE B. CHACE WYMAN.

VALLEY FALLS, R. I., April 19, 1893.

My husband and I regret very much that we can not be with the anti-slavery friends in Danvers on the 26th. Mr. Wyman is now in Chicago, and I am going West on the 24th.

Mr. Wyman was one of the younger members of the group of Abolitionists in Worcester from 1846 or 1847. He was earnestly and enthusiastically devoted to the cause, was a speaker in anti-slavery meetings; and during most of the dozen years preceding the Civil War he was a non-voting Garrisonian. He has many interesting and happy memories of Theodore Parker, Wendell Phillips and Wm. Lloyd Garrison. He served three years in the army, because he believed that the war was an opportunity to put an end to slavery. As Provost Marshal of Alexandria, Virginia, he gave the negroes equal justice with the whites, and was the first United States official in that position, who proved himself the friend of the slave. His last military service was to accompany the body of Abraham Lincoln to its resting place in Springfield, Illinois. It was a real regret to him that he was obliged to leave home before your reunion.

Too young myself to participate in the anti-slavery warfare, I was the inheritor of the traditions of freedom from my father and mother, my grandfather Arnold Buffum, and his father William Buffum, a Quaker Abolitionist in Rhode Island. My earliest memories are of anti-slavery speakers entertained as guests in our house, of fugitive slaves, and of childish indignation at the assault in the Senate upon Charles Sumner. The mild smile of Wm. Lloyd Garrison was one of the benedictions that fell upon my childhood, and the kindness of Stephen and Abby Kelley Foster made me an intimate guest in their home.

I have no words to tell all, in the way of mental and moral education, which I owe to the Abolitionists, and my soul honors their memory. I hope that every thing will pass pleasantly and satisfactorily at your proposed reunion and I wish I could be with you.

FROM MR. AARON M. POWELL.

NEW YORK, April 20, 1893.

It would give Mrs. Powell and myself much pleasure to attend the anti-slavery reunion to which you kindly invite us. I regret that our engagements are such that it will be impracticable for us to do so.

It is not too much to say of the American anti-slavery conflict that it was the grandest moral movement of modern times. To have known and touched hands with its noble, self-sacrificing leaders, men and women, and to have shared to any extent in their labors, gives to those of us who yet linger on this side of the border added significance to life itself. More and more, too, as the years go on, do the early Abolitionists become, as an object lesson, helpers and teachers to younger workers of this generation in dealing with the prevalent evils of our time.

I am rejoiced that just now Boston comes again to the front, and characteristically, to protest against our oppressive treatment and scandalous injustice in dealing with the Chinese; and with a timely demand upon the supreme judicial tribunal of the nation to vindicate their legal rights.

FROM MISS MARY GREW.

PHILADELPHIA, April 20, 1893.

To be with you on this occasion, to listen to your voices and clasp your hands in fraternal greeting, would renew the inspiration of our years of struggle, of hope; when, side by side and heart to heart, we fought, with the sword of the Spirit, the battle of Freedom for the American slave.

The years which have elapsed since we sang together the Jubilee song have been so full of earnest work in other fields, so much has been accomplished in Moral, Social and Political Reforms, that, looking backward to that joyous hour, the interim seems very long. How many ecclesiastical barriers have been broken down, how many more are tottering today! What lessons in the brotherhood of Nations have been taught by World's Expositions! And how marvellous has been the progress of woman's emancipation from the bonds of church and statute law and enthralling customs!

To the American Anti-Slavery Society belongs the honor of being the pioneer in this Reform. Women should never forget that in 1840 that Society stood alone in its assertion of perfect equality of its members, without distinction of sex. It was a very radical, very startling assertion and practice then; and there were abolitionists who could not stand this test; and they "walked no more with us." What would these timid conservatives have thought if they could have looked across these intervening years and could have seen women in the pulpits, at the bar, in professors' chairs in colleges, voting at the polls, and filling state and municipal offices? May we not, respected friends, gratefully and humbly rejoice today that in our arduous work as abolitionists we were permitted to give an impetus to this newer cause now speeding to its triumph?

If I could be with you in person, as I shall in spirit, I think that the audience would seem to me youthful. Should you call the roll of our "Old Guard," how few would be the audible responses! The names of many absent ones (not dead, but more alive than we,) will be in your thoughts, and their faces will be a vivid memory. Let us think of them hopefully, ay, rejoicingly, that they "fought a good fight, and kept the faith;" and having finished their course here, have gone onward and upward to larger life and work. They are enshrined in our hearts:—Garrison, Phillips, May, Lucretia Mott, Lydia Maria Child, and the host of faithful souls who with them endured unto the end. And some still here, but far advanced in years, will doubtless send you greetings. As I write, our venerated Dr. Furness is receiving the congratulations of his friends on his ninety-first birthday. He gave to us the benediction of his presence at a similar Memorial Meeting recently held in this city. And Robert Purvis, tried and true, is too feeble to appear among you otherwise than in cordial sympathy.

Another aged abolitionist, Mrs. Rosanna Thompson, long and well known in Philadelphia, unfaltering in the darkest and most perilous hours of our conflict, wishes to send, from her bed of sickness, greeting to her fellow-laborers, and to say that she has "never ceased to be grateful that she was counted worthy to be a soldier in that thirty years' war;—a war in church and state, in commerce and in society; a war which was not all peaceful in its methods, as the violence and martyrdoms of that period will show."

To the young generation, for whom the work of the twentieth century waits, I would say:—Let the achievements of the past stimulate and encourage you to carry on bravely the work which your fathers and mothers bequeath to you. To each nation, to each period, comes its own task, its own test of fidelity to truth and right; its own peculiar phase of the old conflict between justice and injustice, liberty and slavery; and ever the same assurance of ultimate victory.

FROM MRS. CAROLINE M. SEVERANCE.

Los Angeles, Cal., Apr. 20th, '93.

It is a sore temptation which your kind invitation brings me, to be present at the coming commemoration of the old anti-slavery work and days. Almost no temptation could be stronger. But the time would be too short, since your letter reached me only yesterday, the 19th. Too short time for this to be in season for the occasion, I fear. And so I can only mourn my own absence in the distance which does not lend enchantment to the scene, the beloved faces and voices outdoing all conjuring of the imagination.

You do me great honor in remembering me, who was so late a comer and so feeble a helper, in your noble work. But it was one of the noblest fellowships, and most valuable experiences, of my life,—covering largely, also, the kindred work for woman's education and recognition as citizen. I have just now had the rare pleasure of listening to John W. Chadwick's admirable paper on Theodore Parker and his work, which revived delightfully for me those wonderfully pregnant days under his ministry to all good causes in Union Hall, which was the great awakening to so many blinded eyes, and inspiration to so many hungry hearts.

Ah yes, how tenderly I recall the fine old times, and the beloved friends. Give them my heartiest greeting at this end of their memorable gathering, and my hope to see them face to face before they "join the choir invisible."

FROM MISS MARY J. LORING.

Woburn, Mass., April 20, 1893.

I have received the Society's circular. I think your meeting will be a grand affair. There can be nothing higher for man or woman than to take an interest in humanity. My father and my mother were strong anti-slavery people and by their influence their daughter has ever hated oppression in any form. I intend to be present and shall bring for your Society a fire-screen which the Rev. Peter Clark and his wife Deborah held in their hands many times; and one of their descendants is more than pleased to return it to its old home in Danvers. Hoping to have the pleasure of meeting with you again, I am yours for the elevation of humanity and for the prosperity of the Danvers Historical Society.

[Rev. Peter Clark was minister of the First Church of Danvers from 1717 until 1768.]

FROM MR. FRANCIS J. GARRISON.

4 PARK STREET, BOSTON, April 20, 1893.

It will give Mrs. Garrison and myself much pleasure to accept the invitation of the Danvers Historical Society for the 26th inst., if no unforeseen obstacle prevents, though it may not be practicable for us to remain through the entire afternoon. My business duties make it difficult for me to speak with certainty, but I shall be much disappointed if they prevent my meeting the friends whom you are to gather at your next meeting.

FROM MR. CORNELIUS WELLINGTON.

EAST LEXINGTON, April 20, 1893.

I thank the committee for the kind invitation to be present at the commemorative meeting on the 26th inst.

I will take the train which leaves Boston at 10.45, accompanied by one and perhaps two of my sisters, all members of the Lexington Historical Society, and old active members of the Massachusetts Anti-Slavery Society.

It will indeed be a pleasure to us to meet once more any of the few remaining workers in the anti-slavery field in years gone by, and to meet again and become better acquainted with the members of the Danvers Historical Society which you represent.

FROM MR. JOHN J. MAY.

DORCHESTER, MASS., April 21, 1893.

You have my cordial thanks for the invitation to the gathering at Danvers, which I cannot doubt will be a most interesting occasion.

An accumulation of work, caused partly by confinement at home by the prevailing influenza, will probably prevent my going thither, although I do not altogether forego the hope.

It occurs to me that if you seek for portraits of the anti-slavery heroes whom you commemorate, you may like the loan of a crayon portrait, by Kimberly, the best likeness extant, I think, of Samuel Joseph May, late of Syracuse, (born 1797, died 1871), of whom I always have felt, as Andrew D. White expressed his feelings at the grave,—that he was "the best man I ever knew, the purest, the sweetest, the most like the Master."

If the loan will be acceptable, I will readily, on learning this from you, carefully box the picture and send it by express, as you may direct; and I will bear the risk and charges, glad to be of some small service for the good work.

FROM PROF. GRANVILLE B. PUTNAM.

Boston, Mass., April 21, 1893.

I regret to say that school duties will detain me from Danvers on the 26th. I cannot doubt that you will have a most interesting occasion.

In my early boyhood I used to hear with interest the earnest anti-slavery talks of Deacon Howe, as I visited his shop to get the horse shod; of Mr. Learoyd, and Allen Knight of District No. 4.

I was not old enough to understand the merits of all that was said, but the strong convictions of these men made an impression which will never be effaced from my memory.

FROM HON. MELLEN CHAMBERLAIN.

Chelsea, Mass., April 21, 1893.

I esteem it a great privilege to be invited to participate in the commemoration of old anti-slavery days, to be held by the Danvers Historical Society next Wednesday.

I personally knew some of those in Danvers who were most active by their votes, their gifts, and their personal influence, in bringing on these days in which no slave breathes our air. They were noble men and women, and their lives ought not to be forgotten.

FROM MR. LUCIAN NEWHALL.

Lynn, Mass., April 22, 1893.

Please accept my thanks for your kind invitation to attend the "meeting commemorative of old anti-slavery days."

It will give me great pleasure to be at such a meeting, as I have been familiar, and in sympathy with, the anti-slavery movement for the last half century, having had the pleasure and satisfaction of hearing all the anti-slavery speakers of that period, and the personal acquaintance of many of them.

My wife and myself hope to have the pleasure of attending the meeting.

FROM MR. G. L. STREETER.

SALEM, MASS., April 22, 1893.

I shall be pleased to attend the meeting of the Danvers Historical Society in commemoration of Old Anti-Slavery Days, if I am able to, as I hope to be. Those days I recall with great interest, as do all who were engaged in the bitter struggle with the slave-power, in however humble a capacity. At that time it was necessary for the friends of freedom to stand by each other, shoulder to shoulder, and in that way mutual sympathies were excited and strengthened which have served as a bond of union down to this late day so long after the battle and the victory. This, I suppose, explains your historical meeting, and in this spirit I shall be glad to meet the survivors of the conflict and their friends and sympathizers of the present time.

FROM DR. JAMES C. JACKSON.

NORTH ADAMS, MASS., April 22, 1893.

I would that I were able to take the journey and share with the friends who will be present the pleasures of the meeting. But I cannot go. The invitation has stirred my heart tumultuously. It was in the early autumn in 1838 that I accepted an invitation from the Mass. State Anti-Slavery Society, to become one of its anti-slavery lecturers. My home at that time was in Peterborough, Madison County, New York. I had up to that time for nearly five years been devoting my time as an anti-slavery agent in different parts of the state of New York. I arrived at Boston on the first of October, and met the State Committee at the anti-slavery office in Cornhill street on the afternoon of that day, I think. There I met Mr. William Lloyd Garrison, Mr. Francis Jackson, Mr. Joseph Southwick, *and all of the State Committee*, if I remember rightly. I also met the Rev. John A. Collins, who came to my residence in New York state to engage me, and there I met Mr. Parker Pillsbury, to whom, if he shall be present at your meeting, I desire to have you give my affectionate remembrance.

My first speech in the service of the Society was made at Lynn. If I recollect rightly the meeting was held in the Universalist church; the Congregational church could not be had, objection being made by the pastor, the Rev. Parsons Cook. I went through Essex County that fall, speaking wherever the State Society appointed a meeting for me. One of the places where I spoke was Danvers. I have tried to recollect at whose house I was a guest, but I cannot recall the name of the man. After I had been through Essex county, the State Committee took me out of the general field and placed me under the care and oversight of the Rev. John A. Collins, its general agent. From that time onward till the spring of 1840, I attended meetings with Mr. Collins only, wherever in the state he might be present.

In the spring of 1840 I attended the meeting of the American Anti-Slavery Society, when the Abolitionists divided on the question whether women should be permitted not merely to hold membership, but to hold office. That was the first public meeting, so far as I know, held anywhere in the world to discuss publicly the question whether a woman possesses inherently the right to discuss publicly any intrenched public moral evil.

After I became Secretary of the American Anti-Slavery Society, my public labors in Massachusetts essentially ceased. The friendships which I there formed remain fresh in my memory. I have never ceased for one moment to love Mr. Garrison, Wendell Phillips, Francis Jackson, Joseph and Thankful Southwick, Rev. Edwin Thompson, Hon. George Bradburn, Henry C. Wright, Stephen Foster, Abby Kelly, Parker Pillsbury, James N. Buffum and Ruth his wife, William Bassett, George W. Benson, Charles Lennox Remond, Lewis Hayden, and a thousand other men and women whom I loved and who I feel sure loved me.

So much for matters personal. Now for "*The Cause.*" As representing the rights of the Negro to his freedom, full and entire, as a man, I find nothing in history to equal the devotion of abolitionists of all grades and shades of opinion, in any other direction. That there were differences among them the records which were made and which form the history of the great struggle, plainly show; but these differences were as to methods rather than to principles. I had favored opportunity by my position as secretary of the National Anti-Slavery Society to know that apostasies from the underlying, essential idea that a man is a man wherever you find him, were very uncommon.

I have always felt that the great element of safety to the cardinal principle of the movement, as agitation went on, was the introduction into it, as an essential element, the membership and active labors in every department of it, of women. As I observed what were the conservative effects of their presence in our societies, local and general, and of their wise perception of what should be done and should not be done, I felt sure that the cause would be carried on safely and to ultimate triumph.

The greatest and most subtle element we had to fight was the existence of caste. It took a great deal of the fire of the Holy Spirit to burn up and forever extinguish this wicked, miserable, wretched heresy that one man is better than another because of the color of the pigment that underlies his skin. As the truth, however, is mighty and will prevail, so in time the abolitionists of the country came to regard the man and the woman who were negroes, no less entitled to their honor, respect and love because of their color than they would have been if they were white. How thoroughly interwoven into the fabric of American society this feeling of caste is, can be easily seen in the feelings of southern white men and women toward negro men and women, notwithstanding the latter are no longer by law regarded as chattel slaves. It will take, I fear, a hundred years and perhaps two hundred years to root out from the minds of the southern people the idea that manhood in any person knows nothing detrimental to another's manhood because of the physical differentiations which exist between the two persons. Meanwhile in order that this should be brought about, every human being who prizes his own manhood as of Divine origin, should see to it that in his intercourse with other human beings, he should recognize the Divine origin of their manhood and put himself into fellowship with them on that basis, for it is true that only as men can illustrate in their personal lives their sense of the dignity of their manhood can they be made influential and helpful in the extirpation of caste.

A religion that recognizes and justifies the existence of caste in its members may be successful in securing to itself representatives who will openly profess their belief in it, but it never should be permitted by any of its votaries to be denominated Christian, for in Jesus Christ there is neither Jew nor Greek, bond nor free, male nor female, black nor white, but all are one man in Him.

FROM REV. WM. W. SILVESTER, S. T. D.

PHILADELPHIA, April 22, 1893.

I should particularly like to be present at the commemoration meeting of old Anti-Slavery Days to be held in Danvers on the 26th inst. But I cannot accomplish it.

I never was an anti-slavery man from a political standpoint; always, however, I thoroughly disliked slavery and was as glad as any one that circumstances so fell out that its overthrow became lawfully possible and its *black stain* no longer disgraced our nation or satirized the name of freedom.

I have no doubt you will have an enthusiastic and memorable meeting. Such a meeting some years hence will be impossible and I am glad it has occurred to some one to call together this commemoration assembly.

FROM REV. WM. H. FURNESS, D. D.

PHILADELPHIA, April 23, 1893.

It would be a pleasure beyond words, my dear friend, to meet the first apostles of Freedom for the Slave with whom my friends associate me as one of that honored Band. But I have always considered myself an eleventh hour man in the sacred Cause without the excuse of the men in the Parable whom no one had called to work. I was called by the Divine Voice and I ran and hid myself, for I was a long time afraid. Happily I learned that no one who serves the truth, even if he sacrifice his life for it, can do as much for the truth, no, not by a hundred fold, as the service of the truth will do for him. I learned also that Slavery was as much more hurtful to the white race than to the African as it is to do wrong or abet it than to suffer it. When the War broke out we expected to hear the yell of Insurrection at the South, but there came the plaintive sound of prayers and hymns, and the Slaves continued to work for the families whose heads were fighting to keep the Slaves in bondage.

Emerson said that "eloquence was dog cheap at the Anti-Slavery Meetings before the War;" and for the best of reasons; the Abolitionists had possession of the fountains whence flowed rivers of the waters of life. But I am growing garrulous. May Heaven bless the Meeting on the 26 inst., and make it a season of refreshing to all attending it!

FROM MR. JOHN M. LENNOX.

BOSTON P. O., April 23, 1893.

Please accept my sincere thanks for your kind invitation to the Anti-Slavery Reunion. I feel proud of being one of the old Garrison Abolitionists, and also that my cousin, Charles Lennox Remond, of Salem, was one of the active workers in the cause. I hope and expect to be present on the occasion.

FROM MRS. MARTHA WALDO GREENE.

EAST GREENWICH, R. I., April 23, 1893.

I thank you most sincerely for your circular letter which reached me yesterday, but I am compelled to forego the pleasure it would be to me to commemorate with you the old Anti-Slavery days on the 26th inst.

Those old Anti-Slavery days! There never were such before! There can never be such again! They were days when we forgot ourselves in our wish to serve the poorest and most deserted of all God's creatures, and when to do this cost reputation and life.

But even then, as God so wills it, the law of compensation was true to itself.

In my father's house no pleasure could exceed ours, if S. S. Foster, Parker Pillsbury, Abby Kelly and others, tired from the conflict, could visit us for some days, or even for an hour's rest, and tell us of some new recruit of the Anti-Slavery Army or of the safe escape by the under-ground railroad of some poor fugitive.

I do not forget how the story of Amos Dresser roused my indignation, as he told of the tar and feathers, and his Bibles wrapped in old copies of the "Liberator;" and later on, when Henry B. Stanton hardly escaped a similar fate at the hands of our own citizens, being sent by my father to Providence at an hour when the mob were off their guard, I, as driver, being unsuspected of complicity in the case. Then there were reproaches for riding and walking with Frederick Douglass, stonings by the boys when attending Anti-Slavery Conventions at a neighboring town, and charges of infidelity because of denying the Christianity that bought and sold human beings. Yet none of these things moved us. Never was service rendered more freely in behalf of any truth that brought richer reward. Years afterwards Abby Kelly said, "Talk of what we have done for the Anti-Slavery Cause! What has *not* the Anti-Slavery Cause done for *us!*"

Ye do well, dear friends, to keep the memory green of such times and such men. God bless you!

FROM MRS. FANNY G. VILLARD.

NEW YORK, April 23d, 1893.

I am extremely sorry that I am unable to be present at the meeting to be held in Danvers on April 26, in commemoration of "Old Anti-Slavery Days."

The present generation can hardly be made to realize the intense excitement that attended the anti-slavery movement and the spirit of self-sacrifice and of martyrdom that animated the men and women who saw in the person of the despised slave, Christ himself crucified.

If by frequently recalling the devotion to conscience, the unflinching determination and the heroic forgetfulness of self of the abolitionists, it will be possible to inspire people to imitate their noble example, great will be the gain to humanity.

FROM MR. DANIEL RICKETSON.

NEW BEDFORD, MASS., April 24th, 1893.

While I cordially unite with the "Danvers Historical Society" in the commemoration of "Old Anti-Slavery Days," I regret that my advanced age and its attendant infirmities will prevent my acceptance of your kind invitation.

Among the honored guests named in your circular as expected to be present, I remember Parker Pillsbury, a "true son of thunder," who never spared friend or foe in his eloquent appeals for down-trodden humanity. I remember also in one of our conventions in old "Liberty Hall," he declared that these "cotton aristocrats," then in complicity with the slave holders, "could turn all Heaven into Birmingham, make weavers of the Angels, and drown the music of the morning stars with the eternal din of Spindles;" at which one of the audience, who sat a little before me, rose from his seat and walked out of the hall. Among the older members of our Massachusetts Abolition Society, I remember with respect, Rev. Samuel May, Mrs. Lucy Stone, and Mr. John W. Hutchinson, the last of the "nest of brothers with a sister in it," whose united voices so charmed all, and did such good service for the cause of human freedom. I doubt not the sainted name of John Greenleaf Whittier, whose ringing notes so often sounded the prophetic voice of Freedom, will be among those whose spirit will be recognized as with you. I was but an humble laborer in the great Anti-Slavery struggle, though to the "manner born."

FROM MR. WALTER B. ALLEN.

LYNN, April 24, 1893.

To be reckoned a friend of humanity worthy of an invitation to your proposed commemorative feast, is indeed a compliment. To meet on that occasion a few of the remaining veterans of the great Anti-Slavery Conflict, and to hear their voices once more, will be a crowning joy. I therefore accept your kind invitation with thanks, and shall endeavor to be present.

FROM MR. ROBERT ADAMS.

FALL RIVER, MASS., April 24, 1893.

Having received your circulars, through Mrs. Livermore's kindness, I hereby wish to express my gratitude for the same; also to congratulate your Society in their effort to call together the survivors of that great battle for poor humanity. By this movement you will afford much pleasure to the veterans, and also have a snatch of history, which is daily being buried in obscurity.

The history of the fugitives, if written, would fill many volumes of exceedingly interesting literature, which might form a new series of " fiction founded on fact," for the young generation, who are entirely ignorant of the sufferings of the slave, as well as the hardships endured by the pioneers in the struggle for freedom.

I recently visited " Freemason's Hall," in London, where the First World's Convention was held in 1840, and was shown the gallery where Lucretia Mott, with the delegates from America (my father being one of them), sat, while the question was discussed *whether to admit her as a delegate!*

I will take pleasure in being present at your meeting.

FROM MR. WILLIAM D. THOMPSON.

Lynn, April 24, 1893.

I expect to be at the meeting, as I belong to a family that was early identified with the cause. My father, the late William D. Thompson, was one of the oldest abolitionists, and our house was always open not only to those who were engaged in Anti-Slavery work, but to all other reformers as they came along. My brother, Rev. Edwin Thompson, as every one may know, was one of the first to organize societies, in connection with the Rev. Mr. Torrey who lost his life in a Maryland prison. As many who may be present at the meeting will remember, Mr. Thompson was also an active worker in the Temperance cause. Our house being one of the first to entertain agitators of every sort, I had a good chance to know something of what was done at Lynn. I well remember the mobbing there of George Thompson of England, and was present at the meeting; and I recall the way he got out of the church. As he wore a white hat, of course he would be easily identified; so one of the friends, who took in the situation, removed his own and put it on Mr. Thompson's head. Thus no one knew him as he went out and passed through the lines that were formed to the house of Mr. Henshaw on the opposite side of the street. Lynn was a hot bed of agitations, and it was the first place of the negro car trouble, which began with the putting of Douglass out of the train, an act which led to great excitement. * * * * As the friends of the abolition movement have mostly gone, it is well for the few who remain to meet and talk over the doings of the past and revive the old memories. Their labors were not in vain. A great work has been accomplished. I hope that your meeting will be a success and that those who may be present will have a day of rejoicing. It cannot be long before the last remnant of the Old Guard will have gone, and let those who are now left have a full share of the glory.

FROM MR. GEORGE W. CLARK.

DETROIT, MICH., April 24, 1893.

I have received from your Secretary an invitation to be an attendant upon your contemplated meeting on the 26th inst., in commemoration of "Old Anti-Slavery Days," for which I am sincerely grateful. It would give me great pleasure were I able to attend and participate in what I have no doubt will be a gathering of intense interest. But untoward circumstances will deprive me of the happiness of being one of such a noble company on such an eventful occasion. I was converted to the Temperance and Anti-Slavery Reforms when a boy about 16—by the first address on those questions I ever heard—by that eloquent and powerful orator, that Demosthenes of America, Theodore D. Weld. I entered heart and soul into the Reforms I had thus early espoused. I had inherited from my father and mother—both good singers—a soul for music; and saw its power and influence in social circles where I was called on for "Songs" when a mere boy, and at once conceived the idea of introducing this influence and power in connection with my lectures on Temperance and Anti-Slavery, which I did, and I was not only *not* disappointed, but highly gratified with the effect. Many scores of drinkers and drunkards came to hear the *songs* and were converted. I had set music to the best songs I could then find on these subjects, from Cowper, Mrs. Hemans, Massey, Douglas Jerrold, Pierpont, Whittier, Longfellow and other poets. It took like "wild-fire" as they used to say, and I was invited to all parts of the country to render these songs in the great reform conventions, and at the close of these gatherings was called on for copies of them and was urged to publish them, which I did in "The Temperance Songster," "The Liberty Minstrel," "The Free Soil Minstrel," "Songs of the Free," "Clark's Reform Song Book," "The Harp of Freedom," "Lyrics of the Lodges," "And Songs For The Times," etc.

I have now traveled and lectured, rendering these songs, in 24 of our states and in Canada, and my interest and zeal in these Reforms is as ardent and unabated as ever. I used to be told forty and fifty years ago, if I lived to be as old as that gentleman whose name is so familiar, the venerable Father Methuselah. I would never live to see the day when slavery would be abolished in this Country! Thank God I have lived to see that day and nearly thirty years beyond and am some years behind Methuselah yet! And I congratulate you, fellow workers, that you have lived to see, and now to celebrate, the Glorious but Costly Victory!

I am now as eager in the fray and as anxious to see the overthrow of the liquor power as I was to see the overthrow of the slave power! The same God of justice and righteousness rules and reigns, and—

"Come what there may to stand in the way,
That day the World shall see,
When the *Might* with the *Right*
And the *Truth shall be!*"

And now I desire to be affectionately remembered to my old friends, John W. Hutchinson, Parker Pillsbury and Mrs. Lucy Stone.

FROM DEACON JOSHUA T. EVERETT.

WESTMINSTER, April 24, '93.

I have received your circular inviting me to the gathering of Anti-Slavery friends of the days of "Auld Lang Syne."

It would give me inexpressible pleasure to meet the dear old friends named in your circular next Wednesday. But I cannot do so for two reasons. First, I am just moving and as busy as the honey bee in June. Second, I intend to visit Providence, R. I., on Tuesday or Wednesday this week. And my age, 87 years, would seem to be a barrier, but it would not, as I enjoy pretty good health.

But nearly all our co-laborers in that Philanthropic and Godly enterprise have gone to their rest and reward in Heaven. In my generation nearly all have gone. Sixty years ago I was chosen to represent my native town (my first election). Princeton, in the legislature of Massachusetts. In the lower house there were 540 to 550 members. Today there are only three of us living. I must confess to a sort of loneliness, but not of *melancholy*. I formed the acquaintance of brother Garrison soon after that period and enjoyed his intimate friendship till his death and I attended his funeral. For some fifteen to twenty years I was elected President of the County Anti-Slavery Society. Then we held more than quarterly meetings. And in the north part of the county we constructed a number of unseen highways.

over which the poor slave was helped on to Canada. Yes, *fleeing to Canada* to escape the *infernal* clutches of the slave-holder! I remember one very fine young woman about thirty years old, with her babe nearly a year old, brought to our depot in Everettville by an Abolition friend in the part of our county south of our depot. The woman was almost as white and good looking as a certain very fine lady in our neighborhood, to whom she bore a striking resemblance. And the neighbors were invited in to see how *exactly* the slave woman looked like Mrs. Beaman, the neighbor. Then after giving her a good dinner and some things she wanted, we helped her on to another depot, and so she got on to Canada. I wish I could shake the hands of all the true souls that will gather at the Danvers Convention. I received a long and very interesting letter from John Hutchinson a few months since. And I wish I could listen to his charming songs next Wednesday.

I trust your Convention will be an interesting and happy gathering. I have snatched the half hour from the cares and labors of the day to answer your kind invitation to be present.

FROM MR. WILLIAM STONE.

NEW YORK, April 24, 1893.

I am in receipt of your circular of April 13, inviting me to attend the meeting to be held on Wednesday, commemorative of "Old Anti-Slavery Days."

I regret that I shall be unable to accept your invitation, as I heartily approve of your gathering.

The present generation knows so little of the great movement which prepared the North for its successful conflict with the slave power and which resulted in the destruction of the slave system in this country, it is well that it should, before it is too late, hear the story from the lips of those who were actors in that movement and who endured and suffered for its sake.

FROM MR. DAVID MEAD.

DANVERSPORT, April 24, 1893.

Your kind note of special invitation to attend the meeting "Commemorative of Old Anti-Slavery Days," was gratefully received, and it would give us great pleasure to be able to be present on that occasion. But I fear that neither Mrs. Mead or myself will be able to attend.

The object of the call is truly a laudable one; and as I understand it, it is for an expression of sacred remembrance of the worthy men and women who in times of great peril willingly risked their lives and gave of their means for the abolition of that curse, and sum of all inhuman cruelties—southern slavery.

(Mr. and Mrs. Mead were both present at the meeting.)

FROM MRS. ANNE E. DAMON.

CONCORD, April 25, 1893.

To save you the trouble of a fruitless call on Aunt Bigelow, I write to say that I called there this morning and found she had been ill, and from weakness was unable to hear or see as well as usual. I do not think you could communicate with her at all. I succeeded in letting her know of the celebration at Danvers tomorrow, and she said she would like to send her love to all the survivors of the first organization of anti-slavery workers.

("Aunt Bigelow," now eighty years of age, was Ann Hagar, of Weston, Mass., and Mrs. Damon is her niece. She married Francis E. Bigelow, also of Weston, and removed with him to Concord, where she has continued to reside since her husband's death in 1873. With Mr. and Mrs. Minot Pratt, Mrs. Abiel Wheeler, Miss Sophia Thoreau, Mrs. Emerson, and others, she was a most earnest, devoted, and influential abolitionist from the start and to the end. She welcomed to her house most of the well-known anti-slavery orators and friends, and also many a fugitive slave. It was there that "Shadrach" was secretly brought by Lewis Hayden and a Mr. Smith in the night or very early morning, when he had escaped the clutch of his pursuing master, and of the wicked officers who had arrested him and confined him in the Boston Court House. Through the kindness of Mr. and Mrs. Bigelow, and Mr. and Mrs. Nathan Brooks, he was tenderly cared for and safely spirited away to Montreal, where sometime afterward I sought him out in one of my vacation trips and found him keeping a small store, and bright and cheerful. In a late interview with Mrs. Bigelow, who had come to be more comfortable in health than in April, she gave Mrs. Damon and myself a most thrilling account of all the circumstances of the escape and welcome referred to, and of the remarkable way in which the peeled and hunted bondman gained his freedom by the "Underground Railroad." A. P. P.)

FROM MR. J. M. W. YERRINGTON.

CHELSEA, April 25, 1893.

I thank you most sincerely for the invitation to attend the meeting in commemoration of old Anti-Slavery Days tomorrow.

It would indeed be refreshing and delightful to me to be present and to listen to voices which I heard nearly half a century ago, in the storm and stress of the Anti-Slavery struggle, but I fear I must deny myself the pleasure, as I have been unable to make an arrangement, as I had hoped I might do, by which to escape from official duty on that day. If it is possible for me to get to Danvers, even at the eleventh hour, I shall rejoice to do so. The idea of such a gathering was a happy one and the occasion can hardly fail to be one of surpassing interest and enjoyment.

(Mr. Yerrington, so long the printer of Mr. Garrison's *Liberator*, was present at the meeting, notwithstanding his fear that he might not be able to attend.)

FROM COL. THOMAS W. HIGGINSON.

CAMBRIDGE, MASS., April 25, 1893.

I am sorry to be prevented by another engagement from taking part in your commemoration of Anti-Slavery days. Judging by your list of speakers it will be a good and genuine meeting. I have been invited to several such meetings where some of the most prominent speakers had either known nothing of the Anti-Slavery movement, or had bitterly opposed it.

FROM MR. THEODORE D. WELD.

NORWOOD, April 26, 1893.

Dear Old Abolition Friends:—Beloved brothers and sisters, I send you all my fervent "All Hail" and "God-speed," and am with reluctance absent from your midst.

FROM MR. CHARLES E. GRAVES.

HARTFORD, CONN., April 26, 1893.

Many thanks for your kind invitation, which I was unable to accept. I should have enjoyed seeing you at Concord and joining you for the convention of old abolitionists at Danvers, especially in memory of my father (George Graves, of Rutland, Vermont.) He was an original Anti-Slavery man from about 1840, and was therefore under the political ban through all his earlier manhood. I can remember having my fights when a small boy for being charged by my mates with belonging to the " nigger party." So that the names of all those brave men of principle, the original Anti-Slavery men, were household names with me. I can remember my father's attending a great Anti-Slavery convention at Boston when Samuel Fessenden, of Maine, presided, and his repeating some of the words of his address. When I got to be a young man I used to be rather disgusted with my father's faith—a blind faith as it seemed to me—especially when I once heard him say, "I hope to live to see American Slavery swept from the Earth." I thought his zeal made him rather wild. But he lived to see it, all the same.

FROM REV. S. F. SMITH.

DAVENPORT, IOWA, April 27, 1893.

Your esteemed note of invitation was forwarded to me here and received this A. M. Of course it was out of my power to accept, but I thank you none the less for the invitation. Some of the names on your program are well known to me and highly honored; and it would be a pleasure to me to join them. It is a worthy object to cherish the remembrances of the great past, prophetic of a greater future; and as the names of the workers in those early days grow fewer, with the lapse of years they grow dearer. The lives of such a band have not been in vain.

At your request, I enclose for your use an autograph copy of the hymn, "My country, 'tis of thee." Please present it to the Historical Society, with the assurance of my high esteem.

FROM MRS. HARRIET M. LOTHROP.

("MARGARET SYDNEY.")

BOSTON, MASS., April 28, 1893.

Your invitation to the Danvers Historical Society's celebration of old anti-slavery days on April 26th, was received the day before and should have been answered at once. I could not possibly go, as you know that I am fastened at my desk, but I should have written you a letter, as all my sympathies are with you and your society. I was brought up in an atmosphere that was wholly in accord with this object. Some time I want to tell you how much and how far this sympathy of mine extends to the "old anti-slavery days." I should have written you and the society a letter expressing my sympathies, but I had not a minute at my command. I congratulate you upon the success which I see by the papers that your society achieves, and I trust you will make this an annual affair, as we are too apt to forget the struggle of those early days in the success that has been achieved by it.

Among many other letters, also received by the President or Secretary, were similar communications from Hon. E. L. Pierce,

Rev. Edward E. Hale, D. D., Rev. Charles G. Ames, and Miss Mary Willey, of Boston; Rev. P. A. Hanaford, of New York; Richard H. Dana, Esq., of Cambridge; Miss Elizabeth A. Clapp, of South Boston; Mr. Charles Buffum, of Lynn; Mr. Lewis Ford, of North Abington; Rev. C. A. Staples, of Lexington; Mr. and Mrs. R. P. Hallowell, of West Medford; Henry M. Brooks, Esq., Secretary of the Essex Institute, of Salem; Mrs. Marcia E. P. Hunt, of Weymouth; Rev. O. S. Butler, of Georgetown, &c., &c.

BIOGRAPHICAL AND OTHER NOTES.

Those who took an active part in the proceedings of the meeting had more or less to say, as they had been particularly requested to do, about their own personal experience in connection with anti-slavery work or times. However well known to the public many of them, at least, may be, perhaps it will be grateful to friends who may chance to read these pages, if we give here some brief biographical details respecting them all, partially to supplement whatever accounts they gave of themselves, and so complete, as well as we may, the story of the Reunion. Each one of them had a right to be heard, and it is only to be regretted that that there was not space for others who were present and who also had important testimony to bear.

REV. WILLIAM H. FISH, SEN.

Mr. Fish is a native of Newport, R. I., where he was born on the 25th of March, 1812. His parents were Peleg and Alice (Sisson) Fish, both natives of Portsmouth, near Newport. At the age of 15 he went to Providence to learn the jeweller's trade, and made good use of the library and lectures of the Mechanic's Association in that city. In June, 1835, he married Anna Eliza Wright, daughter of Eben and Penelope Wright, all of Providence. There Mr. Fish, during the previous year, had heard the eloquent George Thompson speak on the subject of slavery, and from that time he dates his active interest in the abolition cause, as the friend, who was to be his wife, could likewise date her own. Mr. Wright having decided to remove with his family to Fremont, Ill., where some Providence friends had already settled, Mr. and Mrs. Fish accompanied them and there taught together in the village a private school. From time to time, earnest discussions of slavery took place in their school-house and naturally had the effect to intensify their zeal for emancipation. Here also Mr. Fish studied for the ministry and occasionally preached as opportunity offered, having some time previously purposed to make that his calling. In 1837, after two years at the west, he returned with his wife to New England, passing through Alton, Ill., only a few days before Lovejoy was shot by a pro-slavery mob, and arriving at the east in time to be in touch with the great indignation meeting at Faneuil Hall, at which Dr. Channing spoke and young Wendell Phillips delivered the maiden speech that gave him immortal fame.

Mr. Fish was soon called to be the pastor of the society of Universalists (of the Restorationist school), in Melville, Worcester County, Mass. The invitation having been accepted, he was duly ordained to the ministry, Rev. Paul Dean of Boston, Rev. Adin Ballou, Rev. Charles Hudson (afterward member of Congress), and Rev. Samuel Clark (Unitarian) of Uxbridge, taking part in the services. The society had been under the fostering care of Mr. Ballou, and was therefore of decided anti-slavery sympathies. Garrison and his more noted co-laborers came from time to time and were gladly heard by the people. Meanwhile Mr. Ballou's Hopedale community was giving promise of its good success as one of the better class of socialistic experiments of the period. Mr. Fish was one of its original members and was conferred with from the first by its noble founder, but still he remained at Melville and continued his work there for 9 years, or until 1846, when he went with his family to reside in Connecticut, where for nine years more he did missionary work and occasionally lectured in the service of the Massachusetts Anti-Slavery Society, sometimes speaking at social gatherings in company with Lucy Stone and other advocates of reform. Then followed still another term of nine years, spent in central New York, while preaching Liberal Christianity, and lecturing on slavery and the Hopedale Socialism in as many as fifty different towns, being aided by the American Anti-Slavery Society, and by Rev. Samuel J. May and his Unitarian friends. His principal point of work and care was Cortland, where he gathered an Independent Liberal Christian Society, but where there was a dominant pro-slavery sentiment of the most bigoted and virulent character, the Presbyterians excommunicating one of their church-members for going to hear on Sundays such "infidels" as Garrison and Phillips and Emerson and Starr King. But other brilliant men came in long succession, to give light in the darkness, Greeley, Pierpont, Beecher, Foster, Parker, Horace Mann, and many more of like spirit and renown, and our Cortland minister's hand is sufficiently seen in what was done to provide such a dispensation where it was so much needed. Yet the New York Presbytery and Synod confirmed the action of the local church and did all that was possible to terrorize the faithful and keep them in abject submission to their will.

Central New York witnessed to the most active, stirring period of Mr. Fish's life. Gerrit Smith wanted him to settle at Peterboro, N. Y., where he had his own home, but he chose rather to make Scituate, Mass., the scene of his next pastorate, and hither he came in 1865 to toil on for Christianity, for Freedom, for Temperance, and for Woman's Rights, for twenty years more, in the same spirit of brave and conscientious fidelity to duty as had marked each and all of his previous terms of service. His ministry has extended over half a century, and the whole of it has been consecrated to Christ and Christianity, to many noble reforms and to the best movements of his country and age. The wife of his youth has gone before him, and he now lives with his son, Rev. William H. Fish, Jr., pastor of the Unitarian Church in Dedham, an object of love and veneration with all who know him, but with none more than with those who faithfully wrought with him in all the "Thirty Years' War" against Slavery. It is grateful to hear their warm and accordant testimony to the high worth of this venerable man, and to his long and arduous devotion to Truth and Right. Few are more deserving than he.

JOHN W. HUTCHINSON.

Mr. Hutchinson was born in Milford, N. H., Jan. 4, 1821. In coming to Danvers to attend the Commemorative meeting, he visited the home of his first ancestors in America. His earliest progenitor in this country, Richard Hutchinson, emigrated from England, and in 1634 settled in that part of the original township of Salem which first took the name of "Salem Village" and afterward the name of *Danvers*, with whose First Parish many of his descendants have ever since been most honorably connected. One of these, Col. Israel Hutchinson, having fought at Lake George and Ticonderoga in 1758 and scaled the Heights of Abraham under Wolfe in 1759, commanded one of the Danvers companies in the Battle of Lexington and served with great distinction through the Revolutionary war. Another descendant, of the fourth generation, bought a tract of land in Middleton, Mass., (adjoining Danvers), and another in Amherst, N. H. A son of the latter, also named Joseph, was born in "Salem Village," but settled in Middleton, and one of his children was Elisha, who was born in Middleton, but removed to Amherst and lived in that part of the town which in 1794 was incorporated under the name of Milford. A son of Elisha was Jesse, who was born in Middleton, in 1778, but went with his father to New Hampshire in the following year. At Milford he married Polly Hastings in the year 1800, and it is said that "it was while she was singing one day in a village choir that she first by her voice attracted the attention of her future husband." Both gave early indications of unusual musical talent, and it is not strange that so many gifted vocalists appeared amongst their sixteen children: Jesse, Daniel, Noah B., Polly, Andrew B., Zephaniah K., Caleb, Joshua, Jesse, Benjamin P., Joseph Judson, Sarah Rhoda, John Wallace, Asa Burnham, Elizabeth and Abby J.

The first quartet of the family seems to have consisted of Joshua, Judson, John and Asa. Very early in life they began to evince a passionate love of music and a real genius for it, and the songs which thus soon they sang in the home and the village church, with violin accompaniments and the added voices of Rhoda and Abby, and doubtless others of the family circle, awakened much interest in the neighborhood and were a presage of their future success. Ere long we find the four brothers engaged in giving concerts in Wilton and Nashua, New Hampshire, and in Lynn, Mass., and in several or more of the eastern towns and cities, Salem, Newburyport, Portsmouth, and Kennebunk, Abby and Jesse joining them in their public performances at some of these places. Paltry returns rewarded them for their exertions and at length they all returned to Milford at the earnest request of their father, except Jesse, who settled down to other kind of work at Lynn. But this was not to be the fate of the Hutchinsons. The way for a more fortunate campaign was bye and bye opened to them, though not unattended with failures and disappointments. They sang in many places in New Hampshire, Vermont, Massachusetts and New York, Abby still being a companion. After another return to their home, their interest in the anti-slavery cause was aroused by a convention held at Milford and conducted by William Lloyd Garrison, N. P. Rogers, and others. They now began to sing for freedom, and thus they entered upon their great life-work. "These songs, in connection with their Temperance Melodies," says a writer, "brought them into great repute, and during a subsequent visit to New York they complied with an invitation to be present at the Anniversary of the American Anti-slavery Society, and afterwards at the Anniversary of the American Temperance Society, where they were greeted with the utmost enthusiasm." Thence they proceeded to Philadelphia and Washington, and subsequently sailed to England, giving concerts in such cities as Liverpool, London, Manchester and Dublin, and making the acquaintance of Dickens, Macready, the Howitts, and other notables. This was in 1845. The delighted crowds that greeted them abroad only added to their fame in America and their hosts of friends and admirers here were only too glad to welcome them back to the service in which they had here enlisted and which never needed their voices more than then.

And still their beautiful work went on, nor is it possible to measure the good they wrought, as they went through the northern states, everywhere inspiring the multitudes with a deeper and more ardent love of liberty by their wonderful power of song. Their verses were of the popular sort, dashed off at once as the occasion prompted or called, and modest in their claims to poetic merit, but admirably adapted to please the people who heard them and kindle their enthusiasm. Popular assemblies never tired of hearing them sung by the Hutchinsons, and the announcement that these friends would be present and sing at any appointed meeting was quite enough to secure a full and eager audience. Abby, whose recent death has touched with sadness so many hearts, was married in 1849 to Mr. Ludlow Patton, a broker and banker in New York, and in consequence ceased from her more public work, but John and Asa and Judson clubbed together anew and still continued their mission in behalf of the slave until 1855, when, with others, they established a new town in Wisconsin and called it *Hutchinson*. In 1862, the settlement was destroyed by a band of 300 Sioux Indians, whereupon the brothers for a time divided their care between farming and giving concerts. The lyre was struck to unwonted music, as John, with his son Henry and his daughter Viola, children by his wife Fanny Burnham, of Lowell, whom he had married Feb. 21, 1843, went down to the Potomac and sang their songs to the soldiers in camp during the war, the younger generations of the family, as the Danvers meeting also bore witness, possessing an abundant share of the divine gift of the elders; and even while we write the venerable and special subject of our sketch, still fresh, and earnest, and active, is plying his loved vocation at the great World's Fair, and is doubtless gladdening human hearts there, also, with new strains of the "good time coming." For more than fifty years he has given voice and pen, body and soul, freely and unreservedly, to the service of humanity.

It was our privilege to be one of his guests as he celebrated the seventieth anniversary of his birthday at his pretty residence on High Rock, Lynn, a commanding eminence which he himself and his brother Jesse were among the first to settle. The wife had died several years before, but the children and grandchildren were there, with Abby and her husband from New York, and a great number of old friends from the city and from places more or less remote, not a few of whom had long been his distinguished associates in his philanthropic labors. The music was as delicious as we had found it a half century before, and the greetings were as hearty as the bright flowers were profuse and fragrant. The host was as genial and buoyant and joyous as ever, and nothing could have been lovelier or more engaging than that picture of the "Hutchinson Family" at their charming home, on that memorable evening. Few of our countrymen who have appeared in public, have given more of pure pleasure to the people, or broken or dissolved more of slavery's chains by the human voice, than has he; and it is the consciousness of a life so spent that makes old age at once happy and interesting.

WILLIAM LLOYD GARRISON.

William Lloyd Garrison, the second son of the great Reformer whose name he bears, was born in Boston, January 21, 1838, and was educated in the public schools of that city. The earlier years of his business life were spent as teller in a bank in Lynn, Mass., which he left to become cashier of a bank in Dorchester. Subsequently he went into the wool business in Boston, and he is still engaged in mercantile pursuits. He was one of the victims of the terrible railroad disaster at Revere, Mass., in 1871 and narrowly escaped with his life on that occasion. Since the death of his father, in 1879, he has spoken and written much on social and moral questions, in the intervals of his busy life, and is ever prompt to bear his testimony in behalf of justice and righteousness. The woman suffrage movement, the temperance cause, the persecuted Chinese residents of our country, all find in him an ardent advocate and ready defender, and he is one of the ablest disciples of Henry George in the agitation in behalf of free trade and the single tax, as was abundantly attested by his addresses on these subjects at the Cooper Institute, in New York, in 1887, and at a dinner given in honor of Richard Cobden's memory, at Cleveland, Ohio, last June. He has written most felicitously, both in prose and verse, in tribute to some of his father's surviving associates. His address on John G. Whittier, delivered before the Brooklyn, (N. Y.) Institute of Arts and Sciences, Dec. 17, 1892, and the poem which he read at a reception given by the Whittier Club of Haverhill, in the old homestead, last October, were in his best vein and were remarkably fine productions, while his address at the Danvers Reunion, as printed in this book, is an admirable specimen of his terse, vigorous and finished style. As one of the veterans present remarked after hearing it, "That in itself would have justified this occasion;" and certainly no better or more compact statement and vindication of the Garrisonian position against a slaveholding Union has been written. To the few yet surviving who labored in the great cause with the elder

Garrison, and to all who revere his memory, it is a profound satisfaction that the son has inherited not merely his name, but his broad humanitarian spirit and purpose, and that he wears his mantel so worthily.

REV. SAMUEL MAY.

No one of the old Guard of Liberty is more universally or deservedly loved and revered than Rev. Samuel May, of Leicester, Mass. He was born in Boston, April 11, 1810, and is therefore now in the eighty-fourth year of his age. His father, who died in 1870, aged 91, was the excellent Samuel May, merchant of Boston, and senior deacon of the Hollis Street Church in that city during the long and determined battle which its then minister, Rev. John Pierpont, formidable foe of Slavery and Intemperance, waged against the rum traffic of some of his wealthy and influential parishioners. His mother was Mary Goddard of Brookline, Mass., daughter of Joseph Goddard. The famous Abolitionist, Rev. Samuel J. May, of Syracuse, son of Col. Joseph May of King's Chapel, was his cousin.

The subject of this sketch was for four years in the school of Dea. Samuel Greele, of Boston, for three at the Boston Public Latin School, and for one at the Round Hill School at Northampton, whose principals were Joseph G. Cogswell and George Bancroft. He entered Harvard College as a Sophomore in 1826, and graduated in 1829. Having passed the next year in preparatory studies, chiefly at Brooklyn, Conn., with his cousin, Rev. Samuel J. May, who was then settled in that place, he entered the Divinity School at Cambridge in 1830, where he had the benefit of lectures by Andrews Norton, Drs. Henry Ware, Senior, Henry Ware, Jr., and John G. Palfrey, and where he graduated in 1833. He was settled in the ministry, Aug. 13, 1834, at Leicester, Mass., where he remained twelve years, being at the same time a member of the "Worcester Ministerial Association" with Dr. Aaron Bancroft, Dr. Joseph Allen, and other eminent clergymen of the county.

Continued intercourse with his cousin had more and more served to imbue him with Anti-Slavery sentiment, until, in the year 1833, he was influenced to take a stand openly with the Massachusetts Anti-Slavery Society by the reading of Mrs. Lydia Maria Child's book, "An Appeal in favor of that class of Americans called Africans." From the first he united with his ministerial work an earnest interest in what was soon to be the great philanthropic movement of the time. He helped to form a town Anti-Slavery Society and was an active member and officer. In

1840 he attended the annual meeting of the American Anti-Slavery Society, in New York, at which took place the well-remembered secession of those who were opposed to women having any active part in such gatherings. The strong and wise testimony which he bore from time to time against the colossal sin of the land gave such offence to several of the members of his Unitarian Society that they withdrew from the church. Another, who was prominent and who fully shared their pro slavery feeling, remained behind, and was so strenuous in his opposition to any treatment or mention of the subject whatever, in the pulpit, that Mr. May, unwilling to divide the Society, and being unable to take any other course as to Slavery itself, resigned his position at the end of the eleventh year of his pastorate. Yet the result of several meetings was a *unanimous* request that the resignation should be withdrawn, his violent opponent joining in the vote. Mr. May accordingly yielded to the wishes of his people for the time, but as the hostility of the person referred to soon became more pronounced than ever, he finally, a year later, surrendered his charge.

Not long afterward he was appointed as the General Agent of the Massachusetts Anti-Slavery Society. He accepted the position, and entered upon its work in June, 1847, after having finished an engagement of about six months with the Brooklyn (Conn.) Unitarian church, of which his cousin had some time before been the minister. His office was at 21 Cornhill, Boston, in conjunction with that of *The Liberator*, and his principal work was to keep the Society's lecturing agents as busy as their strength would allow, to correspond with friendly people in Massachusetts and gradually in other parts of New England, to raise funds, establish county organizations, attend conventions, and to see to the publication and distribution of tracts. Other important Anti-Slavery bodies and gatherings were also included in his official care, and after the passage of the Fugitive Slave Law, his labors were still more extended so as to protect as much as possible the many imperilled colored people, in and about Boston, who had escaped from their thraldom. Mr. May was General Agent for 18 years, and only those who know his conscientious and consecrated fidelity to all duty can have any just conception of the vast service which he rendered to the cause during that most momentous period of the Anti-Slavery struggle. No work was more needed, and no man was better qualified for it than was he. He brought to it eminent ability and the highest character, the best intellectual, moral and religious training, and a supreme love to man and love to God. His sphere of toil was a wide one and his labors were many and arduous. They necessarily required that he should be absent from home for much of the time, his wife meanwhile having the responsible care of the family almost entirely. Their only serious interruption was when his impaired health obliged him to return to Leicester and spend a year and a half in the recovery of his strength. As soon as he was well enough, he was again in the field, nor ceased from its claims upon him until the Anti-Slavery Amendments of the United States Constitution became law and the bondmen were all free. It is enough to say that throughout his protracted term of service he enjoyed the most unbounded confidence and warmest support and friendship of such men and women as Francis Jackson and Edmund Quincy, Mr. Garrison and Mr. Pillsbury, Mrs. Chapman and Mrs. Stone, Mr. and Mrs. Stephen S. Foster and Charles Burleigh, Wendell Phillips, Charles L. Remond, and the rest. *While still in his Leicester ministry*

In 1845, Mr. May, in consequence of a severe catarrhal affection, lost his voice entirely, but regained it by a sea voyage to England, extending his journey to the continent. While in the mother country he embraced an opportunity that was presented to him to bring before the Unitarians there the subject of Slavery in the United States, and while in Geneva, Switzerland, he wrote, in reply to a request from some English Unitarians for information about the American Unitarian ministers and people, a letter which afterward became more widely known, and which, as he was accused of something like treachery, he read on his return home, word for word, before the Berry St. Conference in Boston. Some of the brethren who were most unfriendly to the Anti-Slavery cause were quite embittered against him on account of his courageous and truthful testimony, and Dr. Gannett, so greatly beloved and honored, told him that he was "the most dangerous man in Massachusetts." Today, there is no man of his communion who is more venerated by all who know him, inside of it or outside of it, than Rev. Samuel May, of Leicester. Yet *he* has not changed; but the people, Unitarians and others, *have*.

HON. M. M. FISHER.

Milton M. Fisher, son of Willis and Caroline (Fairbanks) Fisher, was born in Franklin, Mass., Jan. 30, 1811, and through his father and mother is a descendant of several English families who immigrated to this country in 1634-37. The earliest of these were that of Thomas Fisher, of Winston, England, who settled in Cambridge in 1634 and removed with his family to Dedham in 1637, on the arrival of Anthony and eleven others of the same family name from Syleham; and that of Jonathan Fairbanks, of

Tatterford, who removed to Dedham from Boston in 1636-37. With them came, also, Michael Metcalf, the first school teacher in Dedham. Nearly all the families in New England and the Western States that bear these several names trace their ancestral lines back to some of the emigrants above mentioned. Fisher Ames, the eloquent orator of the Revolution, Dr. John Fisher, L. L. D., of Beverly, founder of a professorship in Harvard College, and George P. Fisher, the eminent Professor of Ecclesiastical History in Yale College, may all be referred to the Fishers who first settled in Dedham, while among those who have borne the name in English history there have been such distinguished men as Gen. Osborne Le Pecheur (Fisher), one of the Norman barons of William the Conqueror, 1066, John Fisher, a martyr to his faith who was beheaded by Henry VIII, 1535, and the Archbishop of Salisbury, 1613.

Milton M. Fisher completed his education at Amherst College 1833, and received the honorary degree of A. M. in 1865. In 1836, he married Eleanor Metcalf, daughter of Hon. Luther Metcalf, of Medway. Of their nine children four survive: Dr. Thomas W. Fisher, superintendent of the Boston Lunatic Hospitals, Frederick L. Fisher, Treasurer of the Medway Savings Bank, and two daughters, one of whom married and settled in Harriman, Tennessee, and the other is resident at the family homestead in Medway.

At the early age of seventeen he was a teacher of public schools for eight terms, and for two terms a teacher in a classical school for boys. On leaving college and on recovering from ill health, he was a trader in Franklin and Westborough for five years. In 1840, removing to Medway, he established the straw works, now owned by Messrs. Hirsch and Parks, and retired from the business in 1863. Since then he has devoted himself chiefly to insurance, banking, and real estate. During his long business life of sixty years, for fifty-three of which he has been a resident of Medway, he has been honored with various judiciary trusts and municipal and other public offices, and has taken a leading part in numerous enterprises that concerned the prosperity or welfare of his fellow citizens. In 1855, he was one of the commissioners appointed to divide the town of Danvers (the portion that was set off, first taking the name of *South Danvers*, and afterward that of *Peabody*), and subsequently he was made a special commissioner for other state purposes. For 1859 and 1860, he was elected state senator from the West Norfolk District, and was prominent and influential in introducing and carrying through the Legislature several useful and important measures. From 1863 to 1872, a period of nine years, he was a member of the Board of County Commissioners, and for three years was its chairman, while for many years he has also been officially connected with several religious and benevolent organizations.

In the valuable paper which this excellent and greatly esteemed octogenarian presented at the Danvers Commemorative Meeting, he briefly outlined a part of his extended anti-slavery experience or service; but it remains to add, that, during his long and busy life he has delivered many addresses, not only on the subject of Slavery, but also in the interest of the Temperance cause, and upon political and other topics, at the same time contributing numerous articles for the public press. It is worthy of special note, that he is, so far as is known, the last survivor of the First Public Meeting of the American Anti-Slavery Society, held in New York, May 5th and 6th, 1834, except the venerable Robert Purvis, the highly-cultured and noted colored gentleman, whom Philadelphia claims as one of its worthiest and most honored citizens. And it should also be said, that Mr. Fisher, Rev. Samuel May, and Theodore D. Weld, of Hyde Park, who is now in his 90th year and is of unsurpassed merit as a veteran abolitionist, are the three, still living, of the five persons in Massachusetts whom John G. Whittier, in 1891, called the "*Old Anti-Slavery Guard.*" Mr. Fisher is in his 83d year, and yet in various ways, however moderately, employs himself ten hours a day in useful work and care.

GEORGE BRADFORD BARTLETT.

Mr. Bartlett, who recited at the commemorative meeting some vigorous and appropriate lines which he had written for the occasion, was born in Concord, Mass., July 7, 1833, being the son of Dr. Josiah Bartlett, a practicing physician of that town for fifty-five years, and the grandson of Dr. Josiah Bartlett, of Charlestown, whose practice there extended through nearly the same length of time. Of the former it is related, that he performed the first act of surgery in the American Revolution, on the 19th of April, 1775. The familiar traditions respecting the latter mark him as one of the most prominent and honored men of Concord in his time, and as a conspicuous representative of that noble type of widely known and greatly beloved physicians which is almost peculiar to New England life and history. F. B. Sanborn, in his exceedingly interesting biography of Thoreau, quotes as applicable to him the line from Dr. Johnson, "*Of every friendless name the friend,*" and adds: "He said more than once that for fifty years no severity of weather had kept him from visiting his distant patients,—sometimes miles away,—except once, and then the snow was piled so high that his sleigh upset every two rods."

George, the son, who has inherited abundantly the kindly and helpful spirit of the father, was nearly ready for college when he was but 15 years of age, but was obliged by failing eyesight to abandon study for business, which he left after earning money enough for support in an unostentatious style of life, while engaged in more congenial, though it might be less lucrative employments. His first literary work was for "Our Young Folks," the best juvenile magazine of the time, and he has also contributed largely to the "Wide Awake," for which he is now writing a serial; for the "St. Nicholas," Harper's Young People," and the "Youth's Companion." Some of his articles for these magazines have been collected and published in book form by Harper Brothers, New York.

His verses may be found in Emerson's "Parnassus," Longfellow's "Poems of Places," and in many other publications. He is the author of several pamphlets on Amusements in London and New York, and his book about Concord has passed through many editions and has found a ready sale in Europe as well as in America. Indeed no one knows more about the beautiful old historic and literary town, and the authors who have so much added to its fame, than Mr. Bartlett, and visitors find his Guide a necessary and most entertaining companion as they repair to the many interesting objects and places they want to see. He is a favorite lecturer withal, and has instructed and charmed many an audience, far and near, with his talks about the poets, essayists and transcendentalists of Concord and their haunts, and on legendary lore. One of the most popular of these is his "Footsteps of Thoreau," which he prepared only as, after his previous knowledge of that remarkable "poet-naturalist," he had tracked him in all his adventurous excursions up the rivers and over the mountains, and through the fields and forests. Mr. Bartlett is a zealous antiquarian, and is a life-member of the Pocumtuck Antiquarian Society of Deerfield, Mass., as well as a charter member of the Antiquarian Society of Concord.

HON. PARKER PILLSBURY.

Essex County has had the honor of giving birth to at least three of the most celebrated of the old abolitionists:—William Lloyd Garrison, born in Newburyport; John G. Whittier, born in Haverhill; and Parker Pillsbury, a native of Hamilton. Garrison and Whittier have gone to their exceeding great reward, but Mr. Pillsbury still remains, to the joy of his multitudinous friends and admirers, as bright and seemingly almost as vigorous at the age of 84, as in the years when, as Frederick Douglass writes, he was the one terror of the pro-slavery ministers and churches. Gifted and distinguished sons of "Old Essex," besides, there have been, who rendered noble service for the right in the great conflict; James N. Buffum, of Lynn, who was never weary in well-doing, and who through the long years gave freely and unfalteringly his voice and pen and heart to the work; that colored orator of fiery eloquence, Charles Lennox Remond, of Salem, whose manhood was itself a sufficient argument against the system that enthralled his race; Hon. Leverett Saltonstall and Hon. Stephen C. Phillips, also of Salem, and Hon. Daniel P. King, of Danvers, all of blessed memory, who, in Congress and out of it, strenuously resisted the alarming encroachments of the Slave Power, and in their love of freedom bravely withstood the powerful political party with which they were connected, as it connived at the iniquitous schemes of the southern propagandists and their northern allies ; that brilliant and accomplished statesman, Hon. Robert Rantoul, Jr., of Beverly, whose career was so suddenly and sadly cut off by death just as he had entered upon his more conspicuous labors in the National Legislature, but not until he had brought his acute legal learning and masterly ability to expose the unconstitutionality of the Fugitive Slave Law, and given other gladdening promise of additional blows which, had his life been spared, he would doubtless have struck for the cause of Liberty which at heart he had ever loved ; these too, and other well-known reformers and philanthropists with them, attest that Essex County had no mean share in the general work of emancipation. But of all who have been mentioned, no one was more courageous and faithful in the fight than Parker Pillsbury, no one had a tougher mental or moral fibre, a more unselfish zeal for humanity, a more determined and adamantine purpose to break every yoke, or a loftier standard of truth and righteousness. Perhaps there was no other of them all, whom any apologist or defender of slavery, whether it were priest or politician, would have so dreaded to encounter in open public debate on the one burning question of the time.

He was born in Hamilton, Mass., Sept. 22, 1809. His parents were Oliver and Anna Pillsbury. Oliver was a native of Newburyport and the old house in which he first saw the light and which has seen seven successive generations of the Pillsbury family, still stands upon a lot on High street and near the old Timothy Dexter mansion, where a yet earlier generation of the line lived in a log cabin. In his early manhood he moved to Hamilton and there carried on business as a blacksmith and chaise-maker.

At the Dummer Academy, in Byfield, he had first met his future wife, Anna Smith, daughter of Philemon and Mary (Poland) Smith, of Essex (Chebacco), Mass. In coming to Hamilton, he found himself nearer his fair school friend and the acquaintance easily became more intimate, and ere long ripened into marriage. The first few years of their wedded life were passed under the ministry of the great and famous Dr. Manasseh Cutler. Of their eleven children three were born to them there, of whom Parker was the first. When he was but four years old, his father and Captain Moses Foster of Wenham, (who had married Abigail Smith, Anna's sister), moved with their families to Henniker, N. H., where they bought a large farm and where they fixed their home about four miles from the village and the church, on a high peak of rocks, whence in clear weather they could look afar and see distinctly the White Mountains 120 miles away. The brief winter schools, so poor at best, which he attended as he came to be a lad, or youth, afforded him but the scantiest means of education. Full early in life he knew what it was to work, there on those wild, sterile hills, in removing stumps, building fences and stone walls, and helping to eke out a support for the family from the unwilling soil. Yet it was there, amidst the hard toils, the free winds, and the glorious views of that New Hampshire home, that he acquired the strong, physical frame and the stronger love of liberty, which one day he was to carry with him into his great service of enslaved and outraged millions. The late James Perkins, of Magnolia, who was his cousin, once said to us that he was a remarkably bright, robust, and promising boy. He was very fond of reading, and when he was about twenty he became intensely interested in the speeches of Clarkson and Wilberforce in behalf of West India emancipation. About this time he went to Lynn, Mass., where he was employed for three years as the driver of a baggage and express wagon to Boston, before the age of railroads, little dreaming that ere long he himself, with others like him, was to make the old anti-slavery town and its neighborhood resound with his thunders against the wrongs and woes of his oppressed countrymen.

In 1832, he returned to Henniker, where he again engaged in farming and also became active in the church, and at length decided to prepare himself for the ministry. At the age of 27, he entered a Theological School at Gilmanton, N. H., and graduated there at the end of three years, after which he still pursued his studies for a long winter term at the Andover Seminary. For about a year he preached in his adopted state, chiefly at London, a town adjoining Concord, and now and then, for a Sunday or two at a time, in other places. His sermons were not of the

common-place type, but were striking and full of power, giving
evidence that here was a man who was destined to make his mark
and do his own thinking. He was still of the most unquestioned
orthodoxy, and Mr. Perkins once told us how he heard him
preach a very able and vigorous discourse which was followed with
the hymn,

"There is a fountain filled with blood;"

but his bold and independent utterances in regard to various con-
troverted questions of the day led some of his brethren to give
him the cold shoulder, and their fear or distrust of him was soon
to become more marked and manifest. Like so many of the
earnest and promising spirits throughout the North, he came
under the strong and resistless influence of William Lloyd Garrison, and, abandoning the pulpit in 1839, he returned negative
answers to five invitations which then lay upon his table from as
many country or village churches to become their minister, and
threw himself, body, mind, heart and soul, into the fight against
slavery. That was to be the one supreme work of his life. It
cost him dear. Great were the sorrow of his friends and kindred,
and the sacrifice of personal popularity and reputation. The way
before him was one of struggle and hardship, contempt and persecution. The crown was far in the distance, unseen to mortal
view. But never did soldier of the cross take up his burden and
bear it on, against foes and discouragements, more bravely and
resolutely than he, through all the protracted warfare.

The story is too long for any extended record of it here.
As the General Agent of the New Hampshire Anti-Slavery
Society, or in his more individual, independent capacity, he
traversed the Northern States for a quarter of a century, or until
Slavery was abolished, preaching deliverance for the captives
wherever men would come to hear, in church, hall, school-house,
private dwelling, or in the open air, and denouncing with terrible
severity the guilty secular and ecclesiastical powers for their
complicity with the "sum of all villainies." He was everywhere
recognized as one of the very ablest and most formidable representatives of the Garrisonian platform. He had no fear of man
or devil. He had the real fighting quality. He never minced
matters. He charged upon the enemy with the full force of his
powerful nature, and full often his enraged opponents acknowledged their discomfiture by hurling at him stones and brick-bats
and bad names in return for his trenchant logic, withering wit
and sarcasm, and unanswerable facts. But what were all such
missiles to men like Parker Pillsbury? They were only cheering
symptoms that evil spirits were being exorcised, and that the

process was healthful, however hard, even as a famous revivalist was accustomed to say that the best way to convert some men to Christian faith and life was first to make them mad. Not seldom, in moral as in physical cures, the severest surgical operations are necessary and safest.

Mr. Pillsbury's pen, as well as his voice, has been given unstintedly to the cause. Such productions as his "Folorn Hope of Slavery" ("A brief exhibition of the American church *as it is*, in reference to the Slave System of the United States"), 1847, but especially his later and larger book, "The Acts of the Anti-Slavery Apostles," 1883, not to speak of various pamphlets beside, and numberless articles published in the *Herald of Freedom* and other papers, reveal the spirit and quality of the man and cannot be passed by, by any one who would understand the work of the abolition reformers.

His strong-minded and intelligent father died in 1857, and his remarkably interesting and lovely mother in 1879, at the age of 94. However they might not have shared his bolder anti-slavery or freer doctrinal views, they never lost their faith in their first-born, but rested in his profoundly religious nature and lived to be glad for all that he had done to set at liberty them that were bruised. The aged mother was borne to her burial, at her own request, by her four surviving sons, Parker, J. Webster, Gilbert and Oliver, all of whom rose to honorable distinction. For the last quarter of a century our veteran friend has lived in Concord, N. H., where he married, Jan. 1, 1840, Sarah Hall Sargent. Their only child is Helen Buffum, who married, Sept. 22, 1889, Mr. Parsons Brainerd, now mayor of that city. Wife and daughter are still with him, the solace of his more quiet old age, even as they were the sharers of his stormier past, and any one who should see him there, beloved by all who know him, would hardly realize that he was once the object of wide-spread fear and hatred. His work, however, is not yet done. The same spirit that animated him to battle for the slave, continues him in the advocacy of many another noble reform which he espoused long, long years ago, as each appealed to his understanding and heart, whether Temperance, Peace, or Woman Suffrage. In later years, his Temperance principles cover entire abstinence from all narcotics, and from the flesh of all creatures that walk the earth, fly the air, or swim or dwell in the waters. And he professes to live and hopes to die, true to the *Doctrine of Non-Resistance*, as taught by Garrison, Adin Ballou, Lucretia Mott, and Lydia Maria Child, and other brave men and women of their day. In 1854, Mr. Pillsbury went abroad and was gone about two years, and there, as at home, he preached and practised his cherished views in relation to all these matters. Whoever heard him at Danvers on the 26th of April must have felt that his last word has not been spoken and that his mission is by no means ended. His still more recent eloquent addresses at the celebration, on the 21st of June last, of the First Centennial of the Incorporation of his native town, and at the unveiling of the statue of William Lloyd Garrison at Newburyport, are fresh illustrations of his wonted activity and unwaning power. The twentieth century waits for him and will need him.

REV. GEORGE W. PORTER, D. D.

Rev. Dr. Porter, a descendant of John Porter, one of the original and most prominent and influential settlers of "Salem Village" (Danvers), Mass., was born in Beverly, of the same neighborhood, June 21, 1817. His grandfather, Benjamin Porter, married the widow of Bartholomew Brown, Sarah (Rea) Brown. Of their seven children, the eldest was General Moses Porter, a great soldier of the Revolutionary war, of the war of 1812, and of the Frontiers, while the youngest was Daniel, the father of George. Daniel married Ruth Meacum of Topsfield, a town adjacent to Danvers like Beverly. Both were persons of large stature and robust health, and lived to be more than fourscore years old. They had ten children and George was the youngest of these. When he was in his third year, the family removed to Canaan, N. H., where both the parents died. The son's primary and preparatory education was first in the common schools and subsequently at Orange County Grammar School, Randolph, Vt., at Plymouth Academy, Plymouth, N. H., and at Phillips Academy, Andover, Mass.; but there were intervals when he pursued classical and scientific studies under private tutors. For three years he taught school, in the English Department of Chauncy Hall, Boston. His junior year in theological study was also passed at Andover. At its close, already a candidate for Holy Orders in the Protestant Episcopal Church, he went abroad to pursue his preparations for the ministry at several German Universities. On his return, after an absence of two years, he was admitted to Orders and afterward organized the parish of St. Mary's Church, Dorchester, of which he was the Rector for several years. This was his first parish; and since his retirement from the pastoral relation, his professional life has been passed in New England and in the state of New York, with the exception of the period of his diaconate in Philadelphia, as assistant at St. Luke's Church. He received the honorary degree of S. T. D. from Hobart Free College, Geneva, N. Y.

In 1849, he married a niece of Governor William Eustis of Massachusetts, Elizabeth Eustis Langdon, of Portsmouth, N. H., with whom and an only daughter he now resides in Lexington, Mass., occupied with such clerical and other duty as claims his attention and service, and glad to spend his remaining years amidst the pleasant associations and his many cherished friends in that beautiful old historic town. For the usual term of years, he was lately the President of the Lexington Historical Society; and as a more recent mark of the great esteem in which he is everywhere held, when it chanced that a regular meeting of the Convocation of the Episcopal Churches of Eastern Massachusetts for 1892 fell on his seventy-fifth birthday, his assembled brethren and friends passed congratulatory resolutions, expressive of their affectionate regard and high veneration for him, and of their earnest appreciation of his long and faithful ministry of the Word. An excellent portrait of this distinguished son of "old Essex," as well as another of Gen. Moses Porter, his uncle, painted by Miss Elizabeth A. Clapp, of South Boston, has recently been placed among the pictures of the Danvers Historical Society.

MRS. LUCY STONE.

A very interesting sketch of Mrs. Stone appeared in *The Woman's Journal*, of April 15, 1893, and from it we gather the particulars for the brief story of her life presented here. Born at West Brookfield, Mass., August 13, 1818, she was the daughter of Francis and Hannah (Matthews) Stone, and was the eighth of their nine children. She is of noble ancestry, her great grandfather having fought in the French and Indian War, her grandfather having been an officer in the war of the Revolution and afterward a Captain in Shay's Rebellion, and her father a respected and prosperous farmer. She grew up a bright and vigorous child, truthful, fearless, and very helpful to her parents about the house and in the hard life which they, in common with most New England farmers, knew only too well. Her observing and thoughtful mind early saw around her the very unjust and painful lot of woman and already began to recognize the need of reform. Athirst for knowledge, she wanted to go to college, picked berries and chestnuts for money to buy books with, and, alternately with earnest study, successfully taught district schools at very low wages until she was twenty-five, when she had earned enough to take her to Oberlin College and enable her to begin her course at that institution, the only one of the kind in the country which then admitted women. There she met her expenses by teaching in the preparatory department, and by doing housework, at three cents an hour, in the Ladies' Boarding Hall, during most of the time cooking her food in her own room and boarding herself at a cost of less than fifty cents a week, so scant was her pay and so poor were the circumstances.

Oberlin was an Anti-Slavery stronghold and harbored and assisted many fugitive slaves. A school was started to teach them to read, and it is not without significance, as a testimony to her sympathy for the unfortunates as well as her excellent standing in the college, that she was asked to take charge of it. The colored men at first demurred at being taught by a woman, but were finally induced to yield the point and in due time became so much attached to their instructress that when one day the Ladies' Boarding Hall took fire a whole string of them appeared at the scene, eager, most of all, to save *her* effects. Such, indeed, was the favor with which she was regarded by the colored people of Oberlin, that, while yet a student at the college, she was invited by them to be one of the speakers at a celebration they held in honor of the West India Emancipation. It was her first public speech, made nearly a half century ago. She was summoned before the Ladies' Board the next day, when she was admonished that it was "unwomanly and unscriptural" for a lady thus to appear among men on a platform and speak at a public meeting as she had done, Mrs. Mahan, the President's wife, asking her if she had not felt "embarassed and frightened" in her performance in the very midst of such companions; but the brave little woman quietly gave her the assurance that she "was not afraid of them at all," and, though the act was eminently right and proper, the interview seems to have virtually closed with a hint that she must not do it again! At the end of her course, she was appointed to prepare an essay for the commencement exercises, but when it was made a condition that it must be read by one of the professors, since it would be unbecoming a woman to do it, she declined to present it at all, and awaited another and better opportunity at Oberlin, that was sure to come at length. For nearly forty years afterwards, when she had long been famous as an advocate, before the American people, of the rights of her own sex and of freedom for the slave, she was enthusiastically invited and welcomed back to the college to be one of the speakers at its Semi-Centennial Celebration.

She graduated in 1847, and in the same year gave her first woman's rights lecture in her brother's church, at Grafton, Mass., and afterward lectured regularly for the Anti-Slavery Society, not forgetting, in her devotion to the oppressed colored race at the South, that other great cause which she so early espoused, of which she has been so shining a representative and so noble a leader, and which she is living to see marching surely on to victory. Her labors for the latter as well as for the former met with bitter opposition everywhere. For a long time she wrought, as it were, alone. She herself put up the posters for her meetings, which hooting bands of young roughs were only too ready to tear down. All sorts of rude devices were resorted to in order to break up the meetings themselves. On one occasion a hose was thrust through a window behind the platform and she was suddenly deluged with cold water. "She put on a shawl and continued her lecture." Her mission took her through many parts of the country, where a woman's voice in public had never been heard before, but where, with the strong prejudice that existed against such innovations of established custom or rule, there was at the same time a curiosity to see and hear her that often brought crowds at her call. She had a wonderful way of taming mischievous and violent spirits, by her exceptionally sweet and musical voice, her wise and gracious words, and her pleasant and captivating manner. But the tumult was stilled and the turbulence was shamed into silence, only that her message, in all its plainness and power, might find its surer way into the mind and heart. Many reformers, under such provocations and in such excitements, often lose their temper and self-control, or are betrayed into rashness of speech or folly of conduct, but Lucy Stone, whatever the occasion, invariably maintained her simple dignity and Christian womanhood, and ruled the hour because she *spoke the truth in love.* In all this service, she practiced an economy and self-denial which attested her supreme devotion to her work, but which the world knew little about. "When she stayed in Boston," for instance, "she used to put up at a lodging-house in Hanover street, where they gave her meals for twelve and a half cents, and lodging for six and a quarter cents, on condition of her sleeping in the garret with the daughters of the house, three in a bed."

> "Then to side with Truth is noble
> When we share her wretched crust,
> Ere her cause bring fame and profit,
> And 'tis prosperous to be just."

In 1855, Miss Stone was married, at the home of her parents in West Brookfield, to Henry B. Blackwell, a young hardware merchant of Cincinnati, so long and so well known for his Anti-Slavery zeal and labors and for a like service to the Woman's Rights movement. The ceremony was performed by Rev. (now Col.) Thomas Wentworth Higginson, who was then a settled minister in Worcester. "At the time of their marriage, they issued a joint protest against the inequalities of the law which gave the husband the control of his wife's property, person and children. This protest, which was widely published in the papers, gave rise to much discussion, and helped to get the laws amended." Moreover, "she decided, with her husband's full approval, to keep her own name, and she has continued to be called by it during nearly forty years of happy and affectionate married life." Together they have labored in many states of the Union, and by their lectures, their addresses to the people and Legislatures, and their numerous published articles, they have done much to improve the laws relating to woman, and still more to create a public opinion by which at last her wrongs shall be redressed and her rights secured. In 1866, she helped to organize the American Equal Rights Association, for the benefit of negroes and women both; and in 1869 the American Woman Suffrage Association, serving as chairman of the executive committee of each of these bodies. In this capacity she served the latter for the space of twenty years, desiring "not the post of prominence, but the post of work." In 1872, she and her husband became the Editors of the "Woman's Journal," for the establishment of which she raised most of the needed money in 1870; and they have had charge of the paper from then till now, both of them giving to it, with the aid of accomplished contributors, their signal ability, rare experience, and earnest toil.

Mrs. Stone recently completed her seventy-fifth year, receiving the heartfelt congratulations of a host of her grateful and loving friends. One who sees and hears her finds it difficult to believe that she has lived so long. It is still Spring with her rather than Autumn, except for her full store of garnered wealth of wisdom and goodness, and for the yet more abundant and ever-greatening harvest of her sowing where "the field is the world." Her character and life present one of the brightest and most beautiful pictures in our American history, and there is scarcely one that is more fraught with invaluable lessons for young and old alike.

MRS. ABBY MORTON DIAZ.

Mrs. Diaz, so widely and favorably known for her earnest interest and well directed labors in many a philanthropic work, was born in Plymouth, Mass., and was of the prominent and honored family of the Mortons of that place, among whom Abolitionism early found some of its strongest and most ardent supporters. She is a direct descendant of one of the Pilgrim Fathers, George Morton (brother of Nathaniel Morton, the secretary of the Plymouth Colony and author of "New England's Memorial"), and daughter of Ichabod Morton, one of the truest of Anti-Slavery workers, and a member, with his family, of the famous Brook Farm Community. Of this father, her gifted cousin, Edwin Morton, son of Edwin Morton and author of a volume of very fine poems, has written these beautiful lines, suggested by his uncle's own words, "We can have Heaven here, if we but live rightly:"

> "He dreamed that Heaven should come to Earth,
> And ceaseless toiled the day to view.
> O'erborne he sank before its birth—
> And lo! to him the dream is true!
> O weary heart! O weary hand!
> No more the anxious strife renew—
> A Power above the vision planned,
> And Heaven indeed has come to you!
>
> Sweet May returns—with leaf and flower
> The garden of his love expands!
> Rewarding Autumn brings her dower,
> But gives the fruit to other hands!
> So blest is he, and ever blest,
> Who patient sows where others reap;
> And ever-ripening fields shall best
> His ever-growing memory keep!"

Abby was the only daughter, and there were five brothers. In very early life she came under the influence, not only of the Plymouth Mortons and their kindred friends and associates in the old town of the Forefathers, but also of such men as William Lloyd Garrison and Horace Mann, and of the Brook Farm Fraternity, and it is easy to see how much these privileges and ministries had to do in shaping her character and giving bent to her life. She, too, was caught by the magic power of the great Reformer, and in her pithy and suggestive address at the Commemorative Meeting, she tells of some of her first and later anti-slavery work and experience. In her youth she had been accustomed, in connection with household duties, to write prose and poetry by way of recreation, and her taste for literary composition, as well as her capacity for other kinds of useful service, was to stand her in good stead in the not distant future, when, not long after her marriage to Mr. Diaz, she was left with two little sons dependent upon her efforts for their support. She was quick to turn her mind and hand to whatever sort of honorable toil most readily presented itself, in a certain apt and healthy way that many might well imitate. Now it was teaching a juvenile singing-school, and then acting as a housekeeper or even as a cook at a summer resort; now giving out work from factories to needle-women, and then making soap at home, and again writing stories. Such a spirit as that knows no defeat and is sure of recognition, success and honor, at last. Thirty years ago, Mrs. Diaz began to write magazine articles and books of domestic and public interest. It has been said of her: "She is a Puritan of the Puritans, Plymouth born and Plymouth reared; the Puritan blood that fills her veins throbs for liberty, for virtue, for high attainment in thinking and doing;" and her writings are so strongly marked by these qualities and are altogether so bright and helpful, that we can hardly forbear to give in this connection a list of her books, as published by D. Lothrop & Co., Boston. They are, "The William Henry Letters," "William Henry and his Friends," "Lucy Maria," "Chronicles of the Stimpcett Family," "The Cats' Arabian Nights," "A Story Book for Children," "The Jimmyjohns," "The John Spicer Lectures," "Polly Cologne," "Story Free Series," "The Schoolmaster's Trunk," "Domestic Problems," "Bybury to Beacon Street" and "Only a Flock of Women." These are not very Puritanic titles, to be sure, and it is possible that some of the old Puritans would scarcely have found the pages fully in harmony with their sterner and less sympathetic views and ideas, but what was best in Puritanism is largely here and without it Mrs. Diaz's books could not have been written. They abound in practical lessons and are adapted to the life of today.

The same may be said of her numerous "talks" or "lectures." One of the papers well says of them: "The Gospel of life, as promulgated by Mrs. Diaz, is inspiring the most gratifying attention. It is simply the Christianity of Christ that Mrs. Diaz teaches, applying this higher enlightenment to education, economies, and social progress. No one can listen to even one of her 'talks' without rising to more enlarged and elevated views of human life and destiny." The subjects which she treats are such as these: "Life, or What it is to live," "Waste of Human Forces and Their Wise Direction," "Caste, or Class Spirit in America," "The True Work of Humanity for Humanity," "Ethics of Nationalism," "Missionary Work Among the Upper Classes," "Christian Socialism," "Application of Christianity to Civilization," "Our Philanthropies, Charities and Reforms, considered in the light of Reason and of Religion," "The True Social Science," "Thought as Power," "Progressive Morality," "Individuality," "The Woman Question," "Competition," "Intemperance," "The State's Undeveloped (human) Resources," "Human Nature," "Religion not something imposed on Humanity, but a necessity of Humanity," "Educational Duty of the State to its Future Citizens in regard to its own interests," "Character Work in Schools and at Home," and "The Higher Life."

For twelve successive years Mrs. Diaz was elected President of the Women's Educational and Industrial Union of Boston, which she had helped to establish, resigning the position in 1891, on her removal to Belmont where she now resides, though she still remains a Director of the institution and frequently visits its rooms to aid its practical work. During her residence in Belmont, she has started a "Women's Club" there, for the study of history and literature, and of such subjects as the public education of school children, the punishment of criminals, the improvement of streets, general sanitation, economy in use of public funds, etc. From all such enumerations of her varied themes, publications, and labors, it will be seen what a very busy life Mrs. Diaz has lived and at how many points she touches human life and the world's great need. If she writes charming stories for the young and gives useful talks to poor working-girls and timely sympathy and aid to the friendless and lowly, not the less is her rare talent or broad culture made to reach those who are more highly educated or who are in more favored circumstances; and so it is that the light that blessed the Pilgrims still breaks forth anew, and the mission of the Puritan still goes on for all.

REV. AARON PORTER.

Rev. Aaron Porter was born in Danvers, Mass., Aug. 10th, 1826, and like his kinsman, Rev. Dr. George W. Porter, a sketch of whom has already been given in these pages, is a lineal descendant of the first American progenitor of the Essex County race of that name, John Porter, the largest landed proprietor of that part of the town which was formerly known as "Salem Village," and said by the Colonial records to have been a man of "good repute for piety and integrity," as well as "estate." Aaron's father was Samuel Hathorne Porter, better known as Hathorne Porter, one of the noted abolitionists of Danvers, who was greatly respected for his intelligence and high Christian character, and of whose virtues and Anti-Slavery principles and sympathies the son is a worthy inheritor. The latter received his higher education at the State Normal School at Bridgewater, Mass., and at the Theological School at Meadville, Penn., of whose Alumni Association he is a member. After graduating at the Normal School, he taught in the Grammar Schools of Bristol, R. I., for one year, and for five years in the Grammar School of Fairhaven, Mass.

He was married to Martha Ellen Cassino, at Salem, Mass., March 31, 1857, and since that time has been settled over various churches of different denominations. Having been ordained to the ministry at Somerset, Mass., in 1860, and having been for some time the pastor of a church of the "Christian" sect, in that town, he subsequently removed to Lewisburg, Penn., and was the pastor of a church of the same connection there. He was afterward the minister of the Unitarian Church in Northumberland. Penn., (originally under the charge of the celebrated Dr. Joseph Priestley), and then of Universalist Churches in Gibson, Penn., and Mankato, Minn., whither he and his family went in 1869. In 1871, he entered upon a ministry-at-large, at Mountain Lake and on the neighboring prairies, in Minnesota, but later returned to the East and was settled, successively, over the First Parish (Unitarian) at Mendon, Mass., the First Congregational Church and South Congregational Society (Orthodox), in Grafton, Vt., and the Orthodox Congregational Society in East Alstead, N. H., of which he is now the minister.

His numerous settlements in widely separated parts of the country illustrate his missionary spirit, while the fact that his services appear to have been equally acceptable to the several Christian communions in which he has labored from time to time, without claim to any essential change of his doctrinal views, has been due to the emphasis he has laid upon what is most central in the Gospel of the New Testament and the comparatively small importance which he has attached to matters of less moment. A sincere and implicit believer in Jesus Christ, he has made love to God and love to man the burden of his preaching. As his Danvers address showed, he was familiarly acquainted with the early Anti-Slavery friends and work in that town and is justly proud of them, too, cherishing the old traditions and spirit of the "Seven Stars," yet holding to both the Church and the State.

MR. GEORGE W. PUTNAM.

Few of the living old-line Abolitionists date back their anti-slavery interest and work to so early a period, or have been friends or acquaintances of so many of the leaders of different emancipation schools or parties, as Mr. George W. Putnam, of Lynn. None have toiled in the field with greater fidelity or with a more self-sacrificing spirit. He, too, like others present at the meeting, has a rich storehouse of personal recollections of the old days, which were well worthy of record, however small a part of them may be noted here, in these brief, informal sketches.

He was born Sept. 6, 1812, in Gloucester, Mass., whither his parents, Joseph and Mercy Giddings (Whipple) Putnam, moved from Danvers, their native place. Subsequently, in 1824, the family removed to Salem. The father carried on the shoe business, and also invented the "stone drain pipes" which are now used in vast quantities throughout this country and Europe, receiving, like many such useful inventors, little else than ridicule and abuse for his service. His wife was a sister of Matthew Whipple, the father of the late brilliant and noted essayist, Edwin P. Whipple; and her mother, whose name was Giddings, was a connection of the great anti-slavery leader of the West, Joshua R. Giddings, of Ohio. Joseph Putnam's father was also named Joseph. He was a carpenter by trade, and was a "Minute Man" in the Revolution.

George's education was confined to the town school in Gloucester. After the removal to Salem, he was for several years a clerk in the drug store, and afterward learned carriage and ornamental painting. Later he gave some attention to art, became a pupil of the famous Boston artist, F. Alexander, and wrote many articles, in the same interest, for the *New York Herald*, the *Boston Transcript*, and other papers. More recently, he has been interested in life-saving and other inventions, some or all of which reveal his own faculty and skill in this line. Old as he is— for he is past his fourscore—he is still fully engaged in these pursuits.

But it is his anti-slavery record, which chiefly attracts us. In 1833, *sixty years ago*, he heard for the first time a lecture on slavery. It was given in the South Church, Salem, by that sterling Abolitionist, Rev. Cyrus P. Grosvenor, who was not able to procure for the purpose his own church, the Second Baptist. Rev. Brown Emerson, pastor of the South Church, was not present, and some of his parishioners painted their pews afresh so that the reformers should not use them. It was at the close of that meeting that Mr. Putnam, at the age of 21, signed his name as a member of the "Salem Anti-Slavery Society." During that year and afterwards he carried around Salem, for signatures, "Petitions for the Abolition of Slavery in the District of Columbia." Almost every prominent citizen indignantly refused his name, but Hon. Leverett Saltonstall signed, and said *he would be willing to do it every day in the week*. Mr. Saltonstall did excellent work in Congress for "Free speech" and against the "Atherton Gag Law." Another noble man whom Putnam recalls to mind and whom he knew very well, was "Master William B. Dodge," who requested the authorities to remove him from his place as teacher of a *White School* and appoint him as teacher of a "*Nigger School*," and who afterward opened a free singing school and taught the colored people music. Mr. Dodge often preached in the Alms House, in Salem. Finally he emigrated with his family to Abington, Ill., all of them taking with them their anti-slavery principles.

In 1834, Mr. Putnam met John G. Whittier, Amos A. Phelps, Abner Sanger, and Henry B. Stanton, at the house of Rev. Charles T. Torrey, pastor of the Howard St. Church, Salem, and assisted them in arranging for the circulation of anti-slavery documents. Mr. Torrey, as elsewhere stated, was subsequently imprisoned at Baltimore for aiding in the escape of slaves, and died in his dungeon. It was at Salem, in the "Tabernacle Church," that Putnam first heard Wendell Phillips, Samuel J. May, and William Lloyd Garrison, and among the faithful abolitionists of the city whom he remembers with grateful honor were the intrepid John A. Innis and such Quakers as Josiah Maynard and William H. Chase. With a few friends, he was invited to meet, stealthily at night, George Thompson, on his first visit to America, in 1834, when having been mobbed and hunted for his life at New York and Boston, and also at Salem, he was concealed at the house, in North Salem, of Rev. Mr. Spencer, a retired Episcopal clergyman from England. Some of the party remained outside while they listened with breathless interest to the eloquent foreigner within, as, with subdued voice, he described the terrible conflict with slavery, which was in reserve for our country. But these are only a few of the many strange experiences and exciting scenes with which our old soldier of freedom was familiar in his early manhood.

In 1842, he made the acquaintance of Charles Dickens, on his first visit to the United States, and, at the request of the renowned novelist, he travelled with him as private secretary, and, after his death, wrote an account of their journeyings together, which was published in the October and November numbers of the *Atlantic Monthly*, of 1870. For a time he took up his residence at Nashua, where he first heard the "Hutchinson Family," and where, as at Lowell and other places, he himself taught singing schools. Having married Julia A. Putnam, of Chelmsford, Mass., he settled at Lynn, where he now lives. He was there when George Thompson came again to America, in 1851, and he was present at the meeting in Faneuil Hall when the Englishman and his abolition friends were mobbed and driven from the building, at the hazard of their lives. Putnam afterward heard Thompson at Plymouth, Fall River, and Lawrence, and wrote for the *Liberator* accounts of his speeches. At the request of the Committee of the Massachusetts Anti-Slavery Society, he accompanied Mr. Thompson to western New York, and also wrote accounts of his speeches there, for the *Liberator* as well as the *Anti-Slavery Standard*. He was with Thompson, Phillips and Edmund Quincy, at Springfield, when an immense and furious mob, hung and burned the illustrious visitor from abroad in effigy, and assailed " Hampden Hotel" with eggs and brickbats, and howled and roared till long past midnight ; and he wrote an account of that, too, for Mr. Garrison's paper. But the next day, the gifted orator drew a great crowd to hear him and effected a wonderful revulsion of popular feeling, in his favor. Putnam continued to report his speeches as he spoke in various states, at one time going with him and with Samuel J. May and Frederick Douglass to Canada, where they mustered very large gatherings in Toronto and Montreal. They afterward visited Philadelphia and there met James and Lucretia Mott (in whose parlors they held their meeting, not being able to obtain a hall), and Mary Grew, Robert Purvis and many other distinguished abolitionists.

On their return to Boston. Thompson held a grand farewell reception just prior to his departure for England. For some time Putnam was employed in service as a lecturer—spent two years in Minnesota—and then removed his family to Peterboro', N. Y., where he wrote for Gerrit Smith and prepared his circulars and addresses for publication for several years, accompanying and assisting him as he went to New York City, Canada and elsewhere in anti-slavery work. While living at Peterboro' he wrote and delivered there an address on " The Life of George Thompson." Subsequently he removed with his family to Billerica, Mass., and as the news arrived of the death of that glorious champion of liberty, he repeated his eulogy at a Memorial Service, held at the Ruggles St. Church, Boston, by the " Wendell Phillips Club," Wendell Phillips suggesting him for the service, and many famous anti-slavery representatives being present on the occasion. Others spoke at the meeting, and it was then and there that Mr. Garrison's voice was heard in public for the last time. One of the Boston papers said of Mr. Putnam's address, that it " was of unusual interest and was warmly applauded throughout." It was afterward delivered at various other places.

Besides the leading abolitionists already mentioned, our friend had been associated in his labors with such men and women as Parker Pillsbury, Francis Jackson, Elizur Wright, Oliver Johnson, Rev. George B. Cheever, Charles K. Whipple, B. F. Mudge and the Buffums and Thompsons of Lynn, Harriet Tubman the heroine, Sojourner Truth, the Fosters and the Burleighs, Rev. W. H. Fish, Rev. Beriah Green, Rev. John T. Sargent, Lewis Hayden, Hon. Simeon Dodge, Lewis Ford, and others whose names history will not let die ; while, among his friends and acquaintances, there have also been Rev. Samuel May of Leicester, Rev. Samuel Johnson, Lucy Stone, Antoinette Blackwell, Elizabeth C.

Stanton, Mrs. Mary Richmond, Susan B. Anthony, Giles Stebbins, F. B. Sanborn, Rev. John Pierpont, Rev. Theodore Parker, Theodore D. Weld, and *John Brown!* At the house of Gerrit Smith he once passed an evening with the hero of Harper's Ferry and at Peterboro' attended a meeting for prayer and addresses at the hour of the martyr's execution.

Of Mr. Putnam's connection with a branch of the "Boston Secret Association," which was formed to prevent the capture of fugitive slaves by their masters, and with which such men as Samuel May, Sen., Francis Jackson, Dr. Bowditch, and other worthies were connected, we have not space to write here. Nor of his many other as yet unmentioned labors, speeches, and contributions to the press. He has, moreover, a decided gift for song, as his verses which the Hutchinsons have sung so widely show. His first Poem, prompted by the " Atherton Gag Law," was published in the " Salem Observer," and copied into the " Liberator." Another was delivered at the meeting which George Thompson addressed at Plymouth. Among others which we recall was one of unusual merit which not long ago he wrote on the occasion of the unveiling of the statue of John P. Hale, at Concord, N. H., attesting, if evidence were needed, that the veteran who has written and has wrought so well and so much, is still, in his eighties, the lover of Freedom, for whose sake he has freely spent his life, surrendered ease and comfort, and endured no small share of prejudice and opprobrium.

GEORGE T. DOWNING.

Personal friend of Garrison and Phillips, Whittier and Sumner and Theodore Parker, and nearly all the great Anti-Slavery men, George T. Downing is himself one of the most meritorious of the abolitionists of America. Like Purvis, Douglass, Garnet, Ward, Wells Brown, Charles Lennox Remond, and others of his race, of similar reputation, he is possessed of marked ability and attainments, has felt keenly the wrongs and sorrows of his people, and has been a fearless and heroic fighter in their behalf.

A very interesting account of him appeared in a New York paper some years ago and we cull some of its details for our own brief sketch of him here. Though he was born free, he is descended from a slave. About a century and a half ago, there lived in Jinketig, a little town of Accomac County, Va., a rich and influential slave-holder, whose name was (Captain) John Downing, who became a convert under a religious revival, but who was told by the minister, as he would hardly have been told by a clergyman in that state a century later, that he could not join the church unless he set free his slaves. Accordingly the Captain at once emancipated them all. Among them was a young girl, who, as she grew to womanhood, married and bore a family of children. These seem to have taken the name of the old master, as was so common in the south, and one of them was Thomas Downing, the father of the subject of our story. His mother, the little girl just mentioned, was of commanding presence and of strong character and much consideration. The family moved to New York, where Thomas, after a brief stay at Philadelphia, became interested in public affairs and was well known for his manliness and energy. George, the eldest son of Thomas and Rebecca, was born in that city, Dec. 30, 1819, was reared under Christian influences, and early learned to respect himself and defend his own rights. Negro children of New York, as elsewhere in the North, were then, as also later, frequently insulted and stoned and beaten in the streets. No one was more quick or brave than George Downing to repel the assailants, and, with the aid of his youthful colored companions, drive them away. He attended public schools in Orange and Mulberry streets, and also received private instruction; and among his mates were boys who afterward rose to distinction. One of them was the colored orator, Henry Highland Garnet. Some of the scholars formed a literary society and began to discuss "live subjects," and they passed a Resolution, declaring that they would not join in celebrating the Fourth of July, because the Declaration of Independence was, to the colored people of the United States, "a perfect mockery." It may safely be credited that our youth was among the foremost in this action. Then we find him, as an efficient agent of the "Underground Railroad," helping fugitive slaves to make good their escape, attending Anti-Slavery Conventions, and in numberless ways working to arouse public sentiment against the cruel and monstrous evil that was in the land. He was one of a famous Committee of Thirteen, organized at the time of the passage of the Fugitive Slave Law, to make war against that infamous measure and render it a nullity. At the time of the Anthony Burns excitement, he was summoned to Boston and took the first train for the city, to join the mustering friends of Liberty who had been called to the rescue. Standing in one of the streets, he saw a body of Worcester men marching by with a banner inscribed with the word "*Freedom.*" The account adds: "A number of police assaulted the procession and captured the flag. Mr. Downing's whole nature was aroused. He rushed into the crowd and used his muscles, strength and agility for all they were worth. After a desperate struggle, in which the banner was torn almost to shreds, he captured it from the police, and amidst expressions of admiration at his courage and strength, and applause at his success, he bore the emblem to the office of Robert Morris, which was near by." Mr. Downing's dauntless spirit was manifested, in like manner, in connection with the well-remembered John Brown meeting at Tremont Temple. The assemblage there was broken up by the police and influential pro-slavery parties, but it adjourned to meet in the evening at the Joy Street Baptist Church, " a then stronghold of the colored people." The city authorities warned Mr. Downing and J. S. Martin, who were most prominent in the management of the occasion, that such a gathering would result in bloodshed and that they themselves were powerless to prevent it. They were reminded, by Downing and Martin, of their duty to preserve order and protect the citizens, and the meeting was held and was attended by a dense crowd and was a great success, Downing and other friends of it arming themselves for an emergency and Wendell Phillips making one of his most eloquent speeches. A vast, howling mob gathered without, but the mayor called out the militia, violence was restrained, and " the right of free speech was vindicated."

During the war, Mr. Downing was very active in forming several colored regiments, obtaining from Governor John A. Andrew a written assurance that every soldier should be treated with equal and exact justice, and that there should be no discrimination on account of color. While on a visit to Washington, in connection with such enlistments, he was assigned the charge of the Restaurant of the House of Representatives, and, accepting the appointment, he made the acquaintance of many of the leading members of Congress, but especially became an intimate friend of Charles Sumner, who on his death-bed grasped his hand and said with great earnestness, " Don't let my Civil Rights Bill fail!" In defiance of all objections or scruples on the part of others, he allowed persons of his own race to be served with the rest at the Restaurant, and he and his family were the first of that race to occupy a box in a Washington theatre. He was a man of just the metal to despise and break down the prejudice which had so long debarred his people from such privileges as these. In the exercise of the same spirit he was influential in securing the first appointment of a colored man as a United States Minister abroad, in the person of Mr. Bassett who was sent as representative to the Republic of Hayti. As a citizen of Rhode Island, he labored for twelve years to abolish all distinctions on account of color in the public schools of that state, traversed the state and appealed to the people as well as to the Legislature to remove the unjust law from the statute book, and finally accomplished his obje

In a reorganization of the Rhode Island militia, the Governor commissioned him as captain, but of a colored company. Mr. Downing declined the honor, protesting against the accompanying or virtual discrimination. The Governor renewed the appointment and made it satisfactory.

"Mr. Downing," it is said, "has not only succeeded as a public man, but has also shown marked business ability. He owns a very valuable estate prominently located on the most fashionable thoroughfare of Newport." Able, upright, enterprising, highly intelligent, and eminently useful and benevolent, he is held in high esteem in the city and state of his adoption, and by all who know him, and they are many. He has frequently received noteworthy marks of respect and confidence from associations or from his fellow-citizens, as when he was for several years made Grand Master in the Order of Odd Fellows, or when he was selected to make an address of welcome to the great Hungarian Patriot, Louis Kossuth, on his visit to this country. But it is for his loyal and faithful devotion, through a long life, to his own contemned and afflicted people, and his zealous and persistent efforts still more to elevate and ennoble them after he had lived to rejoice in their emancipation, that he will most of all be gratefully and lastingly remembered and honored. The touching allusion which he made to the recent death of the beloved wife of his youth, at the commemorative meeting, will not be forgotten by those who were present.

REV. PETER RANDOLPH.

Those who were able to comprehend the nature and significance of the commemorative meeting, and availed themselves of the opportunity afforded them to be present, will quite agree with us, we think, in the opinion that one of the most interesting features of the occasion was the presence and brief, simple address of Rev. Peter Randolph, of Charlestown. There were many of those who took part in the proceedings who had rendered greater service to the children of oppression and who were far more widely known to fame than he, but it was meet that there should also be one there who should appear as a representative of the "race redeemed from slavery" and as a living witness to what his whiter brothers and sisters had done in its behalf. As he himself so pithily said, in his speech, *they* might speak of slavery as an "idea," but *he* could speak of it as a "reality." In the course of his remarks, he referred to an account of his own experience, at the south and north both, which he was preparing for the press. The book has since been published by James H. Earle, 178 Washington Street, Boston, and we gather from the volume a few

details of his history for our notice of him here, hoping that those
who may read these pages will get the full story itself and so all
the more know the wrongs and sufferings which were once endured
by the colored millions in "the land of the free." There is much
popular ignorance concerning the subject, especially among the
rising generations of our countrymen; and there is no better
source of information for them than the trustworthy testimony of
those who have themselves tasted the bitter fruit of the deadly
tree. In the latter part of Mr. Randolph's *From Slave Cabin
to Pulpit*," he re-published, with an Introductory Note by his
good friend Rev. Samuel May, his "*Sketches of Slave Life*,"
which was issued as a pamphlet in 1855.

About 73 years ago he was born a slave, in Virginia, and
was owned, with 81 others, by a man named Edloe. Led by his
slave mother, he was directed, at the early age of ten years, to
the Christ, sure refuge and comfort of the hapless and sorrowing.
For a long time he labored under the impression that he was
called of God to be a preacher. But how could he preach unless
he could read and thus be able to study the Bible? His great
desire was to be acquainted with the Book of books. A friend
taught him to spell words of three letters. By slow degrees he
learned the art, so as at last to read without much difficulty what
to him was "the source of all knowledge." Then he learned to
write, obtaining a book and copying its letters upon the ground,
in the absence of slate or paper. He thus became able, at length,
to write his own passes, as he went from one plantation to another.
His father was owned by a Mr. Harrison, of an adjoining plantation, where he was made a slave-driver under a white overseer.
" My father would often tell my mother how the white overseer
had made him cruelly whip his fellows until the blood ran down
to the ground. All his days he had to follow this dreadful employment of flogging men, women and children, being placed in
this helpless condition by the tyranny of his master." The name
of the overseer on the plantation to which Peter belonged was
Lacy. One day a pig was found dead, evidently from natural
causes. No one of the slaves would confess that he had killed it,
and so Lacy flogged them all, taking his raw-hide, with a wire
attached to the end of it, and giving each man 20 lashes on the
bare back. " The blood was seen upon the side of the barn where
these slaves were whipped, for days and months. The wounds of
these poor creatures prevented them from performing their daily
tasks. They were, indeed, so cut up, that pieces came out of the
backs of some of them, so that a child twelve or thirteen years
old could lay his fist in the cruel places. My brother Benjamin
was one of the slaves so savagely beaten."

Benjamin, particularly, was so unfortunate as to encounter the prejudice or dislike of the overseer, who was always watching for an occasion to whip or lacerate him. Ere long he was doomed to even a worse fate, but one, alas, so common to the sharers of his lot. Peter, whose oldest brother he was, writes: " When my father died, he left my mother with five children. * * * * She had to work all day for her owner, and at night for those who were dearer to her than life; for what was allowed her by Edloe was not sufficient for our wants. She used to get a little corn, without his knowledge, and boil it for us to satisfy our hunger," and "sometimes would beg the cast off garments from the neighbors, to cover our nakedness, and when they had none to give, she would sit and cry over us and pray to the God of the widow and fatherless for help and succor. *At last my oldest brother was sold from her*, and carried where she never saw him again. She went mourning for him all her days, like a bird robbed of her young—like Rachel bereft of her children, who would not be comforted, because they were not. She departed this life on the 27th of September, 1847, for that world 'where the wicked cease from troubling, and the weary are at rest.'" *And this was Slavery:*—this the evil and wickedness which the abolitionists contended against with all the power that God had given them, and for their righteous and glorious warfare against which, they were stigmatized as "fanatics," and "infidels," and "blasphemers," and "pests," and were visited with ostracism, violence, imprisonment, and death itself!

Edloe made his will, March 20th, 1838, six years before his decease, providing "for the emancipation of his slaves and for the payment to each one of fifty dollars, whenever they should elect to receive their freedom and go out of the State of Virginia." But though Edloe, like many a master, was not void of all sense of justice and humanity, yet, as Randolph says: "Even if the master was kind, the overseers, whom the law protected, and from whom there was no appeal on the part of the slave, could maltreat and abuse with impunity." But the provisions of the will were not carried out in the spirit of the testator. For three years after their master's death, his Slaves were kept at work as before, not being able to obtain from John A. Seldon, the executor, the money intended for them. At the end of that time, they decided to take what they could get—*less than* $15 *each*—and leave for the North. There were sixty-six of them in all, of both sexes and all ages; and among them were Peter Randolph and his wife and child. They reached Boston, on the Schooner *Thomas H. Thompson*, on the 15th of September, 1847. It being noised abroad that a large number of emancipated Slaves had landed at

Long Wharf, a crowd of persons soon gathered to see them and "congratulate them on their new birth to Freedom." Prominent among those who thus greeted them were William Lloyd Garrison, John A. Andrew, Wendell Phillips and Rev. Samuel May. Some of the strangers went to the office of the *Liberator* in Cornhill and there met other warm-hearted Anti-Slavery friends. Through the kindness of Mr. Garrison and Mr. May and some of their associates, about half of the new-comers soon found situations in the city and its immediate vicinity, and the rest in places more remote. One who, like Randolph, could read and write, was more in demand, but even he received but a dollar and a half a week, with board, until he was employed at the Anti-Slavery Fair, in December. Here he had the pleasure of meeting many abolitionists and hearing lectures and discussions such as he had never heard before. "The language and words used by some in describing and denouncing the Slave Power, were strong and uncompromising. Yet the words were inadequate and too weak to express the barbarity and cruelty to which my brethren in the South were exposed."

Mr. Randolph makes mention of sympathizing firms and business men who gave him employment and who usually entrusted him with their keys: J. C. Elms, President of the Shoe and Leather Bank of Boston, Isaac Fenno, Michael Simpson of the Sackville Carpet Co., William Bond & Son, T. C. Marian, Little & Brown, Dutton & Haskell of the *Boston Transcript*, Henry Callender, Mr. Morey, Merritt & Mullen, Tyler Batcheller, Charles Adams, Wm. B. Spooner, and Ezekias Chase. Daniel N. Haskell, of the *Transcript*, was of much help to him in getting his "Sketches of Slave Life" before the public. Mr. Adams, who wanted him to scrub his floor, was a little surprised, perhaps, that he asked three dollars a day, and, being himself a member of the Legislature, he reminded his colored brother that what he required was more than they got at the State House! "But my work is *worth* more," quoth Peter. The latter seems to have made his first speech at a memorial meeting of the Boston merchants in honor of Mr. George Batcheller. His address was highly complimented and was well reported in a New York paper.

Randolph and most of his companions in the city soon connected themselves with a body of Baptist brethren worshipping in a hall in Belknap, now Joy street. In Virginia he had been a member of that communion. The little society grew and was soon organized as the Twelfth Baptist Church of the city and Rev. Leonard A. Grimes became the pastor. Randolph, who is now the only surviving one of its original members, was licensed by it to be a Baptist preacher and at once began to do missionary work. He visited, for this purpose, St. Johns and other places in New Brunswick, and then returned to Boston and preached in Somerville and Dorchester and Plymouth, and elsewhere. In 1856, he was regularly ordained at Brooklyn, N. Y., and took charge, for a year, of a struggling church of colored people in New Haven, Conn., attending lectures at Yale College. "I departed from New Haven richer in knowledge and experience, if in nothing else." His next settlement was in Newburg, N. Y., and then followed, during the latter part of the war, two years in Boston, where he was engaged in a small newspaper business, and in preaching for the Old Ladies' Home on Phillips street. At last he went down to Richmond to do work in his native state, and was in Baltimore on his way thither, at the time of the assassination and funeral of President Lincoln. He proceeded to Richmond by way of City Point. "The colored people from all parts of the state were crowding in at the Capital, running, leaping, and praising God that Freedom had come at last." On his first Sunday in Richmond he preached at one of the principal camps to a large congregation. Two weeks after his arrival at that city, he was invited to be the pastor there of the Ebenezer Baptist Church. Accepting the call, he became *the first settled colored minister in the South*, only white clergymen having previously been permitted to preach to negroes. He could but realize, most deeply, what a change had come over Virginia as well as over himself, from the time when, only 18 years before, he had trod her soil as a slave. Various perplexing questions confronted him in connection with his work. One related to the marriage question, it being necessary to establish proper family relations among the freedmen, such as could not exist under the system of Slavery. Special legislative enactments were required to remedy, if only in part, the prevalent evil. Then again, at meetings, the men and the women were separated from each other, and the latter had no equal rights or privileges, in the church. This was all broken up by Mr. Randolph, who had the blacks assemble like the whites, and all entitled to vote. Still again, near the close of the war, southern Baptist churches (whites) had passed strong resolutions against their sister churches at the North, but now they wanted their colored brethren to affiliate with themselves rather than to maintain alliance with their northern friends. But they were told that this could be done only on two conditions, viz: that they would take back all they had said against the Baptists at the North and would treat those whose co-operation they solicited as Christian brethren and not as Slaves. Randolph was chosen to represent the latter, but all conferences were of no avail. The whites still held that the colored people had no men who were fit to preach and be pastors, and they were otherwise indisposed to come to satisfactory terms. Those who were the real and only Christians in the controversy felt that they "were justified in coming out and forming a separate organization." A convention of colored Baptists of Richmond and vicinity was called, a permanent organization was effected under the name of the Shiloh Baptist Association of Virginia, and Peter Randolph was elected its President, with John Oliver as its Secretary. "The said John Oliver was formerly of Boston, but went South immediately at the close of the war, and rendered much service for his people. I am proud to say that this Association has been productive of much good among the colored Baptists of Virginia."

After four years and a half of active service in Richmond, Mr. Randolph returned once more to Boston, a city which he had had abundant reason to love. He began work in building up a Baptist church at the South End, commencing with a Sunday school which Rev. Dr. A. J. Gordon and his people had formed at 1210 Washington St. Large numbers were added and the new society not long afterward removed to a more commodious place of worship on West Concord St., secured to them through Drs. Lorimer and Gordon and their friends. "The Ebenezer Church continued to increase in membership and influence, until today it is one of the largest churches in Boston." Subsequently we find our preacher engaged in quite extensive missionary labors, in Providence, R. I., in Worcester, Mass., at Mashpee among the Indians, at Nantucket, in Albany, N. Y., and in West Newton, Mass. After leaving his Baptist church in Boston, he read law for a time in the office of E. G. Walker, Esq., feeling the need of some better acquaintance with matters of civil government. He was made a Justice of the Peace by Governor Washburn, and was successively reappointed by Governor Long and Governor Ames. He now lives at Charlestown, Mass., and we have no apology to make for the considerable space we have given to the story of this humble, but earnest friend, who is now free, but was once a slave, who taught himself on the plantation how to read and write, who was then in thrall and misery, but has since done all this work for God and man.

REV. DANIEL S. WHITNEY.

Mr. Whitney was born in South Danvers (now Peabody), March 4th, 1810. He spent his boyhood in "Upper Beverly" and went to school at the old red school-house that stood at the intersection there of the roads leading from Danvers Plains and Danvers Neck. One winter the school was kept by the sisters,

Hannah and Betsey Putnam of Danvers, who were teachers of considerable local celebrity in their day. Our venerable friend, who was their pupil, has recalled to us the circumstance, that at a time when it was not customary to spare the rod, these ladies put it aside entirely. "Hannah's tongue did the *lashing* for the big boys, and Betsey, with the tenderest of tones, did the *praying*. They kept an excellent school, and the committee gave them the credit of making the best writers the district had ever had." Daniel was early instructed in the art of making shoes, and as the occupation was an important aid to his widowed mother, he gladly followed it until he was twenty-two years of age. In Danvers and Beverly and in the towns of Essex County very generally, may still be seen the little shoe shops (now quite deserted in these days of machinery), in which the friends or votaries of St. Crispin diligently plied their humble vocation and fashioned the prepared stock or material into "pumps" or "brogans" for the larger establishments of the manufacturers, and it was especially during the winter days and evenings when there was but little employment for them out-of-doors, that they were most busily engaged in these small structures, and in connection with their toil at the bench would discuss together, as perhaps no other class of workmen were accustomed to do, all the live questions of the hour. They were a thoughtful and intelligent set of men, were fond of reading, were good patrons of the newspapers, and were in the habit of doing their own thinking. Dr. Channing and the late Dr. Peabody and others have paid fitting tributes to their character and have written of the peculiarly helpful influence of their calling upon the mind and life. Dr. Peabody, himself a native of Beverly, wrote concerning the Fraternity of St. Crispin, that it "has almost vindicated for itself a place among the liberal professions by its high grade of general intelligence, and by the number of eminent men who have issued from its ranks, from Hans Sachs, whose lyrics were among the great forces of the Protestant Reformation, to our own Whittier, whose place in the foremost rank of living poets none can challenge:" and Dr. Channing, in the course of a similar train of remark in his discourse on Noah Worcester, the Philanthropist, says that it is an occupation which Coleridge refers to as "followed by a greater number of eminent men than any other trade." Hans Sachs, Worcester, and Whittier, George Fox and John Pounds, Roger Sherman, Henry Wilson, and William Lloyd Garrison himself, with scores of other great helpers of mankind, were all, at some time in their life, shoemakers. Whittier's jubilant song of "*The Shoemakers*," will be remembered in connection.

We well recall what nurseries of Freedom the little shoe shops of Essex County were in old Anti-Slavery times. It was in such places rather than in the factories and homes of the prosperous or wealthy, or in the learned professions, the colleges and seminaries, or the more titled and influential classes, that the Abolition sentiment first took deepest root. It was there that Garrison and "*The Liberator*" earliest found highest favor, and in Free-Soil days the speeches of Giddings and Mann, and Sumner and Andrew, were read with greatest avidity and delight. The shoemakers understood the question of questions better than did their prouder and more flourishing neighbors, crowded the public meetings and made them enthusiastic for Liberty, and themselves in large numbers were borne on the popular wave into legislative halls and offices of trust and power, to do the work which others had opposed or neglected.

But we need not pursue the digression. No one knows the story better, perhaps, than Mr. Whitney himself, who is doubtless grateful for his early avocation for more reasons than one. At the age of twenty he had joined the Temperance army, with whose cause he has now been earnestly and actively identified for 63 years. About the time he quit the shoe-bench, or shortly afterward, he became more deeply interested than ever in religious matters, having charge of the Sunday school of the First Universalist church in Salem, whose pastor was then Rev. Lemuel Willis. Through the advice of Mr. Willis he was led to prepare himself for the Gospel ministry. After some years, spent at academies in Topsfield and Andover, and in school-teaching, he entered upon his theological studies under Rev. Paul Dean of Boston, and in due time was ordained as an Evangelist by the Massachusetts Association of Restorationists. Subsequently, with yearly engagements, he occupied three pulpits, in Middlesex Village, West Boylston, and Berlin, but was never ordained as pastor of a church.

From early life Mr. Whitney has been a lover of freedom and a friend of many reform movements. We have already instanced his devotion to the Temperance Cause. His profound sympathy with the Anti-Slavery struggle dates especially from the time, when, at the age of 26, he heard Rev. Samuel J. May deliver a powerful discourse upon the subject at the Branch Church, in Salem. In March, 1842, wishing to enjoy more freedom in religion and in philanthropic work than the intolerance of the churches then allowed, he joined Adin Ballou's Hopedale Community, with which Rev. William H. Fish also became connected, as has been stated on a previous page. While there, though not occupied with *tentmaking*, he yet engaged in various useful, practical kinds of labor, aside from preaching, as was his wont, here and there, at home and abroad.

It was during his residence and work at Boylston, in 1858, that he received the honor of being elected as a delegate from that town to the State Constitutional Convention of that year, and had the satisfaction of voting in that body to leave the term *male* out of its amended Constitution, subsequently rejected by the people. At Southboro', where he soon established his home and where he has lived ever since, he shared the risks so many encountered in the terrible Slave-hunting period. He was a street preacher but once in his life, and it was in Boston in the day when Simms, the fugitive, was abducted, and when even the stones of the streets seemed to cry out against the crime of his rendition. During the last years of the war, he went down to City Point and served with the Sanitary Commission under Frank B. Fay. Since the war, he has acted as Postmaster of Southboro' for ten years, resigning the office more than ten years ago, as being too old for the position and its cares.

In 1842, Mr. Whitney married Miss Hannah S. P. Cotton, youngest daughter of Rev. Ward Cotton, of Boylston, and a descendant of that "burning and shining light of the Puritan Church," Rev. John Cotton of Boston. She was one of the constructors of the remarkable patch-work quilt, sent by the Anti-Slavery women of Boylston to Mrs. Chapman's great Fair of more than a half century ago and bought by Anti-Slavery women of Boston and presented to Mr. Garrison. It had a kneeling slave as a central figure and an Anti-Slavery sentiment written in every square. Mrs. Whitney is in good health for one who, like her husband, was born in 1810, but on account of an infirmity of lameness is kept quite at home and was unable to accompany him to Danvers, on the 26th of April. Her bit of property in Southboro' has been owned more than 70 years by women, and still the "Taxation without Representation" goes on, as when Otis thundered against the injustice before the war of the Revolution. It is no wonder that the aged and venerated pair are devoted friends of the cause of woman. For more than 50 years they have unitedly borne consistent and unfaltering testimony in behalf of Freedom, Equal Rights, Temperance and Religion; and now in cheerful hope, they stand "on the very edge of the river waiting to pass over."

MISS SARAH H. SOUTHWICK.

Though not so old as some of the surviving Abolitionists who were present at the Danvers Meeting or were unavoidably absent, Miss Southwick, having been born into an old anti-slavery family circle and having from very childhood shared its active zeal and sympathies, has a rich store-house of memories of the great struggle, and very few now living were present at so many of its more thrilling scenes, or on so many of its more important occasions, as she. In her brief written address, as printed on previous pages, she has given, by request, some account of her ancestors, and also of the Boston mob of 1835, of a part of the attendant circumstances of which she was a spectator, however she may not have witnessed, like Dr. Porter, the brutal and atrocious outrage itself. From her "*Reminiscences of Early Anti-Slavery Days,*" which she has "privately printed" in a small volume within the last few months, we gather other recollections of deep interest, illustrative of her own life, and of stirring events with which, as an abolitionist, she was personally associated.

She was born in 1821, at North Vassalboro, in Maine. Her father, Joseph Southwick, was one of the original subscribers for the *Liberator*, and was a delegate from Maine to the Convention which formed the American Anti-Slavery Society, in 1833. Her mother, Thankful Hussey, was, like Mr. Southwick himself, of life-long devotion to Anti-Slavery work, inheriting her principles from her father, Samuel Hussey, a merchant of Portland, through whose acquaintance and sympathy with the labors of Wilberforce and Clarkson the family were largely made ready to espouse the cause in America and to "welcome Mr. Garrison with open arms." Mr. Hussey was a good friend of fugitive slaves, who often came to Portland concealed in vessels sailing from the West Indies and who on their arrival were lodged in jail for safe-keeping. With the jailer's connivance, effectual means were quite sure to be found for their surreptitious start in the night for Canada.

In the spring of 1834, the Southwicks moved to South Danvers, now Peabody, Mass., where they resided until the spring of 1835 with Isaac Winslow who had married Sarah Hussey, sister of Thankful, and who was also an earnest and prominent abolitionist. Another sister, Comfort Hussey, married Nathan Winslow, brother of Isaac, and "both brothers subscribed for the first copies of the *Liberator*, and supported Mr. Garrison heartily with their money and interest." It was amidst such highly favorable family associations and social advantages that young Sarah Southwick early imbibed her anti-slavery sentiments and learned how to work with the workers. She was thirteen years of age, when, in the winter of 1834, she attended the first of the famous Anti-Slavery Fairs in Boston, being accompanied by her father and sisters. Here she saw for the first time Mrs. Lydia Maria Child, who with Mrs. Ellis Gray Loring managed the Fair.

and whom she wanted very much to see, having been a reader of her "Juvenile Miscellany." Observing, on one of the tables, certain articles which her mother had stimulated her to make for the sale, she asked Mrs. Child the price of one of her own needlebooks, whereupon the good lady said, "It is marked fifty cents, but it is not well made, and you may have it for two shillings." Long afterward Mrs. Child wrote some account of the occasion and remarked: "Our chief purchasers were three Quakers and their families, Isaac Winslow, Nathan Winslow, and Joseph S outhwick, who have all ascended to a higher plane of existence." Miss Southwick attended nearly every succeeding Fair for twenty-five years, and she recalls the circumstance that her uncle Isaac once startled an Anti-Slavery convention by putting into its contribution box the generous sum of one thousand dollars.

In the spring of 1835, the family removed from South Danvers to Boston, where they resided for two years in High street. In the summer she and her mother attended a meeting of the Boston Female Anti-Slavery Society, which they both joined, and during the same season she was present at another meeting, when Mrs. Maria Chapman became a member and spoke of her interest in the cause and of her desire to aid it. At the time of the annual meeting, on the 21st of October, of the same year, "the excitement in regard to George Thompson was at its height." (Miss Southwick's brief account of the "Boston Mob" is given in her address.) Of this celebrated orator and philanthropist who was again and again a guest at her home, she says, "What an enthusiasm I felt for him, what admiration, and how interested we were in everything he said! * * * * He was always eloquent, but when aroused he spoke with such rapidity and flow of words as I have never heard from any one since, except the Rev. Phillips Brooks. * * * * As he seldom wanted to retire till eleven or twelve, he would entertain us, after the Anti-Slavery friends who made a point of coming in the evening had left, with stories and reminiscences of his youth and of English life, which were both charming and amusing." On the day he sailed for England, Sarah was sent to Mr. Garrison's house in Brighton street to tell him that Mr. Thompson was to take his departure at one o'clock. Notwithstanding all precaution to the contrary, his movements got noised abroad and were duly chronicled in the evening papers. "After he left (by a schooner bound for St. John), his wife and three children came to our house, and were comfortably fitted out by friends for the return voyage to England by a regular sailing packet from New York." In 1866, Mr. Thompson, on his third visit to America, was present and spoke at the funeral of his excellent friend and hospitable host, Joseph Southwick, which took place at Grantville.

Miss Southwick first made acquaintance with the Grimke sisters, Sarah and Angelina, in 1837, on their arrival from the South at Boston, where they began their lectures before the Female Anti-Slavery Society. She thinks she first heard these noble women, one afternoon at a very crowded meeting in Amory Hall, which was situated at the corner of Washington and West streets. Having emancipated their own slaves in South Carolina and seen the evil of slavery as others had not, they were all the more competent to interest and instruct northern people in regard to the subject, and wherever they went, in their extensive travels in this part of the country, their lectures were attended, as at Boston, by large throngs of both sexes and did very much to encourage and strengthen the work of the reformers. Angelina became the wife of Mr. Theodore D. Weld.

The Massachusetts Anti-Slavery Society held its annual meeting of January, 1837, in the *Stable* of the Marlboro' Hotel, Boston, and Miss Southwick believes she attended all its sessions which were continued through three successive days. The Hotel stood on Washington street, opposite Franklin street. On the site of the stable, Francis Jackson and others subsequently built the Marlboro' Chapel, in the lower hall of which the Boston Female Anti-Slavery Society, or the Abolitionists, for years held their fairs, and "Concerts of Prayer," and regular or occasional meetings. It was at one of these meetings, called to consider the murder of Lovejoy at Alton, Ill., that Sarah first heard Wendell Phillips and Edmund Quincy on a distinctively Anti-Slavery occasion. But she had, shortly before, had the great privilege of hearing Phillips deliver, at the immense indignation meeting in Faneuil Hall, Dec. 8, 1837, the remarkable speech which at once made the unknown youth forevermore famous. Women at that time were not in the habit of attending political gatherings of any kind, but a handful of them, thirteen in all, made the venture at this time and ranged themselves in the front seat of the right gallery as one enters the Hall. "After that, Anti-Slavery women, certainly, always went when they wanted to. I do not recall the names of all the women. The only ones I am sure of are Mrs. Chapman and some of her sisters, my mother, my two sisters, and myself." And the narrative tells us, also, that when Mr. Phillips, roused by the unexpected utterances of the Attorney-General from the front gallery in denunciation of the Martyr, rose and asked the privilege to speak, he "stood on the floor in front, near the left gallery;" and then, when he was invited to come forward upon the stage, "stood on the same platform with the other speakers, near the left gallery as you face the platform, and with his back to the portraits." These particulars, given by one who was there to see and hear, fifty-five years ago, can hardly be uninteresting to any one who may hereafter visit the old "Cradle of Liberty," for nothing in all its history can quite thrill us with admiration like that maiden speech of the matchless orator of freedom, taken in connection with all the circumstances of the occasion. Says Miss Southwick, "I think nobody in these days can understand the power of that speech over that audience. I was young, but to my mind Wendell Phillips was the impersonation of beauty, grace, and eloquence."

Our friend was present, also, at the ever-to-be-remembered National Anti-Slavery Convention of women, held in Philadelphia, in May, 1838. It was her first visit to that city, and she was accompanied by her mother and her sister Abby, by her aunt, Ruth Hussey, and by her uncle, Isaac Winslow, and his daughter, now Mrs. Emily W. Taylor, of Germantown, Pa., whose letter for the Danvers meeting appears on a previous page of this volume. The hall in which the convention was to be held had been built by abolitionists and others, and had been dedicated to "Free Speech," and it was the largest and most beautiful in the city. For the first day or two, in the daytime, a howling mob surrounded the doors and filled the entries, while, at the evening meetings, stones and brickbats smashed the windows and broke in the Venetian blinds; and rotten eggs and other missiles were thrown in upon the audience. At one of these meetings, as many as three thousand came to hear Abby Kelly, Maria Weston Chapman, and Angelina Grimke. "How bravely they tried to be heard above the tumult outside, and the hisses and shouts inside!" The next evening, the women, as they arrived at the Hall and found a dense crowd surrounding it, were told that the Mayor had closed it and forbidden its use. Returning to their Hotel, they soon heard that their beautiful hall was on fire, and, ascending to the roof, they watched it, with mingled grief and horror, as it burned to the ground.

In May, 1840, the Southwicks and Winslows all went to the memorable annual meeting of the American Anti-Slavery Society, when the division took place on questions relating to women as members and officers, and to the attitude of the churches. The sentiment in favor of women as members preponderated and Abby Kelley was placed on the business committee, whereupon, after much discussion, a large number of the delegates, including the great body of the ministers, withdrew from the old organization and formed "the American and Foreign Anti-Slavery Society," establishing soon afterward, as their organ, "The

National Anti-Slavery Standard" in place of the " Emancipator."
The division, thus consummated, was of vast importance. The
new society, with its exclusion of women, was comparatively
inefficient and short-lived. The old one survived, with the continued lead of Garrison and the powerful aid and sympathy of
those who were sought to be shut out, but whose moral support
and practical help were found to be so necessary to true success.
Hence, too, more and more, the antagonism between the church
and anti-church parties.

In 1839, Miss Southwick heard Frederick Douglass make his
first speech at an Anti-Slavery Convention in Nantucket, whither
he had been persuaded to go and tell his story. " He was green
and awkward and embarrassed. He spoke at first with hesitation, but soon regained self-possession and made a very straightforward and earnest statement of his life and what he had seen of
Slavery. The audience was greatly moved." After an illustrious subsequent career of about fifty years the great orator made
a speech at a breakfast which was given to him by Mrs. Mosher
at Cambridge, at which a large company of notables like Drs.
Hedge and Hale, Mrs. Julia Ward Howe and Miss Elizabeth
Peabody, and Rev. Samuel Longfellow and Mr. and Mrs.
Samuel E. Sewall, were present, when Col. T. W. Higginson
asked him how he had learned to speak so fluently considering
his lack of opportunity in his youth, and whether he never felt a
stage fright in his public address. Mr. Douglass greatly
amused the company with his characteristic reply: " I assure
you, gentlemen, I never felt so near having a stage fright in my
life as at this moment," meaning, as Miss Southwick says, *in the
presence of so many people of cultivation and education.*

Miss Southwick also gives an interesting account of one of
the annual Anti-Slavery picnic excursions in which she was wont
to join, and of her acquaintance with the Westons and Chapmans and the service they rendered to the cause generally. The
Weston family were of marked genius and culture. Mrs. Chapman, who was considered " very handsome," was the eldest of
the sisters and was " the soul of our fairs." And the narrator
adds: " She was queenly in gait and manner, and I think her
sacrifices of social position, when she allied herself to the Anti-Slavery Cause, were very great." They were all frequent visitors at the house of the Southwicks. " I had no young friend
for whom I had the affection that I had for Lucia Weston."
These two, Sarah and Lucia, for successive years, circulated
petitions and attended Anti-Slavery Conventions together, sometimes occupying an attic room when crowded out of their own
apartments by guests who swarmed the meetings. " I went to

school to Caroline Weston" (at her residence on Boylston street where the Public Library now stands), and "I look back to her as a teacher and life-long friend with love and gratitude,—a sensible, cultivated, unaffected, warm-hearted woman, whom everybody respected. How much I owe to her in the way of education, I can never express." She and her sister Anne wrote Anti-Slavery poems and articles for the "Liberty Bell," an Anti-Slavery Annual which Mrs. Chapman edited for the Fairs. Anne, and Deborah "the prettiest," and Emma "the youngest," all died as recently as 1889, in Paris. "For the last thirty years I saw very little of them, as they resided a long time in France."

Miss Southwick, who now resides at Wellesley Hills, Mass., concludes her book by saying, "Sometimes, when I hear Mr. Garrison named with reverence and the abolitionists spoken of with admiration, my mind goes back fifty years, and I wonder if I can be living in the same community and country where Mr. Garrison was regarded with contumely and shunned as a fanatic, and where Abolitionists were excluded from polite society. To Mr. Garrison, the change in public opinion must have seemed nothing less than miraculous. 'It is the Lord's doing, and it is marvelous in our eyes.'"

ADDITIONAL CONTRIBUTIONS.

We append a few later contributions to our book, from some well-known friends who have kindly written them at our request: Mr. Henry B. Blackwell, the veteran advocate of freedom for the Slave and of Woman's Rights, for whose expected speech at the meeting, unfortunately, there was not time; Mr. F. B. Sanborn, of literary fame, who is rich with anti-slavery recollections and lore, and whom it would have been a great privilege to hear, but who was then far away in old classic lands; and Dr. Charles A. Greene, a descendant of Gen. Nathaniel Greene, who presents highly interesting testimony about the "Boston Mob," as did Rev. Dr. G. W. Porter in his address; and Mrs. C. S. Brown Spear, who with her first husband, Rev. Abel Brown, and with her second, Rev. Charles Spear, was long engaged in philanthropic work, and who gives us some reminiscences of scenes and occurrences of which she herself was a witness and "a part."

FROM MR. HENRY B. BLACKWELL.

The interesting anecdotes and reminiscences to which I listened at the Danvers Re-union of Abolitionists, have recalled to my mind many youthful memories of the first ten years of the Anti-Slavery agitation, from 1830 to 1840, the most arduous period of all because carried on at first without organized support and in face of a community in entire sympathy with the slave power.

It was my fortune as a boy to see something of the beginnings of the abolition movement in this country. My father, an English sugar-refiner, came from Bristol to this country in 1832, with the hope that slave-labor cane-sugar might be supplanted by free-labor beet-sugar, as had already been done in Germany and France. He was a sugar-refiner in New York City from 1832 to 1838, erecting in 1834 the first vacuum pans ever used in the United States. In 1832 he became a member of Rev. Dr. Samuel Hanson Cox's Presbyterian Church on Laight St., and had many earnest conversations with his pastor, who was then intensely pro-slavery. An ardent liberal and an admirer of American institutious, my father as a "Clarkson abolitionist," was shocked and amazed at the universal subservience of the American press and pulpit to " the sum of all villainies," and at the low standard of political morals. In a little volume which he printed a few years later under the unpretentious title of "Slavery Rhymes," he thus characterized that era of decadence :—

> Unerring signs proclaim an absent God,
> Unearthly hands have written Ichabod.

In 1831 Mr. Garrison started *The Liberator* on its immortal mission and practically began his anti-slavery crusade. In 1833 a convention of abolitionists met in Philadelphia and adopted a "Declaration of Sentiments," which was signed by representatives of many states. That Declaration, with the engraved autographs of its signers, hung for years in our parlor, and my father used to say that the signers would some day be held in greater honor than the signers of the original Declaration of Independence.

In 1833 Rev. Dr. Cox visited England to attend a great meeting of the "Evangelical Alliance." He there found anti-slavery popular in evangelical circles, and, on his return to New York preached a series of anti-slavery sermons, little dreaming of the storm he would evoke. In one of these he called attention to the fact that Jesus was not of the Caucasian race, the Jews being descendants of Shem. At once it was announced that he had said that the Savior was a "nigger," and everyone was thrilled with holy horror, especially the roughs. Immediately the houses of all the prominent abolitionists of New York were sacked by mobs. Among others Rev. Dr. Cox and his brother, Dr. Abram L. Cox, a leading physician, had to fly for their lives. They took refuge in my father's country house near Newtown, Long Island, where they remained for a week in hiding. I remember the profound depression of spirit shown by the worthy divine; while his brother, the physician, practiced pistol-shooting behind our barn, and put several bullets into the back of our old family carriage. We children were enthusiastic abolitionists. We named one of our horses "Garrison" and another "Prudence Crandall." Whittier's songs of freedom were household words. I remember Dr. Abram L. Cox quoting, with fiery emphasis, the words:

> "Great God! And these are they
> Who minister at thy altar, God of Right!
> Men who their hands with prayer and blessing lay
> On Israel's Ark of light!
> What! Preach and kidnap men!
> Give thanks, and rob thine own afflicted poor!
> Talk of Thy glorious liberty, and then
> Bolt hard the captive's door!"

In 1834 the first New York Anti-Slavery fair was held in Niblo's Garden. As a boy of 9 years I was kept busy writing mottoes for "Sugar Kisses" for that occasion. At that fair in 1834, I first saw Gerrit Smith, then in the bloom of early manhood, a magnificent personality. About that time George Thompson first visited this country and delivered anti-slavery lectures of remarkable power and eloquence. He was at once assailed as a British emissary sent out to sow dissensions and break up the Union. So bitter was the feeling that he was compelled to leave the country. I was present at an abolition meeting in a church on the corner of Thompson and Broome streets when Thompson denounced two agents of the British and Foreign Bible Society who had been seduced by Southern hospitality and written reports white-washing the Patriarchal Institution. Soon brickbats and stones came pouring in at broken windows, and we were driven out by the mob. These events of 59 years ago, when I was a mere boy, seem like yesterday. The prominent New York workers then were Arthur and Lewis Tappan, Gerrit Smith, Beriah Green, Anson Phelps, the brothers Cox, Joshua Leavitt, and a few years later David and L. Maria Child, and Oliver Johnson.

It is hard to conceive the ferocity displayed by the pro-slavery community from 1830 to 1840. It was simply demoniacal. Cuban sugar planters whom my father as a refiner met daily in Wall St., said frankly that they found it profitable to " work out" their negroes every seven years and then replace them by new ones from Africa. The anti-slavery papers were the *Liberator* and the *Emancipator*. Later, about 1840, came the *Anti-Slavery Standard*.

In 1838, misled by the hope of raising beet sugar, we moved to Cincinnati, a ten days' journey from New York. There we found James G. Birney and Dr. Gamaliel Bailey editing and publishing *The Philanthropist* (afterwards merged in *The National Era*). Three times the printing office was mobbed and the type and press thrown into the Ohio river. There, on the slave line, with Kentucky across the river, the bitterness was proscriptive. Every few years border ruffians invaded the city under the pretext of reclaiming fugitive slaves, and in pure deviltry drove the free colored people from their little homes and destroyed their household effects. After the damage was done, the authorities made a show of interfering and called for volunteer "deputy-marshals" to preserve order. This was very enjoyable to the young men, who marched all night through empty streets after the excitement had subsided. The leading Ohio abolitionists were Birneys and Donaldosns, Leir Coffin, Harwood Burnett,

Israel Ludlow, John Jolliffe, and, later, on the Liberty party platform, were Birney, Samuel Lewis, and Salmon P. Chase. The centre of work in Cincinnati was Mrs. Sarah Otis Ernst, who with her brave German husband, A. H. Ernst, had a beautiful home in the suburbs, to which she gathered the faithful few who endured social ostracism for the slave's sake. About 1845, Abby Kelly and Stephen S. Foster, then in their prime as agitators and orators, held a series of meetings in the old Millerite Tabernacle in Cincinnati. There I became nearly baptised in abolitionism, only it took with me the form of Liberty party, then Free-soil party, and eventually Republican party.

The abolition movement was so wide in its area and so varied in its manifestations that no one occasion or locality can do it justice. The value of such local gatherings as that at Danvers is to add, by personal reminiscences, to the memories of the great moral and political movement which abolished slavery in America.

FROM MR. F. B. SANBORN.

CONCORD, MASS., August 17, 1893.

DEAR DOCTOR PUTNAM:—Had I been in America at the time, nothing could have given me greater pleasure than to meet with you and my old friends, the anti-slavery men of 40 and 50 years ago, to listen to their recollections, and, if the word came to one of the younger partisans, to add my word of history or suggestion to the full reminiscences of the veterans, such as Fisher, Hutchinson, May and Pillsbury. Now you ask me to come in as a final course, with some mention of Whittier the Poet, and Sumner the Statesman, both friends, and the former a far-away cousin of mine. I do this the more willingly, because I have somehow heard that, in the copious praise of Whittier as a poet and a man, full justice has not been done to his early and effective service in the anti-slavery cause. None was more earnest, and few more serviceable than he, or for a longer period; he was not quite so early in the field as his friend Garrison, but neither did he mingle with his opposition to slavery so many other fancies and animosities, such as hampered and distracted Garrison not a little, in his noble crusade. As for Charles Sumner,—though the completion of his extended biography, a few months since, by Mr. E. L. Pierce, leaves little to be desired by those who knew and honored that great public character,—yet the tone of some criticisms lately printed gives one to feel that Shakespeare was quite right (as usual) in making Ulysses say to his brother chieftain:—

"Perseverance, dear my lord,
Keeps honor bright: to have done is to hang
Quite out of fashion. * * * Let not Virtue seek
Remuneration for the thing it was,—
For beauty, wit,
High birth, vigor of bone, desert in service,
Love, friendship, charity, are subject all
To envious and calumniating Time."

As it happened, I became familiar with the name of Whittier, as most men did, 40 years ago,—before I heard of the recluse and scholarly Sumner. Born in New Hampshire, where Whittier had many relatives and friends, my earliest anti-slavery recollections are associated with an " Anti-Slavery Almanac," published, I think, by Garrison, at the "Liberator" workshop of such weapons, in which was a cut of my mother's cousin, Reuben Leavitt, a Merrimac County sheriff, arresting Mr. Storrs, an Abolitionist minister, while on his knees, praying against negro-slavery. I hardly knew then what the words meant; nor could I understand what enormity the bland and fine-looking kinsman who sometimes came to our house, could have committed, to be thus held up for reprobation. But as years went by, and I read the newspapers, and Whittier's verses, and came to know a little of another cousin, Moses Norris, then in Congress; of his leader, Franklin Pierce, (whom I had heard, a handsome lawyer, pleading for a criminal at our Rockingham court); and the rest of the New Hampshire Democracy, I followed eagerly the lead of my brother Charles and his friends, in our little town of Hampton Falls (where Whittier died last year) to the support of John P. Hale, when revolting against the pro-slavery dictation of Pierce and Norris. This was in 1845, and the immediate question was the annexation of Texas. I was then but 13 years old; yet my anti-slavery sentiments were as clear and pronounced as they ever have been since; the cause being one which appealed to the emotions, and did not require arguments addressed to the understanding. The next year, 1846, our party, the Independent Democrats, uniting with the Whigs, who had long been a hopeless minority in New Hampshire, carried the State election, in March, and Whittier, from his cottage at Amesbury, poured forth his exultation at our success, in a burlesque poem, put into the form of a letter from Frank Pierce to my cousin Norris, which Elizur Wright printed in his Boston Chronotype (that admirable little hornet of a newspaper), and which had much vogue in New Hampshire. I could once repeat it all, but will spare you all but a few stanzas. Pierce began:—

'Tis over, Moses! all is lost!
I hear the bells a-ringing;

> Of Pharaoh and his Red-Sea host
> I hear the Free-Wills singing.
> We're routed, Moses, horse and foot,
> If there be truth in figures;
> With 'Federal Whigs' in hot pursuit,
> And Hale with all his niggers.

The ' Free-Wills' were the ' Freewill Baptists,' then a strong sect in New Hampshire, and mainly, like the Quakers, on the antislavery side. Pierce, in the verses, then went on to mention the sad omens that had foreshadowed this political overturn,—naming among others our unlucky cousin Reuben, whose assault on free speech could not be forgiven :—

> Our Belknap brother heard with awe
> The Congo minstrels playing;
> At Pittsfield, Reuben Leavitt saw
> The ghost of Storrs a-praying;
> And Carroll's woods were sad to see,
> With black-winged crows a darting;
> And Black-Snout looked on Ossipee,
> New glossed wi h Day & Martin.
>
> We thought the 'Old Man of the Notch'
> His face seemed changing wholly,—
> His lips seemed thick, his nose seemed flat,
> His misty hair looked woolly;
> And Coos teamsters shrieking fled
> The metamorphosed figure;
> 'Jest look! that old stone cuss,' they said,
> 'Himself is turnin' nigger.'

Belknap, Carroll, and Coos are counties in New Hampshire,—while Black-Snout and Ossipee are two mountains, higher than Hymettus or Pentelicus, though with less musical names, between the towns of Ossipee and Sandwich, through which tne Bearcamp river drains down to the Saco, in regions long since made familiar to his readers by Whittier's more serious poetry. The Old Man of the Notch is the "Great Stone Face" that Pierce's friend, Hawthorne, soon after described, in one of his best romantic satires; it overlooks the Franconia Notch, down which the teamsters of Coos county must drive, in the days before the iron horse superseded their slower cattle.

Ten years after this satire, President Pierce was giving Jefferson Davis full power to make Kansas a slave state, if he could; and we were striving (successfully, as it proved), to prevent him. Then it was that *John Brown* made himself known to his countrymen, who never afterward could forget him; and then also, Whittier lent the powerful aid of his verse, singing,—

We tread the prairie as of old
Our fathers sailed the sea,
And make the West, as they the East,
The homestead of the free.

Nor let us forget, while thinking of the grand effort that saved Kansas to Freedom, and gave us our first great advantage in the civil war,—the control of the regions beyond the Missouri,—let us never forget what Charles Sumner did for us in that eventful year, 1856. Had he laid down his life when death came so near him then, he could not have suffered more, nor deserved better of his country. Yet we lived to see mean men, perverted by political hatred (meanest of the small passions), inflict upon Sumner the formal censure of Massachusetts, for one of the most generous acts, even of his most generous life. It is a pleasure to remember how gallantly Whittier, though differing from Sumner in some points, stood by him in that day, and gave his best efforts to have the disgrace of Massachusetts,—for Sumner could not be defamed by such a censure,—wiped off by the men who had incurred it. In the same way, the unworthy voices that have lately piped up to belittle and disparage Sumner, will cease to be heard, as the true measure of that man is taken by posterity,— and he is seen to have stood next to Lincoln in the ranks of civil and political life, during the second and more important American Revolution,—that of 1860—1875.

Yours for truth,
F. B. SANBORN.

FROM CHARLES A. GREENE, M. D.

In 1829, my father published (in a building called *Merchants Row*) a newspaper, entitled "The Christian Herald." The building stood at the corner of Congress and Water streets, Boston, Mass. Another building of the same name now occupies the same site. Hon. Charles Sumner's father was a co-partner of my father in the issuing of the above periodical. In the latter part of 1830, Mr. Garrison moved into the building and occupied one room opposite my father's, on the third floor; and began preparations for the issuing of "The Liberator," and, as my memory serves me, issued the first number on the 1st of Jan., 1831. Of one matter I am confident, my brother Samuel and myself carried to the subscribers of the *Herald* each of its issues in Boston; and to accommodate Mr. Garrison, in his poverty, my father helped him by having my brother and myself deliver his issues. And I well remember quite a number of the subscribers to whom I served the paper, viz: Dr. Abner Phelps, who lived directly opposite the building called *Merchants Row*;

a man who was engaged in the liquor business, named D. Weld, on Washington St., above the Lion Tavern, in a greenhouse that had its end towards the street; and a painter by the name of Green, on the same street. My father had in his employ a printer named Rowland Hart, and he did the press-work for my father on a Franklin Press similar to the one now belonging to the Bostonian Society. Sometime previous to the above issue of "The Liberator," my father became well acquainted with Mr. Garrison, and was in decided sympathy with his work. Knowing his impoverishment, he loaned him types and set up the matter for his first and after issues, and Rowland Hart did the press-work. At that time my father lived on the opposite side of Congress Street, over the Arch. At the time that the Anti-Slavery movement was being talked of, when the mob threatened the life of Mr. Garrison and while he was on his way to the Leverett St. jail, where he could be in safety, my father ran all the way by the side of the vehicle, and as it was turning off Green St. on to Leverett, a man rushed up to the carriage and caught Mr. Garrison by his white neck-tie, and at once twisted it around, endeavoring to kill him, by thus throttling him. It was suddenly done; and when the victim's tongue had been forced out of his mouth by the operation, my father caught hold of the collar of the man (who had a blue coat with brass buttons) and tore it in twain, and loosened his hold at the same time, and Mr. Garrison was taken to the jail. I have heard my father tell the story more than a score of times. He was a very powerful man, weighing 225 pounds, and noted in his youth, and in his collegiate course at Brown, for his great strength. In 1835, my father became a co-partner of Ebenezer Hayward (who was also a subscriber to "The Liberator"), and they opened, in Wilmington, N. C., a store to which they shipped articles from New England, and the vessels returned with tar, shooks, sugar, conch shells, resin, and other Southern commodities. The first year that my father lived there, my brother Samuel taught a few negroes their letters. When about to return to the South the next year, some of my father's Wilmington friends advised him not to do so, as his life would be taken in consequence of the above attempt at the education of the "chattels." So my father sent an agent there and closed up the store.

There comes to mind the name of another strong Anti-Slavery man. I know his name was Clough—I think Ebenezer C. He lived near, or on, Pleasant Street. He was one of the last men in Boston to wear the short pants and silk stockings, and had silver buckles on his shoes. He was a subscriber to "The Liberator."

FROM MRS. CATHARINE S. B. SPEAR.

I never was converted to Anti-Slavery. I never was anything else from earliest childhood. In my spelling book, at seven years of age, I read a poem, commencing "I thank God I was not born a little slave, to labor in the sun," etc. But I don't, for God never made a slave! No one was *born* a slave under the Divine Law. This is of man's device. Hooker says, "Law has its seat in the bosom of God, and her *voice* is the harmony of the Universe."

We had a fugitive slave to live with us and to labor in my father's family. He had escaped from New York, for slavery then existed there. We children were very fond of *Henry* and liked to hear him tell stories. Much attention was afterward given to the subject of Colonization, but I never liked the scheme. I recall, how in my school days I expressed Anti-Slavery sentiments in one of my compositions and what good impressions were made on my mind by the poems of Cowper and Montgomery. Cyrus P. Grosvenor was the first one to give me documents and tracts for distribution. Copies of the *Liberator*, as often as published, were also forwarded to me for the same purpose, by Mr. Garrison and Mrs. Chapman. I soon heard of Frederick Douglass and wrote to John A. Collins to send him "forthwith" to Hubbardston, my native town, where he created a great furor. An effort was made to turn me out of church, not by our good old minister, Rev. Samuel Gay, but by a new preacher from New York. It proved a failure and he himself left the Parish.

We had, previous to this affair, an extensive grove meeting, an Anti-Slavery gathering of sixteen hundred people, at which Mr. Garrison and six ministers were present and on the stand; and abolitionists came from Princeton, as firm as their own Wachusett. We had four banners in the line of march, with a band of music and with a figure of Liberty. The Ladies' banner was a circular one, bearing the inscription "*Universal Liberty*," and decorated with evergreen, with the figure of an eagle, the emblem of our Republic, in the centre.

A little slave boy, *Anderson*, was present on the occasion, under the charge of Dr. Hoyt of Athol, who had recently obtained his manumission from the court in Worcester. Standing on the platform, he was presented with a banner and acknowledged the gift by saying: "I tank you, my brudder, for dis loye-token. It can be mine *now*. I once was a poor little Arkansas slave, but now the flag of the free shall o'er me wave!" The grove echoed with applause.

I was living in Boston at the time of the rendition of Anthony

Burns and have witnessed many affecting scenes in Washington. I have expostulated with slave-hunters under the shadow of the Capitol, and asked them how they dared to take their victims, who were our countrymen, back into Slavery. I could only go to the rendezvous of the poor creatures and tell them of their danger and bid them to hide.

Mr. Spear was appointed Chaplain by President Lincoln and we ever remembered the slave. I was his companion in visiting prisons and in lecturing. We had the pleasure of thanking President Lincoln for his Proclamation of Emancipation, and he said to Mr. Spear, "I am much obliged to *you*," and he would have said the same to every Abolitionist in the land.

My first companion was Rev. Abel Brown, who died a martyr to the cause of Freedom and of Temperance combined—the result of mobocratic violence. I was with him in *five riots*. His resting place is at Canandaigua, N. Y.

FROM A FRIEND OF HON. SIMEON DODGE.

Among those who were present at the Danvers meeting on the 26th of April, were Hon. and Mrs. Simeon Dodge, of Marblehead. Their home, all through the darkest days of the cause, was the shelter of the fugitives who were sent from Boston for safety. A very large number found shelter, food, and clothing there, and were concealed there for days and weeks together, while the pro-slavery spies were constantly watching around the premises. Mr. Dodge prepared, in consequence, a *secret trap-door* for the slaves to use in escaping, in case a raid was made upon the house by the officers of the law. He, in connection with the late John A. Innis and others—Abolitionists of Salem—maintained an "underground railroad" to Canada, and at dead of night Mr. Dodge has carried fugitives to Salem, and with the aid of others sent them on toward the Canada line.

During all the time of the "Fugitive Slave Law," Mr. Dodge kept on with his good work, receiving the earnest co-operation of his excellent wife; and under that "Law" they were in constant danger of arrest and imprisonment, and of fines which would have taken away every dollar they had in the world. William and Ellen Craft were concealed there for a considerable time, when the slave-hunters came to Boston to re-capture them.

It was much easier in those days to make speeches, than to *do the work* and run the *constant risks*—cheerfully done and bravely borne by those noble souls, Simeon Dodge and wife, of Marblehead.

"THE LIBERATOR" IN DANVERS.

Special acknowledgments are due and made to Mr. Francis J. Garrison and other friends who, from their wide acquaintance with the general Anti-Slavery field and its work, have given us much valuable information which we have sought in aid of the preparation of the foregoing pages. Mention has been made of several of the original subscribers for the *Liberator*, in Danvers. At some subsequent date, the names had become much more numerous, as will be seen from the following list which Mr. Garrison has kindly furnished us. They belong to both parts of the old town, before South Danvers took the name of Peabody:—
Ezra Batchelder, Ezra Batchelder, Jr., Daniel P. Baker, Mrs. Gertrude Barrett, Daniel Buxton, Jr., O. A. Buzzell, Eli F. Burnham, Mrs. Mary P. Clough, J. B. Copp, Mrs. Betsey Cutler, John Cutler, Ezra Dodge, William Endicott, William Francis, Jr., Mrs. S. Grout, Augustus H. Hammond, Jesse P. Harriman, Wendell P. Hood, Dr. Ebenezer Hunt, William B. Jenness, Perley King, William A. Legro, Walter S. Lovejoy, Joseph Merrill, Isaac Munroe, Maria S. Page, Isaac W. Roberts, James M. Sawyer, Samuel Staples, Miss Abigail Symonds, Andrew W. Trask, Edward D. Trask, Abel H. Tyler, Putnam Webb, and Rev. Mr. Williams.

At Danvers "New Mills," if not also in other parts of the town, there were a few subscribers, Richard Hood and others, for the *Herald of Freedom*, Concord, N. H., edited by N. P. Rogers. A half-dozen or more of the leading Abolitionists of the "New Mills," or the "Neck," contributed to the pages of both papers, from time to time. "*The Emancipator*," the organ of the Liberty Party, also had its patrons in Danvers.

In connection with the sketch of Parker Pillsbury, it should be stated that his first distinctive anti-slavery work was the editing of the *Herald of Freedom*, for several months during the year 1840, while N. P. Rogers, William Lloyd Garrison, Lucretia Mott, and other prominent Abolitionists were abroad to attend the memorable World's Convention in London, to which various allusions have been made in this volume.

www.ingramcontent.com/pod-product-compliance
Lightning Source LLC
Chambersburg PA
CBHW020248170426
43202CB00008B/276